姚建华 主编

**媒介和数字劳工研究：西方的视角丛书**
SERIES OF MEDIA AND DIGITAL LABOUR: WESTERN PERSPECTIVES

# 制造和服务业中的数字劳工

Digital Labour in the Manufacturing and Services Industries

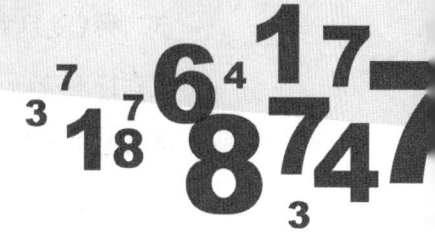

商务印书馆
The Commercial Press
创于1897

复旦大学马克思主义新闻观教学与研究基地资助

**丛书顾问**

童　兵（复旦大学）

文森特·莫斯可（Vincent Mosco，加拿大女王大学）

格雷厄姆·默多克（Graham Murdock，英国拉夫堡大学）

曹　晋（复旦大学）

马　凌（复旦大学）

冯建三（台湾政治大学）

邱林川（香港中文大学）

# 总　序

Vincent Mosco（文森特·莫斯可）

信息技术正在发生巨变，数字世界的下一步革命可能对世界秩序的影响要远远大于之前的互联网。这是因为新的技术带来了三个强有力且相互联系的系统：云计算（cloud computing）、大数据分析（big data analytics）和物联网（the Internet of Things）（Mosco，2014；Greengard，2015）。它们将数据存储和服务集中于众多的数字化工厂手中，用来处理海量的由网络传感器所收集的信息——这些传感器可能嵌置于消费者、生产部门和办公室的设备抑或活着的个体之中。这些改变带来了大量的挑战，尤其是对劳工来说，而很少有学者意识到这个问题。这也是为什么这套聚焦于数字劳工的丛书如此之及时和至关重要的原因。

技术对于工作的影响已经被讨论了很多年，尤其是在第二次世界大战之后，计算机科学家诺伯特·维纳（Norbert Wiener）提出自动化而导致大量工作机会流失，引发了公众对此议题大规模的探讨（Wiener，1948）。不可否认的是，数字技术正在，并可能持续创造出就业的机会，它们包括三个方面：其一，构建连接全球的大型数据网络；其二，数据中心内部的岗位；其三，对由互联网连接起来的实体进行控制、维持和监控所需的涉及传统基础设施的工作。然而，今天新的技术有多得多的机会来抵消人类的劳动，尤其是专业知识劳动。事实上，一位资深的咨询师将云计算定义为"仅仅是你的信息技术运作过程外包的下一步"（McKendrick，2013）。这与一位高德纳研究员简述的信息技术的大体趋势不谋而合，他说道："信息技术长远的价值属性并不在于支持人力资源，而是取代它。"（Dignan，2011a）数字技术正在创造出使得公司即刻就能将其信息技术运行过程合理化的机会。高德纳的研究员再一次强调："首席信息官相信他们的数据中心、服务器、桌面和商业应用软件总体上来说是效率低下的,并需要在将来的十年内对其不断调整,使之合理化。我们相信与这些无效率资产联系在一起的工作人员也会随着这个过程而大规模地被合理化。"(Dignan, 2011a)

依赖于数字技术的公司主张:数字技术的体系会打破商业组织模式,而这种打破随着第一台大型计算机进入工作场所就开始了。从那以后,所有的商业和政府机构坚持运营它们自己的信息技术部门,大公司坚持运营自己的数据中心。现在新体系的支持者认为,当许多大型的数据中心可以以更低的成本和更少的专业人员来满足这些需要的时候,建造和运行这些数以千计、每个组织专门的设备就不再重要。这个过程早已经开始,先期的研究表明即使对信息技术部门进行有限的"瘦身",公司仍可以削减其15%—20%的信息技术预算(Howlett, 2014)。

新技术同样使得对所有知识和创造性劳动普遍的合理化过程成为可能,因为这些职业的工作不断涉及信息的生产、处理和传播。一位观察者发现:"在接下来的40年间,分析系统将取代今天知识劳工所从事的大部分工作。"(Dignan, 2011b)2013年的一份报告指出,当今美国几乎二分之一的劳工正在受到直接失业的威胁,处于失业的高风险范围之内(Frey and Osborne, 2013)。尽管机器和劳工在工作中的具体比例尚未得知,但当今借助软件用机器系统取代知识劳工工作的趋势不可抵挡。我们开始看到这些改变对教育、医疗、法律、会计、金融、销售和媒体领域的影响。私营和公共部门的组织正在被鼓励将其核心业务过程外的所有业务外包给诸如Salesforce.com等公司——它们专门从事管理客户信息庞大的数据,这项工作通常由公司内市场和客服部门负责。

不断外包给计算机的工作的增多对弹性生产的整个全球系统带来了严重的问题。高德纳指出:"这一结果将对所有经济体产生影响——尤其是像印度这样的新兴经济体,现在正主导着技术外包。"(Dignan, 2011a)新数字技术同样扩大了潜在的外包实践的范围。这可能是一句大话,但就像《福布斯》杂志指出的那样,"我们现在都是外包方",且外包可能的形式不断多样化:"外包不再以百万美元大贸易为特征,在这些交易中信息技术部门的运作过程交由第三方负责。相反,许多小事情的点点滴滴渐渐地交由外部的实体负责。"(McKendrick, 2014)数字技术的下一步革命已经改变了劳动的过程。瑞典电影产业的工人将计算机芯片植入其皮肤之下，只需要隔天来办公室上班，以此来提高生产效率和对其管理的控制——这就是对此观点的明证（Cellan-Jones，2015）。

正是因为这种对工作场所和包括办公室工作人员和工厂工人本质上重塑的可能性，这套由姚建华博士主编的"媒介和数字劳工研究：西方的视角"丛书的出版就显得格外"恰逢其时"。首先，建华是最合适在理论上迎接这些议题所带来挑战的学者，因为他对于数字劳工的西方研究视角有着广泛的涉猎且在加拿大接受过系统化的理论训练。他本人对于中国媒介工作者的研究展现了该领域研究者所必需的理论视角和方法论策略。此外，他在将西方视角应用到对当下中国知识劳工所面临的诸多问题的分析方面，具有良好的能力（Yao，2014）。

整套丛书分成四个具体的领域，完整地为读者提供了西方视角下数字劳工最前沿的研究。第一卷《制造和服务业中的数字劳工》（*Digital Labour in the Manufacturing and Services Industries*）聚焦于制造和服务业这两个具体行业中的数字劳工。此卷从阶级、社会性别等一系列社会学的核心范畴出发，这些范畴对于描述西方社会劳工中因信息技术应用的不平衡导致的"数字鸿沟"及其程度十分有益，尤其是工人阶级和妇女在工作场所所遭受由数字技术无规制的应用所带来的大量失业和工作环境的恶化。这在一定程度上导致了特朗普总统任期内美国威权主义政府的兴起。此外，在制造和服务业中，数字技术对工作转型和全面消除工作方面的影响最为深远。

第二卷《媒介产业的数字劳工》（*Digital Labour in the Media Industries*）主要聚焦于西方媒介产业，在这里新的数字技术影响重大：在新闻、广播和广告等传统行业内工作数量减少和权力不断集中于少数大型技术公司。当2016年8月苹果、谷歌、微软、亚马逊和脸书宣布成为世界上最有价值的五大公司时，这种发展得到了最有力的证明。谷歌和脸书现在是世界上最大的广告公司且负责传播世界上大多数的新闻。然而，与诸如《纽约时报》在内的传统新闻业先行者不同的是，这些公司并不雇佣职业的新闻记者。它们仅仅依赖于用户发布自己的故事，然后向用户兜售广告，使得用户不得不尝试区分事实和虚构、真新闻和假新闻、信息和政治宣传。本卷揭示了媒介工作者的重要性。

数字技术带来的最大变化在于生产和消费边界的不断模糊。第三卷《数字劳工：产消合一者和玩工》(Digital Labour: Prosumers and Playbours)强调了这种根本性的变化过程。我们通常将生产者界定为生产产品的工人，而将消费者界定为使用这些产品的用户。但在数字世界中，消费者越来越多地通过使用不同的媒介来创造价值，比如说在以脸书为代表的社交媒体上发布自己的照片、视频和文字。他们与工人不同，因为他们并不因为自己的努力和工作而被支付明确的薪酬；因此，我们将他们称为"产消合一者"(prosumers)。同样地，公司也会让用户通过玩耍的形式，在其闲暇时间内创造价值，我们可以使用"玩工"(playbour)这个术语对其予以界定。虽然这种形式的工作在几十年前政治经济学家达拉斯·斯麦兹(Dallas Smythe)的研究中早已预见，今天的学者对这种工作形式越来越重视——因为这种工作形式在全球劳工中不断扩张。

本套丛书的最后一卷《数字经济中的劳工组织》(Labour Organizations in the Digital Economy)着眼于西方学术界对于数字劳工世界在面临诸多挑战时应对方法的研究。它尤其聚焦于工人组织的两种趋势，第一种是工会合并的趋势；第二种是现有工会的扩张，现有的工会组织已经开始从以某一种技术为基础的行业（比如新闻业），扩张到基于数字技术的新的产业中了。这种产业由数字技术集合而成，具有播送和联合的能力，这种能力将工人与社会运动组织联系在了一起，既宣传了工人的需求，又推动了政治议程。

数字劳工作为一个研究领域，对于许多学科而言正在变得越来越重要，尤其是对于公共政策的研究者来说。本套聚焦于数字劳工的丛书为他们全面地了解西方视角下数字劳工研究的最新成果提供了重要的公共服务。

（姚建华 译）

## 参考文献

Cellan-Jones, Rory. (2015) 'Office Puts Chips Under Staff's Skin.' *BBC News*. January 29. http://www.bbc.com/news/technology-31042477.

Dignan, Larry. (2011a) 'Cloud Computing's Real Creative Destruction May Be the IT

Workforce.' *ZDNet*. October 24. http://www.zdnet.com/article/cloud-computings-real-creative-destruction-may-be-the-it-workforce/.

Dignan, Larry. (2011b) 'Analytics in 40 Years: Machines Will Kick Human Managers to the Curb.' *ZDNet*. October 18. http://www.zdnet.com/article/analytics-in-40-years-machines-will-kick-human-managers-to-the-curb/.

Frey, Benedikt and Michael Osborne. (2013) *The Future of Employment*: *How Susceptible Are Jobs to Computerisation*? Oxford University. September. http://www.oxfordmartin.ox.ac.uk/publications/view/1314.

Greengard, Samule. (2015) *The Internet of Things*. Cambridge, MA: MIT Press.

Howlett, Den. (2014) 'Exclusive: Computer Economics Study—Cloud Saves 15 Percent.' *diginomica*. February 13. http://diginomica.com/2014/02/13/exclusive-computer-economics-study-cloud-saves/.

McKendrick, Joe. (2013) 'In the Rush to Cloud Computing, Here's One Question Not Enough People Are Asking.' *Forbes*, February 19. http://www.forbes.com/sites/joemckendrick/2013/02/19/in-the-rush-to-cloud-computing-heres-one-question-not-enough-people-are-asking/#77260ffd7194.

McKendrick, Joe. (2014) 'We're All Outsourcers Now, Thanks to Cloud.' *Forbes*. August 11. http://www.forbes.com/sites/joemckendrick/2014/08/11/were-all-outsourcers-now-thanks-to-cloud/#6ccd23f967aa.

Mosco, Vincent. (2014) *To the Cloud*: *Big Data in a Turbulent World*. Boulder, CO: Paradigm.

Wiener, Norbert. (1948) *Cybernetics*: *Or Control and Communication in the Animal and the Machine*. New York: Wiley.

Yao, Jianhua. (2014) *Knowledge Workers in Contemporary China*: *Reform and Resistance in the Publishing Industry*. Lanham, MD: Lexington Books.

# Contents

Introduction                                                  Graham Murdock / 1

## I    Digital Labour: Class, Digital Divide and Gender

1. The Underpinnings of Class in the Digital Age: Living, Labour and Value
   Ursula Huws / 13
2. Labouring Under the Digital Divide
   Michelle Rodino-Colocino / 43
3. Gendered Futures? Women, the ICT Workplace and Stories of the Future
   Karenza Moore    Marie Griffiths    Helen Richardson    Alison Adam / 71

## II    Digital Labour in the Manufacturing Industry

4. Foxconned Labour as the Dark Side of the Information Age: Working Conditions at Apple's Contract Manufacturers in China
   Marisol Sandoval / 97
5. 'The Future's Bright, the Future's Mobile': A Study of Apple and Google Mobile Application Developers
   Birgitta Bergvall-Kåreborn    Debra Howcroft / 145

## III    Digital Labour in the Services Industry

6. The Subterranean Stream: Communicative Capitalism and Call Centre Labour
   Enda Brophy / 171
7. Prospects for Trade Unions and Labour Organisations in India's IT and ITES Industries
   Andrew Stevens    Vincent Mosco / 190

# 目 录

导 言
　　　　　　　　　　　　　　　　　　　格雷厄姆·默多克 / 1

## 第一章　数字劳工：阶级、数字鸿沟与社会性别

1. 数字时代的阶级基础：生活、劳动和价值
　　　　　　　　　　　　　　　　　　　乌苏拉·胡斯 / 13

2. 数字鸿沟下的劳动
　　　　　　　　　　　　　　　　米歇尔·罗迪诺-克劳希罗 / 43

3. 性别化的未来？女性、信息和通信技术工厂与未来的故事
　　　卡伦娜·穆尔　玛丽·格里菲思　海伦·理查森　艾莉森·亚当 / 71

## 第二章　制造业中的数字劳工

4. 作为信息时代黑暗面的富士康劳工：中国苹果合同制造商企业中的工作环境
　　　　　　　　　　　　　　　　　　马里索尔·桑多瓦尔 / 97

5. "光明和移动的未来"：苹果和谷歌移动应用程序开发者的研究
　　　　　　　　碧吉塔·伯格维尔-卡里伯恩　德布拉·霍克洛夫特 / 145

## 第三章　服务业中的数字劳工

6. 地下潜流：传播资本主义与呼叫中心劳工
　　　　　　　　　　　　　　　　　　　恩达·布罗菲 / 171

7. 印度信息技术和信息技术化服务产业中工会与劳工组织的前景
　　　　　　　　　　　　　　安德鲁·史蒂文斯　文森特·莫斯可 / 190

# 导　言

Graham Murdock（格雷厄姆·默多克）

当代对于数字技术的评论倾向于将其与过去的"旧"技术进行根本性的割裂，但这种割裂往往忽视了引发技术变革的更为广阔的社会背景和不断朝着有利于资本积累的方向演变的现实。要了解当前数字劳工的组织形式，我们需要将其视为具有剥削性的资本主义制度发展的最新产物，而这种剥削可以追溯到当代资本主义的源头。

维多利亚时期资本主义最为核心的机械化生产依赖于数学制表来进行精确地计算。这些表格由被称为"计算机"的工人手动完成，因此其中通常会存在错误。1822年，英国著名数学家查尔斯·巴贝奇（Charles Babbage）提出通过制造自动计算数值的机器来消除人为的错误。尽管他得到了英国政府慷慨的资助，但他所谓的"差分机"（Difference Engine）从未完成，项目也因此被放弃。然而，他并未气馁，随后着手研究一种新的机器——解析机（Analytical Engine）。这种机器可以通过打孔卡来输入数据，进而编程，并使用了当时另一位"名满天下"的数学家阿达·洛芙莱斯（Ada Lovelace）提出的算法。而洛芙莱斯就是诗人乔治·拜伦（George Byron）的女儿。该项目虽然也未完全成功实施，但是巴贝奇的理念今天被广泛地认为是现代计算机的基础。

巴贝奇对于自动化计算的兴趣并不仅仅是学术上的，而且带有明显的实用和商业意图。1833年，他在对新英格兰工厂中使用机器情况的研究基础上，出版了其代表作《在机械制造和生产中的经济学》（On the Economy of Machinery and Manufacture）——这是他对计算引擎（Calculating Engine）的研究成果之一。该书不但被不断处于上升地位的产业资本家广泛阅读和引用，而且极大地影响了他们对新机器的投资回报最大化的思考。巴贝奇认识到投资回报最大化的价值,从而要求在生产过程中对劳动进行系统的分工。这并不是一个新的观点,因为在《国富论》中,亚当·斯密就已经将劳动分工视为市场经济基本论述的核心。通过以生产大头针为例,斯密揭示了即使完成一个简单的商品都涉及大量不同的劳动过程,将这些劳动过程不断分解为独立的任务,既更为有效又能带来更多的利润。

巴贝奇在此基础上进一步主张:将对工作的执行分解为不同的过程,这些过程要求不同程度的技能。企业主可以更精确地根据特定的流程来匹配工资率,绝不支付超过必要的部分。马克思在《资本论》第一卷对工业生产的讨论中,发展了巴贝奇的观点,论述道:既然各种功能可以是简单的,也可以是复杂的;可以是高级的,也可以是基础的,那么生产过程中就会产生劳动权力的等级结构,并与工资等级相对应(Marx, 1990: 469)。与巴贝奇一样,马克思承认机器生产是纪律和监控新的且强大的来源。巴贝奇认同"机器生产过程中最大的优点就是可以发现在工作中工人的漫不经心、懒散懈怠以及不诚实"(Rosenberg, 2017)。但是马克思有不同的看法,他认为:将手工艺者转变为工人需要一系列的技能,对他们劳动节奏和秩序进行监督,使之成为机器的附属品,这是他们被"异化"的主要原因。诚如马克思所言,"在生产手工艺品的过程中,匠人使用工具;在工厂中,机器使用工人"(引自 Rosenberg, 2017)。

制造一个基于巴贝奇理念的工作计算机直到 1940 年代真空管技术的发展才成为可能。这些早期的机器占地面积巨大,且制造和运营费用昂贵,这就限制了其使用者范围,主要是政府和企业组织。晶体管技术以及制造更小机器可能性的出现才使早期的机器有了进一步的提升。1970 年代中期,个人电脑得到迅猛发展,促使了更多的观察者注意到 1978 年西蒙·诺拉(Simon Nora)和阿兰·明克(Alain Minc)递交给当时法国总统德斯坦的具有开创性的报告,该报告预言基于计算和通信融合基础上的"社会计算机化"(computerization of society)的时代即将来临(Nora and Minc, 1981)。大型计算机在组织企业活动方面继续发挥着重要的作用,但越来越多的关键职能被移交给了台式机。此后,日常计算的能力转移到了手机和平板电脑之上,它们可以随时随地处理大量的数字化文本、数据、声音、语音,以及静止和移动的图像。同时,具有强大处理能力的高端超级计算机的发展催生了新的数据分析行业,使其能够识别基于用户而产生的大量数据的趋势和模式。这种能力为商业模式提供了基础——在这种商业模式中,以谷歌和脸书为代表的西方主要的互联网公司收集和整理用户信息,并将这些信息转售给以满足用户个性化需求为目标的广告商。

新兴经济体在数字价值链的每一个环节都产生了对劳动力的需求,从智能手机部件的日常装配到开发新的操作软件和应用系统,用以回应用户的不同需求和质询。然而,为了理解这种劳动如何被组织起来,我们需要回到巴贝奇最开始的项目所提出的问题,并将数码机器的到来"坚定不移"地放置在大型企业积累资本和追逐利润的语境之下。

马克思关于生产方式的核心概念对生产力和生产关系进行了重要的区分。包括技术在内的生产力的创新可能改变生产的组织形式,但并不能改变资本和劳动之间本质上权力关系的不平等或是剥削的过程。许多关于数字技术的研究忘记了这个简朴的事实,它们并没有意识到数字媒体的兴起实际上强化了而不是分散了资本的力量。

数字技术在资本主义组织和运作中的日益集中,正好与主要资本主义经济体的利润率的结构性危机相契合。20世纪70年代中期,以"福特主义"为标签的标准化商品的大规模生产和消费(如亨利·福特的T型汽车)并不能导致利润率的持续上升——这点已清晰可见。右翼的评论者将这种停滞的增长归咎于国家的干预和管制(进而导致了1929年的华尔街股灾和第二次世界大战)和对企业征收高额的税费用以支持更全面的社会福利制度。同时,这些评论者主张回归自由放任的资本主义,使得企业可以获得最大的经营自由。在由撒切尔夫人领导的英国和罗纳德·里根领导的美国,他们发现有影响力的政治领导人更愿意将他们的想法转化为具体的政策,推广在很多其他国家中所采用的不同程度的自由的市场。限制企业自由行动的法规被放宽;公司需要缴纳的税费被削减——这些市场原教旨主义的干预使得生产和消费发生了重大的结构性调整。

围绕着信息与通信技术融合的新兴产业在这个过程中发挥了核心的作用。学界和政界逐渐达成共识:全球发达经济体中资本主义的基础正从工业制造转向信息业和服务业。数字媒体被视为这一转型的根本驱动力,既为新的网络经济提供必要的基础设施支持,又提供一系列为生产新的数字产品和应用程序而组织起来的新兴经济部门。20世纪90年代后期,巨额收益的预期推动了对新数字公司投机性投资的热潮。大家所熟知的互联网泡沫在2000年破裂。大多数新公司的倒闭使得数字媒体部门越来越集中于少数大型企业。微软公司维持了之前作为软件提供商的优势地位,其他关键运营部门中虚拟垄断公司也不断加入。谷歌在搜索领域、脸书在社交媒体领域、亚马逊在在线零售领域、苹果公司在个性化产品方面优势明显。这个集中的过程极大地增强了这些主导性的企业施加政治影响力和决定市场结构的能力。

为了应对资本主义70年代中期所累积的危机,消费者被鼓励更多和更经常地消费、因为潮流和风格的改变而更快地丢弃他们已有的商品,并通过使用信用卡而不断加剧个人在经济上的债务。消费市场正日益分化为众多以名牌为标志的小众化市场(或称为利基市场,niche market),这些市场逐渐成为自我表达和自我实现的主要舞台。数字媒体,特别是遍布全球的互联网,为广告和产品的推广提供了最为理想的载体和重构消费所需的促销手段。企业迅速抓住了基于互联网的互动性所产生的大量机会。除此之外,因为在线广告几乎完全缺乏监管,这就使得那些受欢迎的网站充斥着促销信息,并与其客户之间建立更为亲密和个性化的关系。

与促进消费同时存在的,是在生产过程中不断降低劳动力成本的诉求。这里主要有四种方法,包括:离岸外包(offshoring)、外包(outsourcing)、使用临时工代替正式工、逐渐削弱劳工组织(和与之相伴随的劳工抗争)。作为"媒介和数字劳工研究:西方的视角丛书"的第一卷,《制造和服务业中的数字劳工》的贡献就在于详细地描述了这些方法的实际运作过程,指出这些方法对于劳工及其生活状况的影响,并探究其对于社会分层和不平等的深远影响。

诚如米歇尔·罗迪诺-克劳希罗(Michelle Rodino-Colocino)在《数字鸿沟下的劳动》一文中所指出的,早期的研究表明,工作场所之外使用计算机并进行有效操作的过程会因阶级地位和教育水平的不同而存在明显的差异。我们将它称为"数字鸿沟",数字鸿沟的存在引起了政策制定者的广泛关注,因为在新的数字经济学中,很少有工人能够使用这些新技术,并有效地发挥它们的作用。劳工的应对方式就是参加培训课程以获得相应技能的提升。将"数字鸿沟"的产生归因于个人的失败遮蔽了在不同劳动力中出现的结构性的"鸿沟"。这种鸿沟具体表现为：特权精英启动并控制数字创新过程；中间阶层负责在现有协议的基础上设计出新的应用程序；大量的数字劳工被安排从事日常的装配和服务功能——这种鸿沟的存在更加固化而非挑战现有的阶级结构。

装配电路板或者是为打电话来呼叫中心的客户提供咨询服务并不需要特别的数字技术能力——在使用标准的文字处理和电子表格软件包的过程中，仅仅涉及最基础的技能。这些任务究其实质，乃是再生产了大量日常体力和文职工作，类似的工作长期存在于工厂和办公室之中，以及存在于面对面咨询的解答之中——从事这些工作的人员同样来自于工人阶级家庭，他们通常只接受过最基础的教育。与其他领域的职业实践一样，在数字产业，占据着高级创意和管理岗位的人员大多具有职业和管理的背景，且接受过精英教育。微软创始人比尔·盖茨的父亲是一位非常著名的律师，他的祖父是一位众所周知的银行家；脸书的首席执行官马克·扎克伯格的父母是牙医和精神病学家；谷歌的联合创始人谢尔盖·布林（Sergey Brin）和拉里·佩奇（Larry Page）成长于由数学和计算机教授组成的家庭之中。

这种熟悉的阶级再生产模式因社会性别分工而变得更为错综复杂。数字劳工的扩张对于女性而言是把"双刃剑"：一方面，数字劳动为女性提供更多的就业机会；另一方面，它强化了对于性别差异在能力和技术上的本质主义的定义。卡伦娜·穆尔（Karenza Moore）和她的合作者在《性别化的未来？女性、信息和通信技术工厂与未来的故事》一文中指出：在数字产业有这样一种普遍的假设，即女性在沟通和协调上具有"与生俱来"的优势，而这些社交能力特别适合与客户或顾客打交道。这在很大程度上排除了女性从事与研究和创新相关工作的考量，因为这些工作需要较高层次的技术和认知能力。不同工作机会的合法性来源于西方文化中根深蒂固的二元论：男性与理性和计算相关联、女性与情绪和感情相联系。女性主义历史学家认为，在创新的历史上男性的成就持续受到关注，而女性贡献的价值往往被低估，这种高度的选择性更为上述根深蒂固的二元论背书。即使在今天，洛芙莱斯的算法所展示出来处理原始数据的能力（这种算法是脸书和谷歌商业模式的基础）仍然很少受到关注——对于她的关注度远远小于巴贝奇研发解析机这个失败的项目。

女性在数字劳动力市场中就业机会的不平等因为她们在社会关系网络中边缘化的地位而进一步被加剧——后者在个体获得工作岗位的过程中发挥了重要的作用。大多数的女性承担着大量照顾家庭和抚养孩子的责任，因此她们很少有时间出来进行工作之外的社交，而这种社交往往对于维系核心的关系网络至关重要。此外，她们很难在产后重新回到快速多变的职场之中。穆尔等学者指出，在全球数字经济重镇的英国，信息技术职业中女性只占16%，她们往往集中在较低薪酬的部门，更多的人选择离开这个行业而不是进入该行业。她进而论述道：这种排他性意味着女性作为家庭和工作场所数字设备的主要使用者，很少投入到这些设备的设计和开发过程中。

乌苏拉·胡斯（Ursula Huws）在《数字时代的阶级基础：生活、劳动和价值》一文中指出，数字劳工不是一种孤立的劳工形式。它目前的组织形式是劳动分工日益复杂化的产物。企业战略将"体力劳动"与"脑力劳动"、"概念"与"执行"、"硬实力"与"软实力"之间的区分不断内化，并将此作为企业扩张的基础，使其遍布全球范围内的价值链之中。

## 离岸外包

根据巴贝奇"将劳动过程最大限度地分解为可以辨识的任务，并对每一个步骤所完成的工作支付最少报酬"的原则，数字公司纷纷转战海外，享受在全球新兴经济体中极其低廉的劳动力成本的优势。罗迪诺-克劳希罗在她的文章中讲述了一个软件测试者的案例：她在西雅图附近的一个数字中心的企业工作，虽然不情愿，但是她在离职之前必须培训离境替代者，这是她得到遣散费的必要条件。开发软件需要更高水平的技能，但是离岸工人的薪酬仅仅是美国工人的一半。越是涉及低水平技能的工作，薪酬的差距就越大。罗迪诺-克劳希罗发现，印度的亚马逊工人仅仅要求190美元的薪酬，而支付给西雅图总部从事相同工作劳动者的薪酬则是1900美元。

离境外包在成本上的优势最显著地表现在日常装配工作的组织之中。桑多瓦尔·马里索尔（Sandoval Marisol）在《作为信息时代黑暗面的富士康劳工：中国苹果合同制造商企业中的工作环境》一文中详细论述道：苹果和其他主要参与制造智能手机和平板电脑的西方企业都严重依赖于亚洲分包商所雇佣的劳动力。在这些劳动者中,女性占据了绝大多数,且她们往往是新生代农民工——她们必须长时间地工作、很少有机会休息,且受到严密的监控,以确保她们完成生产配额的要求。这种剥削的结构被智能手机最终的消费者所遮蔽,因为智能手机会对消费者进行"狂轰滥炸"式的广告营销,这些广告通常呈现出优雅的风格,同时强调产品升级的功能,以及强化手机在消费者日常生活中的价值。

当分包商在非正规的经济环境中运作,那么对于工人的保护就更无从谈起,这进一步强化了对离境劳工的剥削。穆尔和她的合作者援引了来自印度的数据:女性占据了信息技术化服务部门(ICT-enabled services)超过三分之一(37%)的工作岗位,但是其中超过半数的女性(19%)在非正规的部门工作。

## 外包

一直留在全球发达经济体中的工作现在也不停地被外包给了小型供应商或自由职业者。企业从这种外包中取得两个实质性的好处。首先,它们可以避免为劳工提供福利,如带薪假期、病假工资、产假、养老金(企业合同工通过集体谈判而获得的福利)。其次,生产的成本直接转嫁给负责某个具体项目或任务的分包商。他们支付使用或购买仪器和设备的费用,租赁或购买场地的费用,在生产过程中耗费的水、电等费用,以及劳工技能升级过程中所涉及的额外培训的费用等。

这种交换的不平等性在碧吉塔·伯格维尔-卡里伯恩(Birgitt Bergvall-Kareborn)和德布拉·霍克洛夫特(Debra Howcroft)对为苹果或谷歌开发应用程序的自由职业者的研究中表现得淋漓尽致。他们在《"光明和移动的未来":苹果和谷歌移动应用程序开发者的研究》一文中指出:除了承担开发的成本之外,设计应用程序过程中自我雇佣的劳动者和微型企业在确保其劳动回报方面都面临着诸多障碍。苹果公司坚持对所有加载到其设备之上的应用程序进行审批。一旦被苹果公司接受,开发者必须承担额外的工作,如使用社交网络密集地对该应用程序进行推广以确保它位于前100的名单之中,进而被更多的用户所关注。开发者为他们研发的应用程序定价,但是苹果公司收取30%的销售收入,作为使用其平台的"租金"。

有一句老话这样说：你所知道的并不是关键，关键的是你所认识的——这句话同样适用于解释数字资本主义制度下不平等的就业机会。因为外包是基于项目来组织劳工，所以整合到核心社会关系网络之中的重要性愈发明显，它不断地决定个人的职业声誉，进而决定工作的分配——因此，拥有社会资本变得至关重要。对于那些已经通过家庭、共同的教育和合作项目的经历而建立起联系的劳动者，在这方面具有特别的优势，他们可以投入大量的时间和精力发展和维系新的社会关系。对于那些出生在贫穷或少数族裔家庭中的劳动者而言，在社交上他们的劣势异常明显：因为他们的社会背景将他们排除在具有影响力的人物的交际圈之外，所以他们可以动员的社会资本十分有限。

**使用临时工代替正式工**

在由主要的数字公司运营的工厂中，劳动者持续地被划分为：基于长期雇佣合同的劳动者（数量非常有限）以及签订临时或固定劳动期限合同的劳动者（数量不断增多）。这并不简单地意味着工作安全性的不同，更意味着薪酬和工作环境的"天壤之别"。2000年，微软公司西雅图总部运营部门11%的劳动者来自外部机构，且签订临时合同——他们中一些人的收入远远低于标准薪酬水平；而且在工作中，这种特殊的身份很容易被辨识：他们通常被要求佩戴橙色的、可识别身份的徽章，而那些长期雇佣的劳动者则佩戴蓝色的徽章。

**劳工抗争**

本卷中的论文向读者揭示了大部分的数字劳工都处境堪忧且是不安全的。对于很多劳动者而言，在一个既定公司中被长期雇佣或拥有广阔的职业发展前景这种传统的期许已经变得不那么现实。胡斯在她的论文中尖锐地指出：这种变化已然导致评论家们发现工人阶级的概念不再适用于在新的数字资本主义背景下对劳工的分析——进而被"大众"或"无产者"这些更具有"不确定性"的概念所取代。在此基础上，她对马克思劳动价值理论进行了强有力且颇具说服力的辩护，她指出：对于劳动价值理论的分析仍然需要从对劳动的组织入手，因为劳动为资本创造剩余价值。对于在何种工作条件下,用多少劳动时间来换取多少薪酬的抗争将劳动者和他们仅有的劳动力相联系,他们将自己的劳动力出卖给愿意购买这些劳动力的资本家。胡斯将这种结构的对抗性视为连接商品生产核心中各种关系的要件。

从历史上看,工会在具有剥削性的资本主义制度下不断保障工人的基本权益。然而,大部分数字公司一直拒绝承认工会。罗迪诺-克劳希罗在她的论文中提到:成立于1998年的华盛顿技术工人联盟(Washington Alliance of Technology Workers)尝试着联合在西雅图地区为亚马逊和微软公司工作的合同工,但这种尝试最终以失败而告终。

这并不意味着对于恶劣的工作环境就不存在抵制。恩达·布罗菲(Enda Brophy)在《地下潜流:传播资本主义与呼叫中心劳工》一文中,对呼叫中心的员工进行了详细的论述:工人采取了一系列个人游击的战术以赢得更多的空间和表达自身的不满;与此同时,他同样发现集体组织正在不断壮大。他分析了印度的信息技术化服务专业人员工会(Union for ITES Professionals, UNITES),同样安德鲁·史蒂文斯(Andrew Stevens)和文森特·莫斯可(Vincent Mosco)的论文《印度信息技术和信息技术化服务产业中工会与劳工组织的前景》在探讨是否存在新的可能性将个体劳工组织起来的问题时,也使用了该案例。

马克思对资本主义的分析直指该制度中的核心矛盾——劳资关系的矛盾。他敏锐地发现,为了使生产效率最大化而将大型企业中的劳动者组织起来的做法有时会产生意想不到的效果:这让劳动者更清晰地意识到他们共同的处境,并团结起来对他们的处境进行改变。马克思强调铁路系统所产生的新的、更快的通讯网络在组织不同城镇中的工人方面发挥了不可替代的作用,进而使得信件、新闻、对于团结的宣传可以每天进行传播。同样,数字网络加剧了劳资矛盾。一方面,数字网络使得企业能够实时协调日益在地理上分散且不断在范围上拓展的劳动分工。但是另一方面,数字网络为劳动者提供新的组织工具,用以培育进行抗争和抵制的组织。现在的问题是,这些新的传播在多大程度上可以成功地将存在于数字价值链不同环节和面对不同情况的劳工联合起来——这个问题也是本卷所关注的核心问题。

(姚建华 译)

## 参考文献

Marx. Karl. (1990). *Capital*, Vol. 1. London: Penguin.

Nora, Simon and Alain Minc. (1981). *The Computerisation of Society: A Report to the President of France.* Cambridge, MA: MIT Press.

Rosenberg, Nathan. (2017). *Babbage: Pioneer Political Economist.* http://projects.exeter.ac.uk/babbage/rosenberg.htm [retrieved March 16, 2017]

# I

Digital Labour: Class, Digital Divide and Gender

# The Underpinnings of Class in the Digital Age: Living, Labour and Value

Ursula Huws(乌苏拉·胡斯)[1]

[导读]* 在互联网研究中,对于如何界定数字劳工的讨论愈发激烈,这些讨论强调"工作"和"玩耍"、"生产"和"消费"之间越来越模糊的界限——尤其是"无酬劳动"是否也创造剩余价值,是否存在剥削和异化? 在作者看来,对这些问题的回答,需要我们重新审视劳动价值理论(the labour theory of value)。

劳动价值理论是马克思在对资本主义作为一种社会关系分析过程中使用的核心概念,其连接了从劳动中产生的剩余价值、劳动以及工人对生存的需要——离开了劳动,资本就无法积累、资本主义也就无法运作。但是,什么是劳动? 什么样的劳动才能创造剩余价值? 如何界定"必要劳动"? 作者指出,仅仅从是否具有生产性的角度来界定劳动,往往遮蔽了这样的事实:存在着大量创造价值的"无酬劳动",但它们并不改善劳动者的生计。"数字劳动"中普遍存在"无酬劳动";同时,"数字劳工"在整个工人阶级中的比重不断增加,且他们中的一些收入微薄、穷困潦倒。因此,对于研究者而言,理解数字劳工在全球资本主义中的作用、数字劳工的组成,以及数字劳工所表达出的阶级忠诚变得格外重要。

---

[1] 现任教于英国赫特福德大学(University of Hertfordshire),主要研究劳工与全球化问题。Analytica 研究咨询公司负责人;同时,她也是《工作组织、劳工与全球化》(Work Organization, Labour & Globalization)杂志的主编,代表作有《全球数字经济中的劳动:高科技无产阶级时代的到来》(Labor in the Global Digital Economy: The Cybertariat Comes of Age, 2014)、《高科技无产阶级的形成:真实世界里的虚拟工作》(The Making of a Cybertariat: Virtual Work in a Real World, 2013)等。Prof. Huws notes that the original article is from Socialist Register 50: 80-107.

\* 本书中,"导读"均由编者为帮助读者更好地理解论文的观点而专门撰写。

从劳动中产生的剩余价值：在资本主义中，租金、贸易和通过商品的生产而创造的剩余价值是资本家获得利润的三种主要途径。在对新媒体企业的分析中，我们不难发现：(1)租金：来源于广告代理商支付给社交媒体或者搜索引擎公司大量的金钱用以将这些广告传递给用户；用户为信息付费，如使用在线数据库；在线服务平台向服务提供方、使用者，或者广告商收取费用，如eBay；(2)贸易：来源于在买卖过程中赚取差价，如线上对他人知识产权的占有和销售、使用他人免费翻译的网站内容来盈利等；(3)商品生产过程中创造的剩余价值："数字劳工"无处不在，如果根据马克思在《政治经济学批判大纲》(*Grundrisse*)中强调的将"生产性的劳动"界定为使产品出现在市场上的一系列过程，那么现代企业中的诸多功能都具有"生产性"，包括市场营销、物流管理、流通、运输、客服、零售和批发、快递等等——也就是说，从出工厂大门到最后到消费者手中的整个价值循环链都具有生产性，而这些过程中的劳动都创造剩余价值。

劳动："无酬劳动"是一个重要的概念。第一种"无酬劳动"指代那些独立于市场、在家庭中创造使用价值的劳动，如家务劳动等"体力劳动"和记住生日、安排聚会等"非体力劳动"，而后者的大部分存在于今天虚拟的网络世界中，如在线社交网络活动就属于此类范畴。第二种"无酬劳动"指代"消费工作"，消费者承担了市场中原本由"雇佣劳动"所从事的商品流通过程（作为生产过程的重要组成）中的部分劳动，这些劳动往往具有生产性，网络跨越疆域的特征使这类劳动日益普遍。第三种"无酬劳动"指代"创意劳动"，包括写博客、在网上发布照片、音乐和视频等，这些不具有生产性的劳动往往产生"社会使用价值"。第四种"无酬劳动"指代日趋流行的"无酬实习"和"志愿者劳动"。

工人对生存的需要：这里涉及对于"必要劳动时间"的讨论。虽然工人通常以独立个体的形式进入劳动力市场，但他们往往和其他人一同生活，所以对工人必要劳动时间的计算并非易事。这种计算因养老金、福利待遇和减税政策，以及其他形式的补助变得更为困难。对于网络上"无酬的数字劳工"来说，他们维持生计的收入来源可能是多样的：来自父母的经济支持，来自养老金或社会福利，或来自日常工作的工资等。但是有一点十分明确：离开了经济来源（不管是上述哪一种形式），这种"无酬劳动"就无法继续。

在资本高度集中，信息传播技术如此发达，并影响劳动在时间和空间的分工，进而使个人的工作和生活紧紧粘连在一起的今天，我们是否都是没有区别的劳动力，为没有区别的资本创造没有区别的价值呢？答案必然是否定的。资本主义是一种社会关系，而这种社会关系取决于"工人的认同"（workers' consent），因为工人在商品的生产过程中发挥着特殊的作用。这种认同，对于工人之间的共同利益诉求和工人之间的联合异常重要。仅仅因为"无酬劳动"对"雇佣劳动"产生的冲击，而将"无酬劳工"视为"害群之马"，这一想法过于简单——它忽视了催生"无酬劳动"的结构性要素，以及从更广义的现实来看，在"无酬劳动"和"雇佣劳动"中都存在剥削——不管它们以何种形式出现。因此从这个意义上来说，工人阶级是否具有挑战资本的能力成为了劳动价值理论隐含的内核。

最后，作者格外小心地勾勒了未来的阶级结构。为资本家企业所雇佣、从事商品生产的劳工仍然是发展最为迅速的群体。虽然他们中并非所有的人都拥有稳定的工作，但毋庸置疑，他们都从事"生产性劳动"，创造剩余价值。不同地区、不同职业和不同社会身份的工人可能认为他们之间没有任何的相似之处，反而存在着竞争性的利益关系，如何将他们联合起来，分享共同的阶级意识是一个值得探讨的问题；同时，管理的、职业的和技术的工人更多地自我认同与雇主成为联盟而非其他工人阶级，他们的困惑应该如何解决？在资本主义社会关系之外，还存在着许多"工人阶级"：如从事非常小规模商品生产、租赁和贸易者，公共服务机构的工作者，以及大量的"无酬劳工"。揭示全球价值链的复杂性以及将劳动过程的研究和它联系起来是一件劳心劳力的事情，但这对于我们更好地、一起行动起来改变现存的体系，以及开始思考哪些是可以替代的可能性却是亟需的。

As Marxism has segued in and out of vogue, there is hardly a Marxian concept that has not at some time been questioned as anachronistic, in the light of the transformations in economic and political conditions that have occurred over the last century and a half. The current renewal of interest in Marx's ideas is no exception. It is indeed no easy task to apply theoretical concepts developed in the mid nineteenth century to a world where capitalism has penetrated every region and every aspect of life, where the pace of technological change is so rapid that labour processes are obsolescent within months of being introduced and where the division of labour is so intricate that no single worker has any chance of grasping it in its full complexity. Divisions between manual and non-manual work dissolve and are reconstituted, the boundaries between production, distribution and consumption melt away, and, whilst some paid work morphs into unpaid work, new jobs and new economic activities are generated from areas of life which were traditionally seen as beyond the scope of any market. In the suck and blow of commodification, the abstract becomes concrete and the concrete abstract, casting doubt on conceptual categories that formerly seemed self-evident. It may seem that we need new definitions of the most basic concepts used by Karl Marx, including 'class', 'commodity' and 'labour'.

One current idea that has attracted considerable support, especially among the young, is the notion that the idea of a working class defined by its direct relationship to production is outmoded. Since all aspects of life, such arguments go, have been drawn into the scope of the capitalist cash nexus in some way, all those who are not actually part of the capitalist class must be regarded as part of an undifferentiated 'multitude'. In Michael Hardt and Antonio Negri's formulation, this 'multitude' takes the place of a working class, while according to Guy Standing, a 'precariat' constitutes a new class in and for itself alongside the traditional proletariat.[1] Standing does not attempt to locate this 'precariat' with any precision in relation to capitalist production processes. However, many of the followers of Hardt and Negri have engaged in elaborate attempts to do so in relation to the 'multitude'. Two questions in particular have puzzled them: what sorts of commodities are being produced by members of this multitude?[2] And how does the value produced by this labour accrue to capital?

In these debates, particular attention has been paid to the value created online by 'virtual' or 'digital' labour. In the field which is becoming known as 'Internet studies', there have recently been energetic discussions about 'digital labour' and how it should be conceptualised.[3] These debates have addressed the increasingly blurred boundaries between 'work' and 'play' (encapsulated in the term 'playbour'[4]) and between production and consumption ('prosumption'[5] and 'co-creation'[6]); discussed the problematic category of 'free labour'[7] and questioned whether such labour, paid or unpaid, can be regarded as producing surplus value and whether it is 'exploitative' or 'alienated'. With the exception of Andrew Ross, few of these authors have drawn parallels with other forms of labour carried out offline. Yet, many of the questions they raise apply much more generally to labour under capitalism. These debates thus provide a useful starting point for investigating the labour theory of value itself, and how – or, some would wonder, even if – it can be applied in twenty-first century conditions.

This essay argues that it is still possible to apply Marx's theory in current conditions, to define what is, or is not, a commodity, to identify the point of production of such commodities, whether material or immaterial, and to define the global working class in relation to these production processes. In order to do so, however, it is necessary to re-examine the labour theory of value in all its dimensions. I pay particular attention to 'digital' or 'virtual' labour not only because it is currently attracting so much attention, but also because online labour is particularly difficult to conceptualise. It is thus a fertile source of cases against which to test more general hypotheses. If a theory can apply here, then it should be more generally applicable. The aim of doing this is to enable a mapping of the working class across the whole economy by applying the theory more broadly (as Marx did). This is an important task, in my view, because without a clear sense of which workers are engaged directly in the antagonistic relation to capital that characterises commodity production, and without identifying where that point of production is located, it is impossible to identify strategies that will enable labour to confront capital where it is possible to exercise some power to shape the future in its own interests.

## LABOUR AND CAPITALISM

The labour theory of value is the knot at the heart of Marx's conceptualisation of capitalism as a social relationship. It integrally links three things: workers' need for subsistence, their labour, and the surplus value expropriated from the results of that labour, without which capital cannot be accumulated or capitalism perpetuated. The expropriation of labour is the act of violence at the heart of this relationship. It is the worker's labour time which constitutes the bone which is fought over in this relationship, so an understanding of how and under what circumstances this expropriation takes place is critical to an understanding both of capitalism as a system and of which workers can be said to belong to the working class. The knot cannot be undone: each rope is essential to holding the system together. Nevertheless it seems necessary to examine it, strand by strand, so that we can grasp how it is put together, what tightens it, and what enables new threads to be drawn in or existing ones more elaborately entangled.

In its basic form, the argument is remarkably simple: the worker, obliged to do so in order to subsist, works a given number of hours for the capitalist, producing a certain value as a result. Some of this value is essential to cover the cost of subsistence, and the hours worked to produce this value ('necessary labour time') are (usually) reimbursed. The remainder ('surplus value') is appropriated by the capitalist to distribute as profit and invest in new means of production. On close examination, however, just about every element of this simple story turns out to be open to question. What, exactly, is 'labour'?

And, more particularly, what labour is productive of surplus value? How is 'subsistence' to be defined? Does it include only what the individual worker needs to keep going, or does it also include what is required for the sustenance of his or her entire household? If we cannot define subsistence precisely, how can we possibly calculate necessary labour time? And, just because all value within capitalism ultimately derives from the results of human labour applied to the earth's raw materials, does this mean that all value that accrues to individual capitalists is necessarily surplus value?

The current debates around 'digital labour' skim past some of these questions and oversimplify others. This essay will not attempt to rewrite Marx's entire theory, as that would be both hopelessly over-ambitious and misguided. Rather, it will take some of the questions raised in these debates about digital labour as starting points for examining the factors that will have to be taken into account in any modern elaboration of Marx's theory, an elaboration that will, in my view, be an essential precondition for understanding the new class formations that are emerging in the twenty-first century in all their complex and contradictory dimensions. I will do this by attempting to unravel the three strands – *living* (or subsistence), *labour*, and *value* – in order to categorise their separate components. I will do this in reverse order, reflecting the priorities of current debates in this field. These concepts are all well used and difficult to re-employ without bringing along a large freight of associated meanings, both intended and unintended. So it is perhaps useful to begin with two explanatory notes.

The first concerns the terminology. In advanced capitalist societies, not only is the division of labour extremely complex but so, too, is the distribution of wealth. Workers' subsistence is achieved not only as a direct result of waged labour but also via redistribution through the financial system (in the form of credit, private insurance and pension schemes, etc.) and through the state (in a monetary form through tax and social security systems, and in kind by means of state-provided services). In such a context, the direct connection between labour and value can be obscured. It is common for analysts to follow Marx in classifying labour as 'productive' or 'unproductive'. The approach I adopt in this essay draws on insights from feminism and makes a slightly different distinction. This is a distinction between labour which is productive for capitalism as a whole (which can be termed 'reproductive') and labour which is directly productive for individual capitalists (which, for lack of a better term, I have named 'directly productive'). I draw a further distinction between work that is paid and work that is unpaid. I argue that (dependent though it is on other forms of labour for its reproduction) the quintessential form of labour that characterises capitalism is labour that *both* produces value for capital *and* produces the income that is necessary for the worker's survival. This is work whose very performance contains within itself the contestation of labour time between worker and capitalist at whose heart lies the wrench of expropriation, the experience of which Marx described as 'alienation' (a term which has, unfortunately, become so contaminated with other meanings that it can no longer be used with the precision with which Marx employed it). And this is therefore the work that lies at the centre of the accumulation process. The workplace is not, of course, the only place that labour confronts capital. But, because capital cannot be accumulated without workers' consent, it is the site at which labour has the greatest potential power to wrest concessions from capital (without resorting to bloodshed).

*Table 1   Labour: A Schematic Typology*

|  | *Paid labour* | *Unpaid labour* |
|---|---|---|
| *Reproductive (productive for society/capitalism in general)* | **A** public administration and public service work (including NGOs); individually provided private services | **B** domestic labour (childcare, household maintenance, etc., including non-market cultural activities) |
| *Directly productive (for individual capitalist enterprises)* | **C** commodity production, including distribution | **D** consumption work |

The term 'waged labour' encompasses work which Marx would have designated as both productive and unproductive. It also excludes various forms of labour (piecework, freelance work, etc.) paid in non-wage forms, which contribute directly both to capital accumulation and workers' subsistence. Defining labour only in terms of whether it is productive or not, in Marx's sense, ignores the reality that (as will be discussed below) there is a considerable amount of unpaid labour which produces value directly for capital without contributing to the worker's subsistence. Conversely, of course, there is paid labour which contributes to subsistence without creating value directly for capital. After spending some time considering a range of alternatives (including 'contested productive labour', 'alienated productive labour', 'directly productive labour' and 'productive waged labour'), I have, for the purposes of this essay, decided to use a shorthand term to distinguish this form of labour from other forms of productive and waged labour. Drawing on the metaphor I have used to describe the labour theory of value, I therefore refer to it below as labour which is 'inside the knot' (Quadrant C in Table 1).

Labour 'inside the knot', in this definition, is labour carried out directly for a capitalist employer by a worker who is dependent on this labour for subsistence and is therefore a front-line adversary in the struggle between capital and labour over how much labour time should be exchanged for how much money. This may seem like a somewhat narrow definition. It is indeed the sort of definition that was much criticised in the 1960s and 1970s for excluding large groups of workers who often saw themselves as part of the working class, including public sector workers and some service workers, whose relationship to production was indirect. In using it here, I am not arguing that such workers are not productive. On the contrary, many of the tasks they perform are essential for the reproduction of labour. However, these workers' exposure to the coercive logic of capitalism may be somewhat mitigated, either because they are working under older forms of employment (for instance as domestic servants or as petty commodity producers), or because they are employed by the state to provide as yet uncommodified services.

These forms of labour still exist, of course, but, as I have argued elsewhere, in the current wave of commodification, these forms of work are diminishing and the workers who carried them out are rapidly being drawn 'inside the knot'.[8] In other words, the commodification of public services has produced a major shift of labour from Quadrant A in the diagram above to Quadrant C.

This is not the only movement that is occurring.[9] The more general commodification of consumer goods and services has also involved large shifts from Quadrant B to Quadrant D, transforming the nature of some unpaid work from the direct production of use values for household members to the purchasing of commodities in the market, involving a direct relationship with capitalist production and distribution activities. In a further twist, there has also been a shift of labour from Quadrant C to Quadrant D as capitalist production and distribution companies have reduced their labour costs, increasing the exploitation of their paid workers by externalising more and more tasks onto consumers who have to carry them out as unpaid self-service activities. In a parallel process, austerity measures are also leading to a shift of activities from Quadrant A to Quadrant B, which in turn puts more pressure on the further shift from B to C. Thus, whilst labour 'inside the knot' constitutes a sub-set of all labour, it is a sub-set that is rapidly expanding to become the overwhelming majority of paid labour.

My second cautionary note concerns the danger of extrapolation from a typology of labour to a typology of workers, and hence to a class typology. Whilst part of my aim is to classify different forms of *labour* in their relation both to capital accumulation and workers' subsistence, I do not intend in so doing to produce a classification of *workers* that can be read off in any simple manner from this typology. Most workers engage in several different kinds of labour, paid and unpaid, both simultaneously and over the course of their lives, crossing these simple categories. Even more importantly, most workers live in households where different kinds of labour are carried out by different household members, some of whom, at any given time, may be unemployed. Whether or not members of such households perceive themselves, or can be perceived by others, as belonging to the working class is a large question. In my conclusion, I will attempt to sketch out some of the ways that it might be possible to map working classes in the twenty-first century drawing on this analysis. But the analysis of labour constitutes only a small first step in that larger process and this exercise is necessarily speculative.

## 'DIGITAL LABOUR' IN A MATERIAL WORLD

Before embarking on this analysis, it is worth noting that digital labour cannot be regarded as a discrete form of labour, separated hermetically from the rest of the economy. As I argued in these pages, the existence of a separately visible sphere of non-manual labour is not evidence of a new 'knowledge-based', 'immaterial', or 'weightless' realm of economic activity.[10] It is simply an expression of the growing complexity of the division of labour, with a fragmentation of activities into separate tasks, both 'mental' and 'manual', increasingly capable of being dispersed geographically and contractually to different workers who may be barely aware of each other's existence. This is a continuing process, with each task subject to further divisions between more creative and/or controlling functions on the one hand, and more routine, repetitive ones on the other.

Furthermore, whilst there has clearly been an enormous expansion in non-manual work, both routine and deskilled and otherwise, it remains a minority of all labour. As I have argued previously, the growing visibility of apparently dematerialised labour, dependent on information and communications technologies to observers in developed economies has sometimes served to obscure the reality that this 'virtual' activity is dependent on a highly material basis of physical infrastructure and manufactured commodities, most of which are produced out of their sight, in the mines of Africa and Latin America, the sweatshops of China and other places in the developing world. Without the generation of power, cables, satellites, computers, switches, mobile phones and thousands of other material products, the extraction of the raw materials that make up these commodities, the launching of satellites into space to carry their signals, the construction of the buildings in which they are designed and assembled and from which they are marketed, and the manufacture and operation of the vehicles in which they are distributed, the Internet could not be accessed by anyone.

Whilst 20 percent of the world's 100 largest transnational corporations are now service companies, it should not be forgotten that 80 percent are not.[11] And, according to UNCTAD (The United Nations Conference on Trade and Development), in 2012 it was manufacturing companies that were expanding their foreign investment the fastest.[12] The physical production of material commodities is still capitalism's preferred method for generating profit; it is still growing; and it seems likely to continue to employ the largest proportion of the world's workforce. There is, moreover, a continuum between tasks that mainly involve the exercise of physical strength or dexterity and those that involve mental agility, engagement or concentration. There are few jobs that do not require workers to bring their own knowledge, judgement and intelligence to the task in hand, and even fewer that do not involve some physical activity, even if this just entails speaking, listening, watching a screen or tapping keys.

That said, a large and growing proportion of the workforce *is* involved in performing 'digital labour' whose products are intangible, much of it low-paid and menial. And many members of this workforce are descended from or cohabiting with workers who would by any definition be assigned to the working class. It is therefore important to understand what role their labour plays in global capitalism, what the composition of this workforce is, how it is changing, and what class allegiances these workers might express.

## VALUE

Put simply, it could be said that there are three main ways that enterprises generate profit under capitalism, the first two of which also existed under other systems. These are rent, trade and the generation of surplus value through commodity production. Because it is the paradigmatic form of value generation under capitalism, it is commodity production that receives the most attention from Marxian analysts. If value is observably being generated from some activity, the tendency is to search for the commodity at its source. If a commodity cannot easily be identified, or if it does not appear to be produced by extracting surplus value from paid workers, then it is sometimes concluded that this means that Marx's labour theory of value does not apply and is either outmoded or in need of adaptation. However, before leaping to the conclusion that entirely new theories are needed to explain online activities, it is worth analysing them in relation to traditional forms of value generation to see whether they fit these categories.

## Rent

The ways in which commercially-mediated online activities seem to encroach indiscdrawriminately on work, leisure, consumption and personal relationships draw attention to the extent to which capitalist relations have spread into all aspects of life, or as Marx put it, 'in the modern world, personal relations flow purely out of relations of production and exchange', encouraging broad-ranging speculation about how the monetisation of online exchanges can be understood and theorised.[13] The starting point for many of the current discussions about the value that is generated on the Internet is the indisputable reality that online companies like Google and Facebook are hugely profitable. If they are making profits, it is then argued, this must be because some commodity is being produced, which in turn begs the question of what precisely these commodities might be and whose labour is producing them. In the case of Google and Facebook, the main source of income is revenues from advertising, which can be targeted with great precision as a result of the ever-more sophisticated analysis of data generated by users. Here, Dallas Smythe's concept of the 'audience commodity'[14] has been seized on by a number of commentators, including Christian Fuchs.[15] Originally developed as part of a Marxian attempt to understand the economics of advertising in commercial radio and TV, this concept portrays the media audience as the commodity which is sold to advertisers to generate revenue: 'Because audience power is produced, sold, purchased and consumed, it commands a price and is a commodity.'[16] Fuchs applies this logic to the Internet: 'the productive labour time that is exploited by capital ... involves ... all of the time that is spent online by the users'. He goes on to argue that 'the rate of exploitation converges towards infinity if workers are unpaid. They are infinitely exploited'. Other contributors to the digital labour debate suggest that 'reputation'[17] or even life itself (produced by 'bio-labour')[18] have become commodities.

Whilst Smythe's concept has undoubtedly opened up useful insights into the nature of the mass media, it has also led to much confusion. The underlying assumption among Smythe's followers seems to be that the term 'commodity' can be used to refer to anything that can be bought and sold. There is a certain circular logic operating here. Since Marx declares that 'commodities are nothing but crystallised labour' and that 'a good only has a value because labour is objectified or materialised in it', then it must follow, according to this logic, that anything described as a commodity must be the result of productive labour.[19] But how useful is such a broad conception of the term?

It seems to me that in order to understand the distinctive nature of the commodity form under capitalism, a somewhat different definition needs to be used. I have defined commodities elsewhere as 'standardised products or services for sale in a market whose sale will generate profits that increase in proportion to the scale of production'.[20] This definition singles out capitalist commodities as fundamentally different from those produced under other systems. A traditional carpenter making chairs and selling them directly to the public makes more or less the same profit on each chair. The capitalist who opens a factory and employs workers to mass-produce chairs has to make an investment in machinery, buildings and so on and will not make a profit on the first chair, but the more chairs that are produced in that factory, the greater will be the profit on any given one. This gives the chairs produced in the factory a fundamentally different character from those produced individually by a single artisan in relation to their value. There are a number of services, including intangible ones (such as insurance policies or software programs) which have the same character as commodities. It is the social relations under which they are produced (the coerced labour of waged workers, under the control of the capitalist) that gives them this character.[21] Such a definition of commodity inverts the logic of Smythe's followers. It takes as its starting point the nature of the capitalist-labour relationship rather than the fact that something is being sold.

If they do not derive from the sale of commodities, how can we understand the profits made by online social networking or search engine companies? There is an alternative explanation, and it is one that has long antecedents in the offline world: they derive from *rent*. A simple historical example of a similar way of generating income could be provided by a street market where the rent charged for a stall-space is higher in areas where the most customers (or the richest customers) will pass by. Bricks-and-mortar examples can be found in New York's Fifth Avenue, London's Oxford Street, or any other street with a large and lucrative footfall: the more well-trafficked the site, the higher the rent. For well over a century, properties that border busy highways have been able to make money by renting space for billboards. Don't these online companies simply follow the same model, albeit with sites that are virtual rather than paved and rather more sophisticated means of identifying the most lucrative customers and gaining intelligence about their desires? The value that accrues to the social networking and search engine sites does indeed ultimately derive from surplus value produced by labour. But this is the labour of the workers who produced the commodities that are advertised on these sites, not the labour of the people who use the sites.[22]

Some participants in the digital labour debate, such as Adam Arvidsson and Eleanor Colleoni, dispute Fuchs's notion that social media users are producing surplus value.[23] They, too, argue that the value that is generated can be more properly regarded as rent. However, they use the term 'rent' to refer to the value that accrues to financial investors in these companies. But in this respect, they do not say what it is that makes online companies different from any other companies that are quoted on stock exchanges and attract financial investments. In attempting to classify what, precisely, it is that generates the value that attracts such investors, they develop an explanation whereby 'social media platforms like Facebook function as channels by means of which affective investments on the part of the multitude can be translated into objectified forms of abstract affect that support financial valuations'. They further argue that such companies gain their share of 'socially produced surplus value' through 'the ability to attract affective investments ... from the multitude or the global public'.[24] This somewhat convoluted model sidesteps the rather more prosaic question of who is paying whom for what in order to generate the return on investment for the shareholders. It can, in my opinion, be rather simply answered by maintaining that it is the advertisers (producers of commodities for sale) who are paying the social media or search engine companies for the opportunity to advertise to their users. This statement is not to deny that social media sites do not incidentally also facilitate other forms of labour which could be regarded as more directly productive. These will be discussed below.

There are, of course, a number of ways that value is generated online other than through the use of search engine or social media sites. There are many other online activities that rely on rent for the generation of income. These include a variety of other sites that rely on advertising revenue, but also sites that charge rents to their users for access to information (such as online databases), sites from which copyright music or videos can be downloaded (such as *iTunes*), companies that sell software licenses online, and online games for which subscriptions have to be bought (on the same principle as software licenses).

Other sites can be regarded as essentially online equivalents of offline businesses that generate income from rent. These include online marketplaces (such as *eBay*), dating sites (such as *eHarmony* or *Match.com*), online employment agencies which match freelance workers to employers (such as *oDesk* or *Elance*), price comparison sites, online travel booking or accommodation finding sites (such as *Opodo* or *Expedia*) or various forms of peer-to-peer services allowing people to find bed-and-breakfast accommodation (such as *Airbnb*) or car shares (such as *Lyft*). The connection with offline businesses is often evident here. For example, one of the largest of the online peer-to-peer car rental services, *RelayRides*, was launched with funding from GM Ventures (the investment arm of General Motors) in 2011 and has now been acquired by Zipcar, which in turn was acquired by Avis in January 2013.[25]

Whatever the specific mix of sources of revenue, most of the profit of such enterprises comes from some combination of charging usage or commission fees to service providers and/or service users and/or advertisers – in other words, rent. It is interesting to note that some of these sites seem to be enabling the development of new forms of petty commodity production and *rentier* activity or allowing older forms to survive offline. *Etsy*, for example, makes it possible for individuals to sell craft products in the online equivalent of a crafts market. *Airbnb* lets them make an income from renting out rooms in their homes for bed and breakfast (taking a percentage of the cost). Peer-to-peer car rental services enable people to provide taxi services or charge others to borrow their cars.

**Trade**

Trade involves acquiring something at one price (including stealing it) and selling it at a higher price, making a profit in the process. Some forms of stealing, such as the appropriation of other people's intellectual property, may take place online. These include the reselling of captured images or music or the plagiarism of text for sale or some more elaborate forms of theft which are currently emerging, such as the exploitation of the unpaid labour of language learners to obtain free translation of web content by the website *Duolingo.com*, or *reCAPTCHA*'s reuse of users' attempts to decode distorted images of letters and numbers (required for security on many sites 'to ensure that you are not a robot') that cannot be recognised by automatic optical scanning systems.[26]

However, there are also a very large number of companies that sell products online (Amazon being probably the most famous) in a manner that replicates offline commercial trade. Indeed, many established merchants now buy and sell both online and offline. Although there may be some blurring of traditional boundaries between the distribution activities of manufacturers, wholesalers and retailers, and some labour processes may be rather different, there is nothing mysterious about how value is generated by such companies. The scale of many of these companies, and the fact that they have had to put extensive infrastructure in place for processing payments internationally, has meant that some of them have been able to diversify into rental activities which have in turn created the basis for new forms of commodity production, discussed in the next section.

**Commodity Production**

This brings us to the final category: value which is generated from the production of commodities. Here, the analyst seeking to isolate the role of digital labour in value creation is faced with considerable challenges. The spread of computing across most sectors of the economy, combined with the near-universal use of telecommunications, means that there are few economic activities that do *not* involve some element of digital labour, whether they take place in farms, factories, warehouses, offices, shops, homes or on moving vehicles. Furthermore, these activities are linked to each other in complex chains which cross the boundaries between firms, sectors, regions and countries. Tracing the connection of any given activity back to its origins, or forward to the final commodity to whose production it has contributed, is no easy task. Nevertheless, it is by no means impossible. One useful approach here is to analyse economic activities in functional terms.[27]

The functions of research and development and design, for instance, clearly make direct inputs to the development of new commodities (or the adaptation of older ones). Much of the labour involved in these activities nowadays comes into the category of digital labour in that it involves computer-based tools and/or is delivered in digital form to the workers who will take it forward to the production stage. The same goes for activities whose purpose is to develop content for books, films, CDs or other cultural products. Here, some activities may be more directly 'digital' than others: actors or musicians, for instance, may be performing in a manner that is 'live', but if the end result is going to be incorporated into a reproducible commodity, then their functional relation to capital is the same as that of fellow workers sitting at screens or mixing desks.[28] Digital labour is also involved in a variety of ways in production processes, whether this involves the operation of digitally-controlled tools, the maintenance of software, the generation of immaterial products or the supervision of other workers engaged in these processes.

When it comes to 'service' activities, it is useful – though increasingly difficult – to make a general distinction between those that contribute directly to production (such as cleaning the factory floor or servicing the machines); those that contribute to the maintenance or management of the workforce (such as processing payroll data, staff recruitment or training); those that contribute to the more general management of the enterprise (including financial management); those that are involved in activities connected to purchasing, sales and marketing; and those that are involved in distribution. All of these categories include activities that are carried out online and/or using a combination of information and communications technologies. They are, however, becoming more and more difficult to tell apart, for several interconnected reasons.

The first of these is the increasingly generic nature of many labour processes. Workers inputting numerical data on a keyboard, for instance, may be doing it for a bank, a government department or a manufacturing company, for purposes entirely unknown to them. Call centre operators may be using standard scripts to deal with sales, customer services, debt collection, government enquiries, fund raising or a variety of other functions, cutting across any neat classification scheme that would allow them to be sorted into different categories by function. Software engineers may be working on the development of new products, or the maintenance of existing ones.

Closely linked to this form of standardisation is the growing propensity of such activities to be outsourced, often to companies that bundle together a number of different functions for different clients into clusters of activities carried out in shared service centres. The possibility for these and other services to be carried out online has further blurred the distinction between services provided to businesses and those provided directly to final customers. If everyone can order goods online, to be delivered to the door from a central warehouse, then the distinction between 'wholesale' and 'retail' becomes an artificial one. Similarly, there is a growing range of standardised immaterial products, ranging from software licenses to bank accounts to insurance policies that can be sold as readily to individuals as to companies.

The existence of online platforms through which labour can be coordinated has led to the development of an extreme form of subdivision of tasks, sometimes known as 'micro-labour', 'crowd work'[29] or 'crowd-sourcing'.[30] These include 'pay-per-click' work whereby workers are paid by commercial companies to 'like' their Facebook posts or blog entries, or platforms like Amazon's *Mechanical Turk,* whose users are paid a few cents to perform a variety of very small tasks, so fragmented that they are very unlikely to understand what relation any given task has to the final commodity to which it contributes.

If such activities, however dispersed, are carried out by paid workers, in the employ of enterprises set up to make a profit, then they can unproblematically be assigned to the category of work that directly produces surplus value for capital – labour 'inside the knot'. However, as the borderlines between production, distribution and consumption become increasingly fuzzy and the same activity can be carried out interchangeably by paid and unpaid workers, this simple position needs some modification. Marx was somewhat ambivalent about distribution labour, regarding transport workers as productive but not retail workers. However, at one point in the *Grundrisse*, he asserted that the whole process of bringing a product to market should be regarded as productive labour: 'Economically considered, the spatial condition, the bringing of the product to the market, belongs to the production process itself. The product is really finished only when it is on the market'.[31] Following this logic, a wide range of functions to be found in a modern corporation can be assigned to this directly productive category, including marketing, logistics management, distribution, transport, customer service, retail and wholesale sales (whether online or offline) and delivery – in short, the whole value chain from factory gate (or software development site) to the final consumer should be regarded as productive labour. But what happens when the customer's unpaid labour is substituted for that of the productive waged worker? What if, for instance, you go and fetch a purchase yourself from the store or warehouse? Or design your own product, selecting a unique combination of standard features from a website? And what, exactly, is the difference between booking your own holiday via a website, keying in your own data, and doing so over the phone to a (paid) call centre operator who keys it in on your behalf? In the latter case, the labour falls comfortably into what is traditionally regarded as the 'productive' category. But what about the former? In my view, all these activities should be regarded as productive. However, only those carried out by paid workers fall 'inside the knot' whereby their relationship to capital is both direct and, actually or potentially, contested.

## LABOUR

Any attempt to categorise different forms of labour has to begin by confronting the extraordinarily difficult question of what labour actually is. The word itself covers a vast spectrum of meanings from the physical exertion of giving birth at one extreme to formal participation in employment, or the political representation of people who do so, at the other. If we take it to refer to activities which are actually or potentially reimbursed by wages in a 'labour market', then we have to include a large range of activities which most people carry out without pay, including sex, caring for children, cooking, cleaning, gardening, singing, making people laugh and holding forth on topics that interest us.

If we apply a more subjective filter and try to exclude activities that are carried out for pleasure, then we are confronted with the awkward reality that the same activity may be experienced as a chore or a joy under differing circumstances and, furthermore, that some activities, paid or unpaid, may be both onerous and enjoyable simultaneously. The baby, for instance, may give you a beaming smile whilst its smelly diaper is being changed; a truck driver's long lonely journey may suddenly bestow a heart-stoppingly beautiful glimpse of landscape; hard physical work in harsh surroundings may engender a camaraderie between workers that leaves a warm glow long after the muscle ache has subsided; solving a tricky problem may release a sudden gush of satisfaction, even if the problem is not one's own.

Another dimension that might help to distinguish between 'labour' and 'pleasure' is whether or not the activity is carried out voluntarily or by coercion, under the direction of another person or organisation. Here again what seems a simple distinction becomes remarkably difficult to apply in practice. One difficulty results from the historically determined ways in which such things as gender roles, concepts of duty or even caste-based divisions of labour are internalised, rendering patterns of power and coercion invisible to all parties and, indeed, giving many acts of service the subjective quality of freely offered gifts of love even when objective analysis might suggest that they involve the exploitation of one person's labour by another. Coercion may also be exercised in more indirect ways. An addicted gambler, for instance, may perceive his or her compulsion as internally generated, not recognising the societal pressures that impel it. The same could, perhaps, be said of many of the online activities that people spend so much time on, including online gaming and interacting with others on social media sites. It is perhaps some inkling of these social pressures that leads so many commentators in the digital media debates to insist that these unpaid activities are a form of 'free' labour.[32]

Unpaid labour is not, of course, a new phenomenon. It has however received only rather fitful attention from Marxian scholars, except as a kind of vestigial repository of pre-capitalist social relations from which waged labour later emerged. Apart from debates about slavery among historians, most of the attention paid to unpaid labour until recently was in the context of what could loosely be called 'reproductive labour', in particular in feminist debates during the 1970s. In these discussions, the main question raised was whether unpaid domestic labour or 'housework' could be regarded as producing surplus value because without it capitalism could not exist. The reproduction of the workforce depended crucially, it was argued, on unpaid labour in the home, not only for bringing up the next generation of workers, but also to provide the nutrition, cleaning and bodily maintenance services that allow the current workforce to perform effectively in the labour market. In 1976, Batya Weinbaum and Amy Bridges published a ground-breaking article in which they argued that, under monopoly capital conditions, much of this labour did not only involve producing services in the home but also consuming commodities produced in the market.[33] The concept of 'consumption work', in which unpaid labour is substituted for what was formerly the paid labour of distribution workers, is one that I developed further in the late 1970s and, I argue here, is relevant for understanding some of the new forms of unpaid labour that take place both on and offline.[34] Drawing on some of this work, I propose here a somewhat rough-and-ready typology of unpaid labour in the hope that it can provide a starting point for a categorisation that will bring some clarity to these debates.

The first category is the labour that is carried out independently of the market to produce use values in the home, the category of labour located in Quadrant B in the diagram above. It is 'unproductive' in the sense that it produces no direct value for capital in the form of surplus value from somebody's direct labour, but 'reproductive' in the sense that it is necessary for the reproduction of the workforce. It includes many of the tasks traditionally carried out in subsistence agriculture and housework. If someone is employed to do this kind of work by the direct user of the service (e.g. a domestic servant, nanny, cleaner or gardener), that worker is, in Marx's opinion, an unproductive worker, although if he/she is employed via a capitalist intermediary (e.g. a commercial childcare, cleaning or gardening company), then he/she moves into the category of productive worker (in terms of the diagram above, from Quadrant A to Quadrant C).[35] However, we are concerned here with unpaid labour. To the extent that maintaining the emotional health of a family and sustaining the social networks in which it is embedded is a necessary part of ensuring the survival of a household, then a range of non-physical activities can be included in this category, including such seemingly trivial tasks as remembering birthdays, writing letters of condolence or arranging social get-togethers which help to produce and reproduce the solidaristic bonds that may be necessary for survival in times of crisis. It also includes acquiring the skills and habits that enable someone to be employable. Even courtship can be regarded as a necessary prelude to this family maintenance project. Many of these activities are carried out online these days; thus, at least a part of online social networking activity could be assigned to this category (represented by Quadrant B). Whether or not the person carrying out this labour is exposed to advertising in the process of carrying it out is as incidental to the productivity of the labour as whether or not he/she might pass a billboard on the way to visit his/her sick grandmother or be exposed to cinema commercials whilst on a date.

The second category of unpaid labour is what I have referred to above as 'consumption work' (Quadrant D). This involves the consumer taking on tasks in the market that were previously carried out by paid workers as part of the distribution processes of commodity production. Since these tasks are necessary to the distribution of these commodities, and increase the profits of the commodity-producing companies by eliminating forms of labour that were formerly paid for, there are strong arguments for categorising this kind of work as 'productive', even when it is unpaid. However, because it does not generate income directly for the worker, it has to be treated differently from paid labour in relation to its contribution to subsistence, a topic to which I will return below. It is in other words 'outside the knot'. As already noted, increasing amounts of consumption work are carried out online, with the Internet having opened up a range of new ways of externalising labour over distance.[36]

The third category involves creative work. Here, Marx made his position clear:

> Milton, for example ... was an unproductive worker. In contrast to this, the writer who delivers hackwork for his publisher is a productive worker. Milton produced *Paradise Lost* in the way that a silkworm produces silk, as the expression of *his own* nature. Later on he sold the product for £5, and to that extent became a dealer in a commodity. ... A singer who sings like a bird is an unproductive worker. If she sells her singing for money, she is to that extent a wage labourer or a commodity dealer. But the same singer, when engaged by an entrepreneur who has her sing in order to make money, is a productive worker, for she directly *produces* capital.[37]

According to this conception, to the extent that it is carried out for the purposes of self-expression, unpaid artistic work, such as blogging or posting one's photographs, music or videos on the Internet comes straightforwardly into Marx's category of 'unproductive' labour (which I would prefer to regard as unpaid reproductive labour, producing social use values). If the product of this labour is subsequently sold, or stolen, to become the basis of a commodity, then this does not change that status. It is only if the worker is hired to do the work for a wage that it becomes productive labour in Marx's sense of the term (i.e. it moves from Quadrant B to Quadrant C). As Ross has pointed out, many artistic workers may oscillate between these forms: 'Creatives have been facing this kind of choice since the eighteenth century when the onset of commercial culture markets offered them the choice of eking out a living with the scribblers on Pope's Grub Street or of building a name-recognition relationship with the fickle public'.[38] The fact that the same person does both kinds of work does not, however, invalidate the distinction between them. Creative work thus has to be seen as straddling a number of different positions in the labour market, including self-employment, paid employment, and petty commodity production, leading, very often, to contradictory identities for creative workers.[39]

The same logic applies even in the much-discussed case of the 'free labour' that built the Internet, much of which was designed by idealistic software developers who donated their labour for nothing in the belief that they were creating a common benefit for humankind (in other words, they were producing social use value without pay, placing them in Quadrant B). As Marx said, 'labour with the same content can be both productive and unproductive'.[40] In this case, it seems that although the results of their labour were appropriated by capital to incorporate into new commodities, their original unpaid labour cannot be regarded as productive in the sense of producing surplus value for capital under coercive conditions (i.e. it is not 'inside the knot'). Rather, the value that was produced from it should more properly be put into the category of trade, which, as I noted above, also includes theft.

A fourth – but overlapping – form of unpaid labour, which is increasingly discussed, is the widespread use of unpaid internship or 'voluntary' labour.[41] This, too, seems to have precedents in various forms of apprenticeship labour, such as the production of 'show pieces' to impress potential employers. Situated ambiguously between education and self-promotion, it is undoubtedly used in highly exploitative ways by employers as a direct substitute for paid work. Sometimes, direct coercion is involved to oblige the worker to undertake unpaid 'work placements', for instance by state job search agencies which threaten the withdrawal of unemployment benefit from those who refuse to take them. Nevertheless, like the unpaid consumption labour already discussed, whilst clearly contributing value to commodity production, this form of labour plays no part in generating present income for the worker and must therefore be regarded as 'outside the knot', even if it is producing value indirectly for the unpaid worker in the form of 'employability'. It is clear that in order to make sense of the relationship of unpaid labour to capital, we have to take into account the third rope in the knot that constitutes the labour theory of value: the worker's subsistence, or 'living'.

## LIVING

The question of how the worker pays for the cost of subsistence is surprisingly absent from most of the debates about 'free' digital labour. Perhaps because they themselves often have secure academic jobs, the majority of the authors who have contributed to these discussions fail to ask how those dedicated workers who built the Internet with their free labour actually made a living. Nor, among those who advocate a 'Creative Commons' on the Internet, to which all authors are supposed to donate their work for free, is it ever made clear how these authors are supposed to pay their rent and provide for their families?

Yet, the labour theory of value cannot be operationalised without this information. In order to know how much surplus value is generated, and how, from any given unit of labour, we need to know the cost of that worker's reproduction, and how much of his or her working time is the 'necessary labour time' required to sustain life. Only then can we see how much of the remainder is left over to be appropriated as surplus value and begin to formulate demands for its redistribution. This is not, of course, a mechanical calculation. It is perfectly possible for workers to be employed below the cost of subsistence. What does the employer care if they die, if there are plenty more where they come from? Equally, it is possible for well-organised groups of workers with scarce skills to punch above their weight and claim back from capital a higher wage than that required for bare survival – even one which allows them to employ other workers as servants. Nevertheless, capitalism as a system, in

Marx's model, requires a working class that is compelled to sell its labour in order to survive, just as it requires capitalists who are able to employ that labour to produce commodities whose collective value on the market exceeds the total wages of the workforce required to produce them. And it is the direct experience of being obliged to contest ownership of workers' labour time with the employer that produces the alienation likely to lead to class consciousness. The question of 'necessary labour time' cannot therefore be ducked.

But even in Marx, this is quite a problematic concept. One reason for this is that although workers normally enter the labour market as separate individuals, their subsistence takes place in households where several people may co-habit.[42] Because these households vary considerably in size and composition and in the number of members who engage in paid work, the same wage may have to stretch to cover the subsistence of varying numbers of people. Marx and Engels discuss the 'natural' (sic) division of labour in the family, which they regard as a form of 'latent slavery' that can even be regarded as the origin of all property.[43] From their premise that women and children are the property of the male head of household, it is possible for them to conclude that, when women and children enter the workforce, 'Formerly, the sale and purchase of labour-power was a relation between free persons; now, minors or children are bought; the worker now sells wife and child – he becomes a slave-dealer'.[44]

In the twenty-first century, when women make up nearly half the workforce in most developed countries and only a minority are economically inactive, such an explanation will not suffice. Every worker who enters employment needs to be separately accounted for as an individual with his or her own cost of subsistence to be raised. The fact that people co-habit with other workers can, however, mean that this 'necessary labour time' should be regarded as producing a fraction, rather than the whole, of any individual's cost of subsistence. Or, in other words, that the concept of a 'family wage' is redundant in most circumstances. A number of other factors have also intervened to make it difficult to identify a simple correspondence between what a person earns and what it costs him/her to survive, at least in situations where that person is co-habiting with, or responsible for, economic dependents. These complicating factors include societal transfers in the form of pensions, welfare benefits or tax credits, intergenerational transfers within families, remittances from migrants working abroad and other forms of subsidy for some (or drains on the resources of others). Tax credits, the favoured neoliberal model of social transfer, have played a particularly pernicious role in disguising not only the extent to which many jobs pay wages that are well below subsistence level, but also in concealing from public awareness the reality that a large and growing proportion of social benefit payments go not to unemployed 'scroungers' but to workers in employment.[45]

Such transfers could thus be seen as having played an important role in blunting class-consciousness and diverting workers' energy away from direct conflict with their employers.

Despite very real difficulties of precise calculation, it is possible to analyse the income of any given individual in any given household and produce some estimate of how this is generated. In the case of 'free labour' on the Internet, it is likely that a number of different income sources may be involved. Some of this labour may be contributed by people who are economically dependent on their parents, some by people drawing pensions or receiving some other form of welfare benefit, some by people with regular salaries from jobs that leave them with enough leisure time to blog, surf the net or write Wikipedia entries; some might be done by people (such as freelance journalists, consultants, or academics) whose jobs require them to engage in self-promotion. And others might be being supported from rents, gambling, the proceeds of trade, crime or other activities. What is clear, however, is that these unpaid contributors could not engage in this unpaid activity without some kind of subsidy from somewhere. Otherwise, how would they eat? Arguments that postulates the production of surplus value at a societal level from their labour seem untenable. Such arguments could also be seen as playing a similar role to societal financial transfers in diverting workers' attention away from confronting the employers directly expropriating their labour towards expressing their anger and sense of exploitation towards abstract targets (such as 'globalisation'). In failing to organise at the point of production, they give away their strongest weapon: the power to withdraw their labour.

## CLASS CONFIGURATION IN THE TWENTY-FIRST CENTURY

We live in a society where capital is highly concentrated, with most commodity production carried out by companies whose fates are largely shaped by financial investors. The commodities that they produce, whether material or immaterial, are made available to us in a global marketplace, delivered through complex value chains in whose operation our own unpaid labour as consumers is increasingly implicated. Information and communications technologies have so affected the spatial and temporal division of labour that for many of us, the boundaries between work and private life are inextricable muddled and few relationships are unmediated by them. In such a situation, are the kinds of distinctions made in this essay ridiculously nit-picking? Should we not just accept that all of us are, in some way or another, part of a huge undifferentiated workforce, producing undifferentiated value for an undifferentiated capital?

I argue that we should not. Capitalism is a social relationship in which workers play specific roles in relation to the production of specific commodities. This relationship relies crucially on workers' consent. If we cannot understand this relationship in its specificity, we cannot identify the critical points in the processes of production and distribution where workers' agency can be implemented to some effect. And if we cannot identify these points, workers cannot understand their powers to consent to, or refuse, the specific deal that is on offer to them. This prevents them from actively renegotiating the terms of the deal – their only option for improving their situation. Neither, without this knowledge, can we see which groups of workers have interests in common, how these common interests might become mutually visible, or how their labour may be interconnected?

Each of the different forms of unpaid labour described above has an impact on paid labour, opening up the potential for tensions and fissures within the working class. Interns, working for nothing to make themselves employable, erode the bargaining position of paid workers in the same roles. Carrying out unpaid consumption work affects service workers by reducing overall employment levels and intensifying work through the introduction of new forms of standardisation and Taylorisation, leading to deteriorating working conditions. Writing Wikipedia entries, blogging or posting video clips or photographs online without payment threatens the livelihoods of journalists, researchers or other creative workers who lack a subsidy from an academic salary or other source and rely on their creative work to provide an income. In many cases, the same people occupy several of these paid and unpaid roles in different capacities. Even more commonly, different members of the same household may be doing so. To regard unpaid workers as scabs who are undermining paid workers is of course much too simplistic, ignoring the imperatives that propel these behaviours and the broader reality that exploitation takes place in all of them, albeit in different forms. But an analysis that equates a common exploitation with an identical role in the generation of surplus value, and collapses all these separate positions into a common collective identity as a 'multitude' makes it impossible to identify the point of production: the point where workers have the power to challenge capital; 'the centre of the knot'.

Starting from a detailed analysis of how value chains are structured, it is possible to begin to sketch out the lineaments of the class configuration that might confront us in coming years. However, this exercise has to be embarked on with extreme caution because, as noted earlier, many of us are engaged simultaneously or consecutively in a number of different forms of labour, with different relations to capital, or live in households where multiple forms of labour take place.

Leaving aside the rural populations that still subsist, at least in part, from their own direct labour on the land, in this emerging labour landscape, the largest, and by far the most rapidly-growing group is that of workers 'inside the knot': those who are employed by capitalist enterprises producing commodities, both material and immaterial. Many of these have been sucked into directly capitalist labour relations comparatively recently, coming to this work as migrants from the countryside or from other countries, being transferred from public sector employment, or recruited from a previous existence in petty commodity production. Not all of these workers have the status of permanent employees, with many paid by piece rates or employed on a casual or temporary basis. They are, nevertheless, productive workers, directly producing surplus value. However, the ways in which their labour processes connect to each other are not obvious.

A product like a smart phone contains within it the results of the labour of miners, assembly-line workers, chemical workers, designers, engineers, call centre workers, invoice clerks, cleaners and many more. Scattered in different countries, with different occupational and social identities, these workers may not perceive themselves as having anything whatsoever in common. Indeed, they may believe their interests to be directly opposed to each other. If and when they organise themselves, this might be on the basis of skill, occupation or the company they work for, but it might also be on the basis of a shared regional, linguistic or cultural identity, a shared political history or a response to a shared form of discrimination. What forms of solidarity or shared consciousness might emerge from these forms of organisation is an open question.

Another open question is the extent to which managerial, professional and technical workers within these value chains will identify with other workers rather than aligning themselves with the employer. These are volatile groups, made up of people who, in the accelerating speed of technological change and economic restructuring, find many of their labour processes undergoing standardisation and deskilling even whilst new opportunities to become managers are emerging. On the one hand, their employers want to nurture them as sources of innovation; on the other, they want to cheapen their labour and drive up their productivity. Caught between these two contradictory imperatives, these intermediate workers may be put into a position where they have to decide whether to continue to internalise management priorities and take the pain, to leave, to look for individualistic solutions, or to throw in their lot with other workers and resist.

Alongside, and overlapping with, this explosively growing body of workers 'inside the knot' of capitalism are other groups less directly involved in capitalist social relations. These include people patching together a living out of petty commodity production, small-scale rent or trade, a class which Marx assumed would die out but which appears to have been given a new lease of life by the Internet, although it is doubtful whether such sources of income can ever supply a sustainable livelihood for more than a minority of the population. In many cases, it seems likely that this way of earning a living, often cobbled together from several different kinds of economic activity, is a transitional one, adopted by people who have been displaced from the formal labour market, or have not yet managed to enter it. It is not new. Working-class biographies have always thrown up many examples of people making ends meet by taking in lodgers, child-minding, pet-breeding or making small items for sale. But it cannot be taken for granted that all such people will necessarily identify their interests with those of workers 'inside the knot'.

Groups that are 'outside the knot' also include people involved in paid reproduction work: public sector workers working in the increasingly rare fields of service provision that remain uncommodified, domestic servants, and other forms of service work that are not directly involved in the market (such as work in the voluntary sector). Their work is, of course, necessary for the reproduction of capitalism, but it is 'outside the knot' according to my earlier definition. Again, these groups cover a diverse range of social identities and may not perceive themselves as having interests in common, either with each other or with workers 'inside the knot'.

Added to these are large numbers of people who are not paid workers but who nevertheless also produce value, either in the form of reproduction, such as unpaid childcare or housework, or (externalised) production, in the form of consumption work. Many of these will be women, and their unpaid status may place them into relations of dependency on paid workers or on the state. History has given us many examples of reproduction workers throwing in their lot with the production workers to whom their lives are linked (for instance in the organisation of miners' wives in the UK coalminers' strike in the 1980s) and of consumption workers acting in solidarity with production workers, for instance in the consumer-based Clean Clothes Campaign which organises petitions and boycotts to improve working conditions for garment workers.[46]

These are broad categories and a much more detailed mapping of the composition of these groups and their interrelationships with each other will be necessary to predict the class configuration that will confront us globally in the twenty-first century. Tedious though it may be to unravel the complexities of global value chains and position our labour processes in relation to them, this seems to be an absolutely necessary task if we are to learn how this system might be changed, act collectively to change it, and start to imagine what alternatives might be possible.

## Notes

[ 1 ] M. Hardt and A. Negri, *Multitude: War and Democracy in the Age of Empire*, New York: Penguin, 2004; G. Standing, *Precariat: The New Dangerous Class*, London and New York: Bloomsbury, 2011.

[ 2 ] Hardt and Negri, *Multitude*; T. Terranova, 'Free Labor: Producing Culture for the Digital Economy', *Social Text*, 18(2), 2000, pp. 33-58.

[ 3 ] See for instance, M. Andrejevic, 'Exploiting YouTube: Contradictions of User-Generated Labor', in P. Snickers and P. Vonderau, eds., *The YouTube Reader*, Stockholm: National Library of Sweden, 2009; A. Arvidsson and E. Colleoni, 'Value in Informational Capitalism and on the Internet', *The Information Society,* 28(3), 2012, pp. 135-150; J. Banks and S. Humphreys, 'The Labor of User Co-Creators', *Convergence,* 14(4), 2008, pp. 401-418; C. Fuchs, 'Labor in Informational Capitalism and on the Internet', *The Information Society*, 26(3), 2010, pp. 179-196; C. Fuchs, 'With or Without Marx? With or Without Capitalism? A Rejoinder to Adam Arvidsson and Eleanor Colleoni', *Triple C*, 10(2), 2012, pp. 633-645; D. Hesmondhalgh, 'User-Generated Content, Free Labour and the Cultural Industries', *Ephemera*, 10(3/4), 2011, pp. 267-284; A. Ross, 'On the Digital Labour Question', in T. Scholz, ed., *The Internet as Playground and Factory*, New York: Routledge, 2012; Terranova, 'Free Labor,' in Scholz, *Internet as Playground and Factory*.

[ 4 ] J. Kücklich, 'Precarious Playbour: Modders and the Digital Games Industry', *The Fibreculture*, 5, 2005.

[ 5 ] Alvin Toffler coined this term in his 1980 book, *The Third Wave*, published by Bantam Books. It has since been taken up by a number of other writers working in a Marxist framework, including Christian Fuchs and Edward Comor.

[ 6 ] Banks and Humphreys, 'The Labour of User Co-creators', using a term derived from C.K. Prahalad and V. Ramaswamy, 'Co-Opting Customer Competence', *Harvard Business Review*, (January/February), 2000.

[ 7 ] A term coined by Tiziana Terranova in her influential article, 'Free Labor'.

[ 8 ] U. Huws, 'Crisis as Capitalist Opportunity: The New Accumulation through Public Service Commodification', *Socialist Register*, 2011, pp. 64-84.

[ 9 ] U. Huws, 'Domestic Technology: Liberator or Enslaver?', in U. Huws, *The Making of a Cybertariat: Virtual Work in a Real World*, New York: Monthly Review Press, 2003, pp. 35-41.

[ 10 ] U. Huws, 'Material World: The Myth of the Weightless Economy', *Socialist Register*, 1999, pp. 29-56.

[ 11 ] UNCTAD, *World Investment Report*, Geneva, 2008.

[ 12 ] According to UNCTAD, 60 percent of manufacturing transnational corporations were planning to increase their FDI (foreign direct investment) in the next year, compared with 45 percent of firms in the primary sector and 43 percent of those in services. See *World Investment Report*, 2012, p. 19.

［13］ K. Marx, *Grundrisse*, available at http://www. marxists.org.

［14］ D. Smythe, 'Communications: Blindspot of Western Marxism', *Canadian Journal of Political and Social Theory*, 1(3), 1977, pp. 1-27.

［15］ C. Fuchs, 'Dallas Smythe Today – The Audience Commodity, the Digital Labour Debate, Marxist Political Economy and Critical Theory, *Triple C*, 10(2), 2012, pp. 692-740.

［16］ D. Smythe, 'On the Audience Commodity and Its Work', in M. Duncan and D. Kellner, eds., *Media and Cultural Studies*, Malden, MA: Blackwell, 1981, p. 233.

［17］ A. Hearn, 'Structuring Feeling: Web 2.0, Online Ranking and Rating, and the Digital "Reputation" Economy', *Ephemera*, 10(3/4), 2010, pp. 421-438.

［18］ C. Morini and A. Fumagalli, 'Life Put to Work: Towards a Life Theory of Value', *Ephemera*, 10(3/4), 2010, pp. 234-252.

［19］ K. Marx, *Capital*, available at http://www.marxists.org.

［20］ Huws, *Making of a Cybertariat*, p. 17.

［21］ This point is made a little differently in a discussion of the distinction between productive and unproductive labour by Marx in *Capital*, Chapter 4.

［22］ There are exceptions in some special circumstances, such as when workers are paid to go on Facebook and click 'like' on commercial websites in the 'pay per click' model. But here they are not employed by Facebook but by companies linked to these commercial websites which have some commodity to sell, so they should more accurately be regarded as belonging to the value chain of these commodity-producing companies.

［23］ Arvidsson and Colleoni, 'Value in Informational Capitalism and on the Internet'.

［24］ Arvidsson and Colleoni, unpublished manuscript.

［25］ 'All Eyes on the Sharing Economy', *The Economist*, March 9, 2013.

［26］ I am indebted to Kaire Holts for drawing my attention to this explanation of the business model of *reCAPTCHA* by its originator, who also founded *Duolingo*, available at http://www.willhambly.com. See also the related video, available at http://www.inmyinnovation.com.

［27］ I have discussed the concept of the 'business function' and its relation to Marxist analysis in several publications. See for instance, U. Huws, 'The Restructuring of Global Value Chains and the Creation of a Cybertariat', in C. May, ed., *Global Corporate Power: (Re)integrating Companies into International Political Economy*, Boulder, CO: Lynne Rienner, 2006, pp. 65-84; U. Huws, 'The Emergence of EMERGENCE: The Challenge of Designing Research on the New International Division of Labour', *Work Organisation, Labour & Globalisation*, 1(2), 2007, pp. 20-35.

［28］ I have analysed the relationship of creative labour to capital elsewhere. See, for instance, U. Huws, 'Expression and Expropriation: The Dialectics of Autonomy and Control in Creative Labour', *Ephemera*, 10(3/4), 2010, pp. 504-521.

［29］ A. Kittur et al., 'The Future of Crowd Work', 2013, available at http://hci.stanford.edu.

［30］ K. Holts, 'Towards a Taxonomy of Virtual Work', Hertfordshire Business School

Working Paper, 2013.

[31] Marx, *Grundrisse*. It should be noted that this interpretation of this passage is disputed. Marx is often considered to be making a special exception of transport workers (perhaps because they were a group with strong potential trade union organisation – a potential that was more-than-realised in the twentieth century when transport workers played a key role in industrial action). It is my view that his argument applies equally to other forms of labour involved in getting products to market, many of which were inconceivable at the time when he was writing.

[32] Terranova, 'Free Labor'.

[33] B. Weinbaum and A. Bridges, 'The Other Side of the Paycheck: Monopoly Capital and the Structure of Consumption', *Monthly Review*, 28(3), 1976, pp. 88-103.

[34] See for instance, Huws, 'Domestic Technology'.

[35] See K. Marx, *Economic and Philosophic Manuscripts of 1844*, available at http://www.marxists.org.

[36] I use the term 'externalising' here to refer to the ways in which employers increase the productivity of paid staff by transferring some or all of their unpaid tasks to unpaid consumers in the form of self-service, whether through the operation of machines such as ATMs or self-service supermarket or online activities such as booking tickets, filling in tax returns or ordering goods.

[37] Marx, *Economic and Philosophic Manuscripts of 1844*.

[38] A. Ross, 'In Search of the Lost Paycheck', in Scholz, *Internet as Playground and Factory*, p. 15.

[39] I have anatomised these in greater detail in Huws, 'Expression and Expropriation', pp. 504-521.

[40] Marx, *Economic and Philosophic Manuscripts of 1844*, 'Productive and Unproductive Labour'.

[41] See, for instance, R. Perlin, *Intern Nation: How to Earn Nothing and Learn Little in the Brave New Economy*, London: Verso, 2011.

[42] I have written more extensively about this in U. Huws, 'The Reproduction of Difference: Gender and the Global Division of Labour', *Work Organisation, Labour & Globalisation*, 6(1), 2012, pp. 1-10.

[43] K. Marx, 'Division of Labour and Forms of Property – Tribal, Ancient, Feudal', *The German Ideology*, 1845, available at http://www.marxists.org.

[44] F. Engels, *On Marx's Capital*, Moscow: Progress Publishers, 1956 [1877], p. 89.

[45] For more on this, see my blog post on 'Hunger in a Supermarketocracy', available at http://ursulahuws.wordpress.com. In the UK, according to HM Revenue and Customs, 'the number of families without children receiving Working Tax Credits-only has risen over time, almost doubling from 235,000 in April 2004 to around 455,000 in April 2009 and now is just over 580,000 in April 2012' and 'the number of families benefiting from the childcare element has consistently risen over time, from 318,000 in April 2004 to around 493,000 in April 2011'.

By this date, tax credits (paid to workers in employment) already accounted for 27 percent of all benefit spending – by far the largest single component. By comparison, Job-seekers Allowance (paid to the unemployed) accounted for only 4 percent. In the US, similarly, many large companies rely on government-provided benefits, such as food stamps and Medicaid, to subsidise below-subsistence wages. For instance, Wal-Mart employees are estimated to receive $2.66 billion in government assistance every year, or about $420,000 per store. See HM Revenue and Customs, *Child and Working Tax Credits Statistics*, Office of National Statistics, UK, 2012; and P. Ryan, 'Walmart: America's Real "Welfare Queen"', *Daily Kos*, 2012, available at http://www. dailykos.com.

[46] See http://www.cleanclothes.org.

# Labouring Under the Digital Divide

Michelle Rodino-Colocino(米歇尔·罗迪诺-克劳希罗)[①]

[导读] 对"数字鸿沟"的第一次和第二次研究浪潮强调了数字技术的获取和数字技能的培养,但都忽略了数字劳工之间的差异性——这导致了"数字鸿沟"研究所内含的民主性议题没有得到有效的挖掘,简单地将"数字鸿沟"问题视为传播不平等的问题,缺乏结构性的批判。

具体来说,在兴起于20世纪中后期的对"数字鸿沟"的第一次研究浪潮中,学者一致认为:对于信息技术获取之间的不平等性将不断恶化因为阶级、种族、社会性别和地理位置所带来的不平等,而弥合"数字鸿沟"将消除更广阔意义上的经济和社会的不平等。对电脑的物理占有、网络连接、经常性接触到这些技术可以给个体带来经济上和政治上的回馈,并共同分享新兴数字经济的"红利"。

21世纪初期对"数字鸿沟"的第二次研究浪潮批判对于技术获得性的过分强调,研究者更少地从"技术所有权"(the ownership of the technology)的角度来理解"数字鸿沟",而更多地从"与技术的关系"(a relationship with the technology)的角度来分析,并强调技术应用的社会背景,从而批判第一次研究浪潮中的"技术决定论"(technological determinism)。在他们看来,不断提升人们的技术能力对于个体本身的职业发展至关重要,因为技术能力越来越成为就业的必备条件;个体因此需要通过技术培训而获得体面的

---

[①] 现任教于美国宾夕法尼亚州立大学(The Pennsylvania State University)传播学院。她的研究方向聚焦于女性主义媒介、批判文化研究、新媒体和劳工问题,曾在《传播、文化与批判》(Communication, Culture and Critique)、《媒体传播批判研究》(Critical Studies in Media Communications)、《新媒体与社会》(New Media and Society)、《女性主义媒介研究》(Feminist Media Studies)等期刊上发表学术论文多篇。

工作。对于雇主而言,让个体接受技术培训即可(并非四年的高等教育),因为他们只需要具备为工作服务的技能,并不需要具有分析、综合、批判和掌握知识的能力。

"数字鸿沟"第二次研究浪潮的学者同时强调信息与通信技术和社会融合(social inclusion)之间的关系。研究社会融合和技术之间的关系更有意义,因为社会融合不仅强调对资源的充分分享,而且强调对个人和集体生活决定的参与——技术的作用是更好地对个体和社会组织进行赋权。从这个意义上来说,整体性的政策挑战并不是弥合"数字鸿沟",而是促进信息与通信技术的获取和使用,以加速社会融合。总之,与第一次研究浪潮中学者强调信息技术获取这种"硬性"的技术决定论(hard technological determinism)不同,第二次研究浪潮中的学者强调信息技能及其与社会融合之间的关系,具有"软性"的技术决定论(soft technological determinism)的色彩。

对"数字鸿沟"的第一次和第二次研究浪潮都忽略了数字劳工之间的差异性。以西雅图地区的技术工人举例,他们之间存在着高收入、稳定工作和低收入、临时工作的明显的两极分化现象:1999年西雅图地区收入最高的1%的软件工作者(大约260人)的时薪为12000美元,而最低的5%的软件工作者(大约1300人)的时薪为15美元。最底端15%的信息技术工人的工资还不足以维持生活,且随着高科技泡沫的破灭,他们加薪的机会变得异常渺茫。此外,在福利待遇上,西雅图地区仅有少于11%的临时信息技术工人享受医疗保险。和其他合同工人一样,信息技术合同工也很少享受到带薪假期、公司职工持股计划、养老金和病假等福利待遇。

对于数字劳工劳动力的考察不能忽视对外国劳工的剥削问题。大量廉价的外国劳工正在通过H-1B签证(特殊专业人员/临时工作签证)项目和离岸外包等方式取代美国的工人。在美国加州戴维斯地区的移民程序设计员和工程师往往比具有永久居留权的程序设计员和工程师在收入方面少15%—20%;在计算机领域,持有H-1B签证工作者的工资比平均工资少20%;五分之一的H-1B签证持有者的实际薪酬少于签证申请表中企业所允诺的数额。除此之外,H-1B签证项目还具有规范和管控劳动力的效果。在离岸外包方面,初级工作甚至一些高级的技术职位不断被外包,且薪酬不断被缩减,如亚马逊将自己的客服部门外包至印度。与此同时,通过将包括软件开发在内的高度技术性的工作进行外包,雇主可以极大地节约劳动成本(通常节约比例在 50% 左右)和延长工作时间(通常在 16—18 个小时)。甚至在华盛顿州,国家机构中的很多高度技术性的工作也不断地被外包——其对于美国本土工人薪酬和士气的影响不言而喻。

"数字鸿沟"是结构性的,因此对于"数字鸿沟"的弥合我们需要思考的是更广泛的社会变革而非个人的改进,如对于公共教育的投入、建立制度性的渠道以听到更多信息技术工人的声音,这些也是在新媒体和传播领域的学术研究和实践过程中非常有价值的议题。

> For all the quality assurance engineers reading this, your jobs are gone ... Make sure on Monday you welcome your replacements with open arms, because your company has chosen them over you. – 'Saddam Hussein'

This quote provides the elusive and certainly illusive evidence that Saddam Hussein possessed weapons of mass destruction. In this case, however, the weapons are pink slips, the war is on high-tech workers, and the 'Saddam' in question foretells dismissals. Further illustrating that the new millennium is marked by what Paul Smith calls the 'Saddamization of all conflict' (Smith, 1997: 8), one yahoo group poster nicknamed 'Saddam Hussein' leaked news that WatchMark, a software firm in Bellevue, Washington, was planning to layoff workers, offshore their work, and withhold full severance packages for those who refused to train their replacements. For Myra Bronstein, one of the laid off software testers forced to train her offshore replacement, the posting elicited a 'feeling of horror and panic because there's nothing to be done' (Reingold, 2004). According to the logic of digital divide discourse, Bronstein's story was not supposed to turn out this way. Bronstein was a highly educated and paid software engineer, a 'symbolic analyst' who, as former Labor Secretary Robert Reich argued, was well-positioned to reap the windfall of 'information age' work (Reich, 1992).[1] For a while she did. Capping off a 14-year career, her three years at WatchMark demanded 12 to 18-hour days in exchange for a $76,500 salary plus bonus. But if the electronic posting from 'Saddam Hussein' foretold the humiliation that Bronstein and 16 co-workers would endure in the coming weeks, it also told a larger story. Her plight is indicative of the structural barriers IT workers face in today's economy. Further training in and wider access to information technology cannot eliminate these obstacles. Bronstein, after all, trained her replacement. Bronstein's story illustrates what debate around the digital divide has overlooked: the digital labor force divide.

Early and late digital divide research underemphasizes the digital labor force divide as it overestimates the impact of access to and skill in digital technology. Such emphasis deprives digital divide scholarship of its democratizing potential by muting structural critique and recasting the divide as a problem of diffusion. To the extent that it promotes diffusion over equality, the digital divide debate serves marketing rather than socially constructive ends.

Although first wave digital divide scholars in the mid-late 1990s disagreed about how to operationalize the gap, consensus gathered around the assumption that disparities in access to information technology exacerbate inequalities constituted by class, race, gender, and geographical location. Coined by Lloyd Morrisett, former president of the Markle Foundation, the 'digital divide' posed a problem and solution for the untrained, unwired, and unWAPed (Hoffman et al., 2001).[2] As one early study put it, since the 'Internet holds the keys to the vault of the riches of the Information Age' (U.S. Department of Commerce, 1995), closing the gap would eradicate wider economic and social disparities.

Second wave digital divide research critiques the literature for its technological determinism, specifically, for overemphasizing technological access (i.e., the physical presence of a computer or internet connection). Second wavists call for projects that expand notions of the divide beyond the point of access. Titles of second wave research underscore authors' desire to 'rethink' (Light, 2001; Warschauer, 2003), 'redefine' (Gumpert and Drucker, 2002), and go 'beyond' the digital divide (Jung et al., 2001; Mossberger et al., 2003). Typical are studies that foreground different types of 'literacy' (i.e., technical, verbal, and mathematical knowledge), qualitative differences in the use of technologies, and the relationship between such use and wider economic and social tendencies and trends (Mossberger et al., 2003; Sevron, 2002; Warschauer, 2003). Second wave scholarship, however, does not entirely eschew the technological determinism it critiques. Consequently, the second wave's emphasis on improving technological skills is not much of an improvement over the first wave's focus on access: both fail to guide policies that redress disparities in the IT workforce.

This article argues for a third perspective, one that backgrounds instead of foregrounds technology. Light (2001) begins such work in her treatment of digital divide research as 'discourse' that promotes technology as a solution to social problems. I join with Light and other critics of technological determinism in arguing that technology too easily appears as the solution to the structural problems that surround the digital divide. The following analysis contributes to the 'critical turn' in digital divide scholarship, following similar moves in communication research in communication and cyberculture studies

(McChesney, 1997; Silver, 2000).[3] More specifically, this critique taps the democratizing potential of digital divide research by focusing on wider socio-economic disparities that the divide, as previously constructed, overlooks and at times metonymizes. This article provides a critical overview of the digital divide by analyzing key moments in the debate, outlining the contours of the digital labor force divide, and considering the challenges and opportunities that lie ahead for digital divide scholars.

Given the debate's recent turn to skill, the present study investigates this development more extensively than it examines first wave scholarship. However, an overview of first wave research is fruitful for our purposes, because it illustrates the debate's evolution. The second wave's focus on skill articulates a soft technological determinism that springs from the first wave's preoccupation with access to technology. In addition, despite emphasizing skill, digital divide research has not abandoned concerns about access. Commenting on a study of access by the National Center for Education Statistics (NCES), Education Secretary Roderick Page recently argued, 'We need to address the limited access to technology that many students have outside of school ... Closing the digital divide will also help close the achievement gap that exist[s] within our schools' (Roach, 2003). Rather than supplant concern for access, then, the second wave's turn to skill presupposes it.

## DIGITAL DIVIDE I: THE FIRST WAVE

Early digital divide analyses illustrate what we might call a 'hard' technological determinism. Before analyzing these texts, let us unpack this concept and its sibling, 'soft' technological determinism. Both hard and soft technological determinism privilege technology as an agent of social, political, and economic change (Slack, 1984; Williams, 1992[1974]). Borrowing from Raymond Williams (1974), hard or 'pure' technological determinism views technology as 'a self-acting force which creates new ways of life', whereas the softer view deems technology 'a self-acting force which provides materials for new ways of life' (p. 8). Hard technological determinists view technology as directly affecting social change; soft determinists consider technology either as influencing social phenomena or as symptomatic of them. Social theories that consider the effects of technology do not necessarily commit the error of technological determinism. What distinguishes a theory as technologically determinist is its filtering out of relevant non-technological variables to explain a particular phenomenon. The technologically determinist tendencies of digital divide research constitute an intellectual and political problem for new media scholars, because the discourse drives policies and limits debate in ways that foreclose discussion of underlying inequities.[4]

The National Telecommunication and Information Administration's (NTIA) first investigation of the digital divide constructs a hard technologically determinist logic that views information technology as a social motor and, more specifically, as a means to attain wealth (U.S. Department of Commerce, 1995). The NTIA bases its study of 'information haves' and 'have-nots' on the assumption that the US has become 'a society where individuals' economic and social well-being increasingly depend[s] on their ability to access, accumulate, and assimilate information' and that 'while a standard telephone line can be an individual's pathway to the riches of the Information Age, a personal computer and modem are rapidly becoming the keys to the vault' (U.S. Department of Commerce, 1995).[5] Accessing information technologies, in other words, unlocks the new economy's coffers.

From this hard determinist view of computer technologies as vehicles for social mobility, the NTIA fashions a new demographic category of oppressed individuals, 'the information disadvantaged', whom the report seeks to 'empower'. Policy interventions, NTIA asserts, require 'identifying those who are truly in need [so that] policy makers can prudently and efficiently target support to these information disadvantaged ...' The notion of information have-nots is innovative for serving as a euphemistic synecdoche for what causes and constitutes poverty. While filtering out questions of race, class, and gender as explanations for economic disadvantage, 'information disadvantaged' constructs lack of access to information technology as a deficit in social resources. Expanding diffusion of telecommunication media, then, promises to eliminate such disparity. However, boosting computer consumption not equality is the telos of NTIA's study.[6] Therefore, whatever connection to a civil rights movement the study means to invoke by calling for empowerment of 'the information disadvantaged' collapses when we recognize that consumption serves as the criterion for judging equality. Such vocabulary, moreover, serves marketing ends rather than the public interest.

As the 'new economy' wore on and its outlook brightened, the NTIA maintained its hard dividist position by crediting computer technology with creating wealth. According to the NTIA's 1999 report: 'The Internet is a nascent, rapidly diffusing technology that promises to become the economic underpinning for all successful countries in the new global economy' (U.S. Department of Commerce, 1999). Under George W. Bush, the NTIA again underscores information technologies' contribution to economic growth: 'The expanding use of new technologies continues to strengthen our economy ... As [new electronic] connections open new economic opportunities for more Americans, it is important that all segments of our Nation are included in this ongoing information revolution' (U.S. Department of Commerce, 2002). Despite the onset of a national recession in 2001 and a 'jobless recovery' the following year, extending internet access promises prosperity on a global and individual level.

Like the NTIA studies, academic analyses of the first wave of digital divide research assume a hard technologically determinist view that information technologies enable economic advancement. One widely referenced study, Hoffman et al.'s (2001) 'The Evolution of the Digital Divide: Examining the Relationship of Race to Internet Access and Usage over Time', operationalizes the digital divide as the extent to which individuals access and use the internet.[7] Hoffman et al. analyze the 'evolution' of internet access and use among African Americans, whites, and Hispanics in the US from 1997 to 1998 and further break down use patterns according to income, gender, student status, level of education, presence of children in the home, and home computer ownership. Operationalizing the digital divide in this way evinces a hard technological determinism, as it implies an overarching concern with the physical presence of computers, net connections, and the frequency of access to such technologies.

Furthermore, the authors suggest that technological access brings economic and political rewards: 'the internet may provide for equal economic opportunity and democratic communication, but only for those with access' (Hoffman et al., 2001: 50). Hoffman et al. intend their study to 'stimulate discussion among scholars and policy makers interested in how differences in internet access and use among different segments in our society [affect] their ability to participate and reap the rewards of that participation in the emerging digital economy' (ibid). Closing the gap in access and use between whites and African Americans requires support for community, school, and other public access terminals, content that entices African Americans, and policy changes that encourage cable and satellite internet delivery, because African Americans' consumption of cable and satellite services is increasing. Since internet access and use are correlated with education, the authors also advise: 'To ensure the participation of all Americans in the information revolution, it is critical to improve the educational opportunities for African Americans' (Hoffman et al., 2001: 94). Education, in other words, is a vehicle for, rather than an effect of, more widely diffusing internet technology.

If the goal is improved living standards, however, scholars and political officials should advocate expanding job opportunities so that education and technological access can benefit have-nots. Since workers are forced to train their foreign replacements, it is misleading to argue that 'the United States economy may also be at risk if a significant segment of our society, lacking equal access to the internet, wants for the technological skills to keep American firms competitive' (Hoffman et al., 2001: 50). Even with adequate training and access, without secure jobs, the US economy seems destined to remain 'at risk'. But what does it mean to put the US economy 'at risk'? Whose fortunes are at risk if we lack an ever-expanding pool of trained labor? Hoffman et al.'s work reveals a rhetorical legerdemain in digital divide research that we will see again in Sevron's (2002) study: acceptance of euphemistic language that benefits the computer industry or more specifically, computer industry executives. For what is really at stake or 'at risk' is computer industry executives' ability to stay 'competitive'. A large, domestic labor pool extends executives the option of employing inexpensive labor at home or abroad, and thus, helps them 'compete' with companies employing cheap labor. Workers, in turn, 'compete' against each other when companies threaten to move jobs to the lowest bidder. Hoffman et al.'s warning implies concern with labor discipline and bottom lines rather than rising living standards for workers.

## DIGITAL DIVIDE II: THE SECOND WAVE

Later digital divide scholarship takes a softer turn. An article appearing in *Communication Research*, 'Internet Connectedness and Inequality: Beyond the "Divide"' (Jung et al., 2001), objects to the technological determinism of first wave research. Jung et al. critique early divide work for too narrowly defining the digital divide as one that can be captured through access and time measures:

> When exclusive emphasis is placed on owning or having access by using these dichotomous have/have-not comparisons, the assumption is that either all haves will incorporate the technology into their everyday lives in the same manner and to the same degree or that the difference in the quality of Internet connection among the haves is unimportant. In other words, these measures introduce an element of technological determinism that ignores the social context in which the technology is incorporated. (p. 509)

By operationalizing 'connectedness' rather than 'access' and considering the digital divide less as 'a problem of ownership of the technology' than as 'a problem of developing a relationship with the technology,' Jung et al. seek to avoid descending into technological determinism. The study measures quality of internet use by developing the 'Internet Connectedness Index (ICI)'. Among the nine items that constitute the ICI are years of home computer ownership, number of tasks for which a person connects to the internet, and number of places where a person connects to the internet. In contrast to 'access', which first wave research operationalized as a technological binary, Jung et al. use a continuum to measure 'connectedness' to the internet. By evaluating 'connectedness', the authors aim to avoid 'such dichotomous comparisons ... [which] are not sufficient when discussing the social consequences of the technology's diffusion' (ibid). Thus, Jung et al. distinguish their work from hard digital dividist studies that measure access (Hoffman et al., 2001; U.S. Department of Commerce, 1995, 1999) and amount of time online (Hoffman et al., 2001; Nie and Erbring, 2001). By investigating 'the social context in which the technology is incorporated' (Jung et al., 2001: 509), and approaching the divide as 'a problem of developing a relationship with the technology' (p. 514), Jung et al. hoped to evade the technological determinism of first wave research.

However, Jung et al.'s study does not entirely jettison technologically determinist assumptions. Measuring the more nuanced divide of internet connection screens out other variables, like the coercive employment strategies of the high-tech industry. Such factors form an important part of the terrain Jung et al.'s study wants to problematize, namely, 'whether there is an ability to maximize the utility of [internet] technology for pursuit of various goals' (Jung et al., 2001: 508). Focusing on individuals' 'relationship' with the internet to the exclusion of structural trends in employment seems inspired by the belief, shared by the NTIA, that internet technologies are keys to the vault of Info-Age riches. As Jung et al. put it, 'When a technology becomes a resource for attaining or maintaining higher status in society, as computer-based technologies have increasingly become, unequal access to such technology becomes more than a question of ownership' (ibid). Articulating a soft technological determinism, where technology is a 'self-acting force which provides materials for new ways of life', Jung et al. imply that latent productivity and freedom enhancing abilities of internet technologies is ready for users 'to maximize'. Underscoring this point, the authors add that the digital divide is not comparable to a 'Mercedes divide' (as Bush's former FCC chair Michael Powell famously quipped), because 'even when compared with other resource-rich media, such as television, radio, or newspapers, computer technologies and the internet vastly expand the available resources that are central to career development'. In other words, diffusing internet access and more importantly, diffusing internet skills are 'central to career development' because digital technologies and skills provide means to employment.

Like Jung et al., Sevron's *Bridging the Digital Divide* seeks to push the definition of digital divide beyond the problem of access. Arguing that 'access is one dimension of the issue', Sevron (2002: 7) contends that two interrelated yet neglected aspects of the divide include training or 'IT literacy' and content that 'disenfranchised groups' create and utilize. With this expanded notion of the divide in mind, Sevron critiques past research, the 'evolution of government rhetoric', public policies, programs aimed at closing the divide, and the role of community technology centers (CTC) in diffusing access, skill, and content.

Of the digital divide research reviewed here, Sevron's comes closest to foregrounding the job market IT workers face. Her chapter, 'Training Disadvantaged Workers for IT Jobs' considers broad economic shifts and their impact on the IT job market. Moreover, in place of the more narrow notion of 'information disadvantaged' that reflects the NTIA's brand of technological determinism, Sevron (2002: 141) uses 'disadvantaged' to describe workers 'who have been largely detached from the labor force, who lack requisite skills, who may face discrimination in the labor market and/or who are currently unemployed or employed in jobs that fail to pay a living wage'. Such vocabulary attends to the ways in which workers are materially disadvantaged (lacking jobs or are paid sub-living wages) and considers information skills they need.

Sevron's take on the IT job market, however, reflects the business community's point of view. Without much critique, Sevron cites industry association data pointing to a labor shortage in IT industries during the boom. Sources for such information include industry group Information Technology Association of America (ITAA), who represents tech giants like Microsoft and IBM, outsourcing firms like WIPRO and Satyam, and the industry-heavy Council on Competitiveness that polls CEOs. According to these sources, 'disadvantaged' workers need IT skills to improve their chances of finding living waged work. As Sevron puts it, 'Workers who do not have IT skills have access to much less opportunity in the labor market than those who do' (ibid). Those without such competencies might become victims of a 'skills mismatch' who cede 'opportunity' to more highly trained workers. The tricky words here are 'access' and 'opportunity'. Certainly, individuals with less technical skill qualify for fewer jobs. And since 'access' to 'opportunity' implies possibility or perhaps, the possibility of possibility, Sevron is quite right to assert that possessing requisite technical skills makes winning a job possible. But as critique of the IT labor market demonstrates, technological proficiency and even mastery do not ensure stable, living waged work.

At times, Sevron appears poised for such a critique. After describing the skills mismatch, Sevron (2002: 144) discusses the 'spatial mismatch' wrought by info-tech's growth in a society segregated along race and class lines:

> Advances in IT have lessened locational constraints enabling firms offering low-skill jobs, particularly in manufacturing and routine services, to leave the inner city for the suburbs and, in some cases, overseas locations where production costs are lower. Meanwhile, segregation and discrimination have prohibited the poor and minority populations from following these jobs to the periphery, creating a spatial mismatch

between low-income urban residents and employment opportunities.

By Sevron's account, skill cannot overcome the lure of cheap labor markets. Poverty and racial discrimination conspires to prevent inner city residents from moving to employment centers. Sevron (2002: 144) also acknowledges that education does not necessarily expand job prospects: 'many jobs experiencing high growth do not require a four-year college education ... [as few as] one of eight higher than average growth occupations will require a college degree'. Such revelations imply that certain structural factors outweigh the significance of IT education and skills in today's job market.

Having discussed limited job opportunities for skilled and educated IT workers, Sevron contends, nevertheless, that tech training is necessary if workers are to 'lift themselves into living waged work'. On the one hand, 'new technologies have made it easier for corporations to move many of their operations to the suburbs', but on the other, 'addressing the digital divide is essential to ensuring that the entire range of workers can benefit from the opportunities the new economy provides' (ibid). The following paragraph best illustrates Sevron's glide from structural critique of the job market to embracing IT training. With only a grammatical transition between arguments, Sevron moves from acknowledging that high growth jobs do not necessarily demand education and training nor pay well to defending the claim that individuals need IT training to land decent jobs:

> Although not all of these high growth jobs are in IT or in well-paying sectors, many entry-level IT jobs also require less than a four-year college degree. *At the same time*, entry-level IT jobs do require specific skills, and the rapidly changing nature of the IT economy requires that IT workers continually upgrade their skills. (ibid, emphasis added)

In other words, high growth entry level IT jobs demand skills, not four-year college degrees.

Sevron's position is significant not because it is contradictory (it is not) but because it distinguishes between training and education. 'Furthermore,' Sevron adds, 'if we look at other occupational sectors we see that technology literacy is now viewed as part of the bundle of skills a worker must bring to the workforce' (ibid). In other words, today's employers want trained but not necessarily educated workers. As Noble (2001) argues in his work on the automation of higher education, the distinction between education and training is important. Education, Noble (2001: 2) argues, is an intensely interpersonal process in which individuals analyze, synthesize, criticize, and integrate knowledge into their being, for their use. Education, furthermore, demands the 'utter integration of knowledge and the self, in a word, self-knowledge'. 'Training,' in contrast, 'involves the honing of a person's mind so that his or her mind can be used for the purposes of someone other than that person' (ibid). Rather than advocating worker's self-growth and ability to participate in a democratic society, Sevron's embrace of training represents employers' interests in developing a work-ready labor force.[8] Perhaps Sevron's position in the field of management explains her uncritical support of business interests.[9]

*Virtual Inequality: Beyond the Digital Divide* (Mossberger et al., 2003) does an impressive job of expanding the definition of the digital divide beyond access. Like Sevron (2002), Mossberger et al. make the soft dividist argument that access is an essential element of the digital divide. They extend this argument by considering how gaps in technical skills and literacy interact with the access divide and demographic differences to produce an 'economic opportunity divide' and a 'democratic divide'. The authors define 'economic opportunity' as 'the ability to subsist above the poverty level, to enjoy some choice and mobility in the labor market, and to realize higher returns for additional experience, skills, and training' (Mossberger et al., 2003: 79). This basic level of subsistence and mobility, the authors note, is hardly guaranteed. The 'democratic divide' refers to discrepancies in participation in internet-mediated elections, accessing government documents and services electronically, and attitudes about using the internet for voting, gathering government information, and participating in town meetings. Mossberger et al. find that income, education, age, race, and ethnicity affect access to and skill in using computers and the internet. The authors conclude that lack of computer skills and literacy in reading and math impedes one's ability to use digital technology to become economically and politically empowered.

Although it expands the notion of digital divide, *Virtual Inequality* does not fully examine the structural changes necessary to extend 'economic opportunity.' Illustrating soft digital dividism's advocacy of skill over access, Mossberger et al. (2003: 67) argue that 'computer skills are best viewed as part of a package of basic skills, along with literacy and numeracy, which can enhance an individual's employability for a broader range of occupations'. Computer skills, furthermore, help workers complete job training and educational programs. More specifically, computer skills assist adult 'lifelong learners' to acquire basic literacy skills. Such programs seem educational, since individuals appear to put such skills to their own use (Noble, 2001). This 'education', however, is intended for exchange on the labor market. Through different language, Mossberger et al. (2003) follow Sevron in emphasizing the value of work-ready skills. In addition, by affirming Lester Thurow's characterization of 'knowledge as "the new basis for wealth" in the information age', Mossberger et al. (2003: 82) support the NTIA's position that such preparation extends economic benefits. It is not clear, however, that workers gain as much as do employers. *Virtual Inequality*'s focus on worker training expands the notion of access, but does not discern problems workers encounter once in the labor market, problems that constitute and reproduce significant economic and political divides.

Finally, although Mossberger et al. (2003: 136) cite Light's argument that 'Americans have a tendency to seek technological fixes for complex social problems', *Virtual Inequality* does not think far enough outside the box. They articulate a technologically determinist explanation of economic change by attributing it to IT. The authors credit information technology with boosting productivity in the late 1990s, enabling 'broader innovations in production processes and products that will continue to affect the economy', bringing about 'rising skills requirements in the labor force and changes in the opportunity structure for American workers' (Mossberger et al., 2003: 62). In the closing sentences of the book, the authors vacillate between hard and soft technological determinism:

> As computers, databases, and the internet have transformed processes of production and the dissemination of information, they have replicated – and, in some cases, exacerbated – long-standing inequalities. Computers and internet access will not remedy problems of racism, segregation, unequal education, unequal political participation, and economic inequality, but they represent one dimension of the problem of providing equal opportunity in a democratic society. Public policy that promotes access, skills, and the empowering potential of technology should represent one dimension of the solution as well. (Mossberger et al., 2003: 138)

After establishing the magnitude of computers' impact on our economy, the authors acknowledge other variables that account for socio-economic inequalities. While computers have 'transformed' production, they cannot solve the problems of racism, segregation and unequal education, political participation, and distribution of resources alone. 'The role of technology,' the authors conclude, 'should not be viewed in isolation from other challenges to full participation in society' (Mossberger et al., 2003: 138). To this, I would add that we should not privilege the promise of technology above other challenges.

Doing so, however, proves difficult even for the softest digital divide investigation. Warschauer's (2003) *Technology and Social Inclusion: Rethinking the Digital Divide* argues against the hard digital dividism of first wave government studies and academic research. Like Mossberger et al. (2003), Sevron (2002), Jung et al. (2001), and Light (2001), Warschauer urges communication scholars to rethink the digital divide by focusing on non-technological variables that interact with technological, social, economic, and political problems. Warschauer (2003: 6) doubts 'digital divide' can capture the nuances of the problem, because 'the original sense of digital divide ... attached overriding importance to the physical availability of computers and connectivity'. Facility with technology trumps its possession: 'What is most important about ICT (information and communication technology) is not so much the availability of the computing device or the internet line, but rather people's ability to *make use* of that device and line to engage in *meaningful social practices*' (Warschauer, 2003: 38). The argument that the 'essence of meaningful access to information and communication technologies' boils down to competency with rather than availability of ICTs distinguishes *Technology and Social Inclusion* as a second wave divide research.

Instead of examining the 'digital divide,' then, Warschauer (2003: 8) investigates 'the intersection of ICT and social inclusion'. For Warschauer, 'social inclusion' gets at problems that define the relationship between society and technology by signifying 'the extent that individuals, families, and communities are able to fully participate in society and control their own destinies, taking into account a variety of factors related to economic resources, employment, health, education, housing, recreation, culture, and civic engagement' (ibid). Investigating the relationship between social inclusion and technology is more fruitful than researching the presence of computers and network connections since 'social inclusion is a matter not only of an adequate share of resources', but also, borrowing from Stewart (2000), of the '"participation in the determination of both individual and collective life chances"' (ibid). Reconceptualizing the problem as one between 'technology' and 'social inclusion' enables analysis of technology's role in empowering individuals and social groups. Warschauer evaluates the extent to which programs in first and third world countries stimulate inclusion and argues that the point of policies and programs is not to overcome the digital divide, but to use technology to foster self-actualization and civic action around the world. His case studies are sensitive to the ways in which social forces affect a program's success in achieving inclusion. An analysis of Irish towns with technology grants demonstrates that the infusion of technology does not necessarily improve inclusion: the winning town, flush with a $22 million technology grant, failed to make meaningful social improvements, while three runners up awarded one-fifteenth of the winnings succeeded in doing so.

Despite attending to important social variables, *Technology and Social Inclusion* articulates a soft technological determinism typical of second wave digital divide research. Warschauer constructs technology as an engine of history. In 'Economy, Society, and Technology: Analyzing the Shifting Terrains', a chapter that depends heavily on Manuel Castells' work (Castells, 2001), Warschauer (2003:

12) argues that transistor-based technology has transformed production: 'The third [industrial] revolution came to fruition in the 1970s with the diffusion of the transistor, the personal computer and telecommunications'. Since the internet is becoming 'the electricity of the informational era', ICT 'can be a multiplying factor for social inclusion' (Warschauer, 2003: 29–30). As a result, Warschauer (2003: 211) argues, 'the overall policy challenge is not to overcome a digital divide but rather to expand access to and use of ICT for promoting social inclusion'. Despite supporting Jarboe's (2001: 8) call to 'focus on the transformation, not the technology', *Technology and Social Inclusion* abstracts technology from society, a hallmark of hard and soft determinism (Williams, 1992: 7). Describing ICTs' effects as indirect and symptomatic of other social phenomena softens Warschauer's determinism, but does not compensate for failing to consider how a lack of secure, living-waged jobs impacts inclusivity. As the next section suggests, making societies more inclusive demands more than intervention in development issues around technology. Building a truly equitable society requires the expansion of economic security and equality.

Although keen to push the debate beyond the digital divide, second wave scholarship does not adequately estimate the significance of the labor force divide. The following section examines the digital labor force divide around the exuberant close of the 20th century. Analysis focuses on discrepancies in pay, benefits, job security, and dignity workers experience in Seattle and other high-tech regions. Closing these gaps would promote the goals of second wave digital divide research by helping individuals 'attain or maintain higher status in society' (Jung et al., 2001: 508), 'access economic opportunity' (Mossberger et al., 2003), move into 'good jobs' (Sevron, 2002: 141), and increase 'social inclusion' (Warschauer, 2003).

## LABORING UNDER THE DIGITAL DIVIDE

The persistence of a divide in the sector promoted as boosting productivity and wealth, in a metropolitan area that epitomized the possibilities of the new economy, suggests that computer technologies are neither 'keys to the vault' of riches nor means to an 'Information Age Commonwealth'. This digital divide is expansive and has grown wider since the tech bust. Workers living in the Seattle metro area, near Bronstein's hometown, suffered heavy job losses during the recession. From February 2001 to April 2002, the high-tech sector shed an average of 640 jobs per month, for a total loss of 9,600 jobs over the 14-month period (Doussard and Mastracci, 2003). Consequently, Washington state technical workers have experienced a double-digit unemployment rate of 10.6 percent, nearly twice that of other employees in the state. The high-tech workforce in Seattle and the rest of the US is further divided into permanent and temporary, full and part time, and living and sub-living wage fractions (Doussard and Mastracci, 2003; Henwood, 2003; Worker Center, 2001).

These gaps predate the tech bust. During the boom Seattle-area techies worked in a bifurcated market of well-paying, permanent jobs and low-wage, insecure positions. In 1999, the top 1 percent of Seattle-area software workers (about 260 people) earned $12,000 an hour, while the bottom 5 percent (about 1,300 workers), earned $15.00 an hour.[10] Additionally, the top 10 percent of all 66,000 area IT workers earned $79.00 an hour or more, while the bottom 10 percent earned less than one-fifth of that; the median wage was approximately $31.00 an hour (Worker Center, 2001).[11] With the living wage in 1999 ranging between $17.00 and $20.00 per hour in the Seattle area (for a family of two children and one adult), a significant portion of IT workers earned incomes at or below living wage levels. The bottom 15 percent (about 7,200 people) earned less than a living wage, while another 5 percent made less than $19.00 an hour. Since the high-tech bubble burst, prospects for wage growth for IT workers have further soured. Nationwide payroll cuts (10%) between 2001 and 2002 were greater than net employment losses (4%), suggesting that remaining IT jobs pay less post-boom (Doussard and Mastracci, 2003: 8).[12]

Official wage estimates, however, are likely to be too generous because of gaps between accounting methods and labor practices. Washington State calculates hourly wages from payroll reports for 40-hour workweeks, but IT workers widely report working longer hours 'off the clock' and, therefore, off calculation sheets. Official data also excludes contingent workers like agency and independent contractors, who are classified as 'help supply service' along with non-IT contract workers from various industries. This move is significant because of the prevalence of contingent workers and their average wage. In 2000, agency temporaries accounted for more than 10 percent of Puget Sound's entire IT workforce and 11 percent of Microsoft's workforce.[13] Agency temps' hourly pay is less than permanent workers'. The mean quarterly wage for IT agency workers for the second quarter of 2000 was $12,772. Amounting to an annual wage of $51,088, this figure is less than 79 percent of the permanent worker's annual median wage of $65,000 (Worker Center, 2001).

Yet, this estimate is still inflated, because it disregards temps' downtime. Agency temps do not enjoy steady work, although 'permatemping', the practice of contracting long-term temporary workers, has been banned. For IT workers, however, the ban is more revanchist than helpful. In reaction to a class action lawsuit that Microsoft permatemps brought against the company (*Vizcaino v. Microsoft*), IT firms instituted mandatory layoffs of up to three months.[14] Further complicating calculations of temps' income are 'non-compete' clauses included in signing contracts. These agreements prohibit workers from easily changing agencies when unemployed between assignments. The same practice that frustrates contingents' search for steady work complicates the calculation of their annual income.

In addition to disparities in pay, Seattle-area tech workers also experience benefit gaps. Like other contract workers, IT contractors are routinely denied benefits like health insurance, pensions, and family and sick leave. Including individuals who make exorbitant co-payments, less than 11 percent of Seattle's contingent IT workers received health insurance through their employer (Doussard and Mastracci, 2003).[15] Vacation benefits are also difficult for temporaries to access. During the mid 1990s, when vacation benefits were more common, agencies required at least 1,500 hours of work to qualify for one week's bonus pay. Temporaries have also been excluded from employee stock option plans (ESOPs), a discrepancy named in the permatemps' suit against Microsoft.

Benefit and income estimates, however, cannot render the full spectrum of disparities that divide digital workers. Contingent high-tech workers suffer the double injury of low pay and a high work discipline. Some describe pressure to show appreciation for having a job. One IT call center worker earning $13.00 an hour claims coworkers routinely decline lunch breaks to prove they 'deserve' or feel 'grateful' for having jobs. The worker explains: 'People are grateful to work [at the call center] to get the experience, and then expect to move ... and make $90,000 a year ... Their attitude is ... they're unhappy because of low pay, but they'll get theirs in a year or so' (Worker Center, 2001). Doing unpaid work, in other words, performs thankfulness; it demonstrates that workers feel deserving of employment, and perhaps, promotion.[16]

Temporaries are also marked in ways that alienate them from full timers. Microsoft temps wear orange instead of the blue identity badges that signify permanent work status; temps' emails bear agency markings; they are denied access to softball fields and are prohibited from attending family barbecues. Not surprisingly, Microsoft temporaries complain about being treated as second-class workers:

> People don't talk to me. Blue badges don't talk to orange badges. They went skiing, I didn't get to go; they went to the movies, I didn't get to go ... you say 'hi' and they don't say hi back. It may sound silly, but it hurts my feelings – they don't let me join in any of the reindeer games. (Worker Center, 2001)

Other Microsoft temps agree: 'Temps are treated like lawn furniture to be allocated among offices' (Shapiro, 1999). One contractor puts it more bluntly, 'As a group they [Microsoft managers] think "we have to treat you like shit because you're a temporary employee'" (Worker Center, 2001).

The digital workforce is also increasingly divided by the exploitation of foreign labor, a trend that escalated during the boom and shows little sign of abating in its wake. Cheaper foreign workers are displacing US workers through the H-1B visa program and offshore outsourcing. Ostensibly designed to grant temporary work permits to technically skilled workers who fill jobs left vacant by a shortage of skilled US workers, the H-1B program provides employers access to uniquely skilled foreign workers on a temporary basis. Employers, however, have used the program during downturns in employment, often while laying off skilled workers. Abuse of the program is depressing wages in the US and will likely contribute to a global 'race to the bottom' (Tonelson, 2000). Estimates of visa holders' under-compensation vary. Immigrant programmers and engineers at UC Davis are paid 15–20 percent less than are permanent residents (Matloff, 2002). Nationally, the INS (Immigration and Naturalization Service) reports that H-1B visa holders in the computer industry are paid 20 percent less than the average prevailing wage; UCLA calculates guest engineers are paid 33 percent less, and the Department of Labor finds nearly one-fifth of H-1B holders are paid less than the salaries promised on visa application forms.[17] The appetite for guest workers has persisted after the boom. In response to industry lobbying, Congress raised the annual H-1B limit from 65,000 to 195,000 in legislation, covering FY 2000-FY 2002 and again in 2003. After the 65,000 visa limit for 2004 had been reached, corporations unsuccessfully lobbied for another extension (Matloff, 2002). The cap was extended for graduate students in 2005.[18]

If reduced labor costs make H-1B holders attractive to employers, so do the labor disciplining effects of the program. Specifically, the program enables contracting workers who are less likely to complain about long hours and underpayment than those who have established permanent residency in the US. Since expulsion from the US is a punishment workers want to avoid, H-1B visa holders appear more 'willing' than their permanent counterparts to work longer hours, for less pay, without complaint. This tacit rule, that guest workers must accept longer, perhaps even unpaid hours, also screens out older workers who are less able to work extended hours because of family demands. As one H-1B visa worker puts it, 'the younger guys, they'll work 15-hour days easily' (Bjorhus, 2002).

Another cost-cutting strategy, offshore outsourcing, also pits workers against each other. Offshore outsourcing sends work 'offshore', overseas to contractors who employ locals typically at a fraction of US workers' pay. The practice contributes to job flight and wage depression for entry-level and more senior, skilled positions. Amazon.com illustrated the benefits and costs of offshoring low-skill work when it sent customer service work to India. Striving to impress Wall Street by achieving profitability (or by achieving the appearance of striving for profitability), Amazon.com laid off 150 workers with one hour's notice weeks before the tech stock bust. Seven months later, amidst a union campaign, Amazon disclosed plans to outsource the same number of workers to India where it would send up to 80 percent of its customer service work. Amazon intended to pay workers less than one-tenth of Seattle workers' wages. Earning less than unionized customer service employees nationwide, a Seattle Amazonian earned $11 an hour or $1,900 per month of 40-hour workweeks. The same worker in India, however, cost between $109 and $179 per month. Seeking to drive down wages and head off a workers' union, Amazon announced dismissals of nearly all of its 400 Seattle-based customer service workers in January 2001 ('Amazon.com to Begin Outsourcing ...', 2000; Cohn, 2001; 'Layoffs: One Click Away', 2000).

Offshoring highly skilled work like software development also helps employers reduce labor costs and expand work hours. Claiming 'times are changing' at a July 2002 meeting, Microsoft senior vice president Brian Valentine told other managers: 'You CAN do it outside of Redmond ... outsourcing is not just for non-critical work ... Redmond is not the center of the universe.'[19] The global labor force has numerous advantages, or as Valentine put it, 'Going global gets you development leverage ... [to] ... extend the effective workday to about 16–18 hours.' Offshoring enables a virtually endless shift, since code can be input in one time zone and checked in another. Valentine singles out India, where Microsoft can 'leverage the Indian economy's lower cost structure ... [and] ... virtually any technical resource can be had'. Moreover, India boasts a 'large and technically qualified talent pool of 450,000 software engineers', a cheap, exploitable labor market that grows by 70,000 workers a year. In rather dehumanizing terms, Valentine concludes that Microsoft can get 'quality work at 50–60% of the cost ... that's 2 heads for the price of 1'. It appears that Valentine's plans are coming to fruition. Seattle-based labor union WashTech, the Washington Alliance of Technology Workers, has disclosed that Microsoft is sending work on its next operating system to India, and is doing so at more than twice the rate than the company publicly admits (Bishop, 2004).

Washington state agencies are also sending highly skilled IT work offshore. The Washington Healthcare Authority, which provides over one half million residents with access to health insurance, awarded a $3 million contract to update its eligibility and accounting programs to Healthaxis, a contractor that outsources a significant portion of the project to Satyam Computer Services in India. Meanwhile, the Washington Department of Corrections has signed a $25 million contract with IBM for a new offender management system. IBM is sending the work to its Indian facility (Beckman, 2003; Cook, 2003). Washington is not alone, as most state governments offshore work to some degree (Mattera, 2004).

National statistics also point to a 'great job exodus' in the IT industry (Beckman, 2003). From August 15, 2003 to August 15, 2004, US corporations offshored 214,022 jobs. Consequently, the US economy lost 120,521 jobs (Offshore Tracker, 2006). Gartner forecasts that 25 percent of all IT jobs will be offshored by 2008 (Reingold, 2004), and Forrester Research predicts that over the next 15 years, US companies will offshore 3.3 million service jobs, 1 million of them in IT, totaling $136 billion in lost wages (Frauenheim, 2004; Gaudin, 2002; Geary, 2004). Although such estimates might prove overly pessimistic, nearly one-fourth of those responding to a high-tech worker survey claimed their employer had already offshored work, and one-fifth had either trained their foreign replacement post layoff or knew someone who had ('A Survey of Information Technology Workers', 2004; Beckman, 2004).

While offshoring's contribution to job loss has attracted substantial media coverage, an equally disastrous though under-reported effect of offshoring is its impact on the wages and spirits of US workers. Jared Bernstein of the Economic Policy Institute attributes 15–25 percent of wage declines in the US to globalization (Doussard and Mastracci, 2003). The psychological effects are also significant. Bronstein, the Seattle-area software engineer forced to train her offshore replacement under threat of being denied severance, testified before the Washington State Legislature in early 2004 that she experienced such demands as demeaning, especially after working so hard for the company (Bronstein, 2004).

## WORKING THROUGH THE DIGITAL DIVIDE

Our analysis of the digital workforce divide suggests that first and second wave digital divide scholars remain overly optimistic that access to the newest technology and acquisition of technical skills provide passage out of low-wage, temporary work. Technical skills and access cannot guarantee such rewards, because the digital divide is structural; it exists in the labor market, in the hiring practices of IT and contract employers, not in the wires, chips, or ether. Nor does it exist in the minds and hands of those accessing them. When workers like Bronstein train their offshore replacements, it is not lack of IT skills that costs jobs; it is the employer who embraces offshoring to keep costs low and discipline high. Although digital divide programs promise to help some improve their lot, first and second wave digital divide research implies that it is the individual's responsibility to do so. This message contributes to the 'politics of the self' (Cloud, 2001) that spotlights individual improvement over broader social change. Focus on the self frustrates the wider structural critique in which we need to engage to close gaping socio-economic divides and avoid contributing to management and marketing agendas.

In shifting the focus of the debate, however, critics of the digital divide should consider the strategic challenges we will encounter. Perhaps the most significant of these is the need to critique the terms of the debate without further instigating social welfare funding cuts. Recent years have not been kind to digital divide remediation funding. The FY 2004 budget slashed two programs designed to close the access and skills divide. The CTC (community technology) budget shrank from over $32 million to $9.9 million, and the $62 million PT3 ('preparing tomorrow's teachers to use technology') was eliminated ('Legislative Update', 2004). We should not read these cuts, however, as a lack of commitment to closing the digital divide or as a vulgar brand of Luddism. Rather than signifying flagging enthusiasm for diffusing digital technology, such reductions signal a broader retreat from publicly supported education. George W. Bush's 2005 budget eliminated 38 federal education programs totaling $1.4 billion, in addition to $9.4 billion in cuts to his own 'No Child Left Behind', and $247 million to a program that teaches parents and children in poor households to read (Gilson, 2004). We must also recognize that the decrease in commitment to public education is not new to the post-boom, post-Bush moment. During Washington state's technology boom, increases in undergraduate tuition exceeded growth in the state's per capita personal income by 50 percent and grew twice as fast as inflation. Also during this period, the state's contribution to higher education funding shrank from more than five times that generated by tuition and fees to less than three times the amount (Washington Higher Education Coordinating Board, 2002).

Widespread retreat from publicly funded education and reductions in programs aimed at closing the digital divide suggest that we engage in constructive criticism of the divide debate. What I mean by this is that in addition to analyzing the debate (i.e., doing 'criticism'), we should create an alternative plan to eliminate underlying social disparities (i.e., being 'constructive'). We should begin by including current and prospective IT workers whose voices have been left out of the debate. A conversation between IT workers and those on the losing end of recent budget cuts, including instructors and CTC and PT3 administrators, would allow interested parties to draft funding proposals for programs that directly serve IT workers' needs. Freed from the constraints of earlier conceptions of the divide as a problem of access and skill, participants can consider alternatives beyond those that use digital technology to redress inequities.

Constructively critiquing the digital divide debate also promises a fruitful project for the field of communication in general and new media scholarship in particular. Like so many disciplines in the age of dwindling public funds for education, communication needs to differentiate itself from other fields to avoid the appearance of duplicating research and course offerings. Robert McChesney argues that our unique critical abilities boost the prestige of our discipline. Not mincing words, McChesney (1997: 572) warns, 'If we accept the turn to purely market-driven communication as legitimate, we almost certainly undermine any justification for the field's existence'. That public support for education has dwindled during the seven years since McChesney's admonition should provide more not less grist for our critical mill.

Thus, as I have been arguing throughout this article, we need to expand the debate to focus on the digital labor force divide. New media scholars in communication departments are well positioned to engage in a more thorough-going critique than are others who have called for broader thinking. Working outside management and marketing departments, we can explore the ways in which past digital divide research has served management ends by supporting production of a large labor pool with work-ready skills. We are free to investigate how expanding the H-1B visa program, offshoring, and a US labor market with IT skills, creates a global labor pool for employers to exploit. We can examine how employers use cheaper segments of this large labor pool against each other to drive down wages. In this instance, 'competition' is not between the best products or most talented companies, but between the cheapest workers. New media scholars can also consider how debates like the digital divide serve marketing ends by promoting the diffusion of technology instead of the expansion of democracy. Without intervention, the debate will continue to operate as a discourse that fuels consumption rather than fosters equality.

Studies that combine textual critique of the rhetoric that promotes digital technologies with structural critique of the labor market both advance new media research and support the underlying principles of digital divide scholarship. Summing up these ideals, Jorge Schement argues that closing the digital divide is the key to a vibrant democracy, 'As we breathe life into the Republic, we will demand access so that all citizens may participate in the economic, political, and social life of a democratic society that is also a good society' (Schement, 2001: 307). Contributing to this project means closing the wider gaps that the digital divide, as previously constructed, metonymizes.

Our teaching and service can also serve democratizing ends. After all, many of us train tomorrow's and today's IT employees. By including critical explorations of IT work in our courses, we alert students to challenges they face; by providing opportunities for them to take action, we encourage their political participation. Critical analysis of the digital divide promises to strengthen our work as teachers and scholars. Thus, closing the divides that cleave the IT labor force into haves and have-nots is an important intellectual and political project. Eliminating such disparities requires us to work through the digital divide rather than labor underneath it.

## Notes

[1] According to Reich's taxonomy, symbolic analysts engage in problem-solving, problem-identifying, and strategic-brokering. They manipulate symbols (data, words, oral and visual representations) and hold jobs that require conceptualization, analysis, and communication. They include engineers, scientists, lawyers, and 'even university professors' (Reich, 1992: 177). When not working with their teammates, 'symbolic analysts sit before computer terminals,' manipulating symbols (p. 179). Reich later revised his argument. In *The Future of Success: Work and Living in the New Economy* (2000), Reich dispels the notion that tech-related jobs necessarily employ symbolic analysts (p. 100).

[2] Morrisett acknowledges using the term 'digital divide' but has expressed doubts that he coined it (Compaine, 2001, p. xiv).

[3] Silver considers digital divide research, including early NTIA (The National Telecommunication and Information Administation) studies, as constitutive of the critical turn in cyberculture studies. However, I find that the hard technological determinism of digital divide scholarship precludes the kind of structural critique (i.e., of employment trends under late capitalism) necessary for eradicating the gap between the haves and have-nots.

[4] See Noble (1984) for further discussion of technological determinism's political import, especially, its use in the defense of capitalism.

[5] The Commerce Department uses 'information haves and have-nots' to describe what it later calls the 'digital divide'.

[6] In a similar vein, Apple Computer has promoted its strategy to reach black urban youths in public schools as a philanthropic rather than marketing campaign (Sterne, 2000).

[7] Use is measured by asking respondents when they first used the web, last used the web, how frequently they used the web, and where they used the web. The number of responses for categories like 'in past two years' and 'at home' are presented in tables (Hoffman et al., 2001: 62–63).

[8] The distinction between education and training constitutes a division of labor, like that between head and handwork, which preoccupied an earlier phase of industrial capitalist managers (Braverman, 1974; Head, 2003; Noble, 1984).

[9] When her book was published, Lisa Sevron was Associate Professor of Management and Urban Policy, and Associate Director, Community Development Research Center, Milano Graduate School of Management and Urban Policy, New School University, New York.

[10] These figures exclude Bill Gates and other chief executives.

[11] The category 'IT workers' includes programmers, indexers, and data entry clerks

in sectors ranging from aircraft manufacturing to government.

［12］ Doussard and Mastracci (2003) argue that since wage data does not include the withered value of stock options that direct-hire IT workers received during the boom, total compensation has further declined. Doussard and Mastracci (2003) and the Worker Center (2001) use Washington State Employment Security Department wage data reported for Computer Industries (Standard Industrial Codes 737), wage data for the sub-industry of Prepackaged Software (SIC 7372), and wage data for Help Supply Services (SIC 7363) for 1999. The 2003 study also analyzes data from the US Current Population Survey (CPS) to describe trends, demographic and structural, in Seattle's high-tech workforce. The 2001 study supplements analysis of statistical data with interviews of IT workers in Seattle's King County. The Worker Center's study and the present analysis use 'Seattle area' and 'Puget Sound region' interchangeably to signify the three counties surrounding Seattle: King, Pierce, and Snohomish.

［13］ M. Courtney, personal communication, July 3, 2002; Worker Center, 2001.

［14］ After working more than 364 days, Microsoft temps must take a minimum 100 day 'leave' before being rehired. Other companies have 100 day 'leave' policies. WashTech President Marcus Courtney describes the policy as retaliation against temps for the lawsuit (M. Courtney, personal communication, July 3, 2002: Worker Center, 2001: 16).

［15］ One agency that provides health insurance requires prohibitively expensive monthly contributions of $150 (Worker Center, 2001).

［16］ Showing appreciation for having a job seems to have become a commonplace feature of the labor discipline for workers in insecure positions. One Lehman Brothers worker reports that, after surviving several rounds of layoffs, management asked her to smile more often so she appeared grateful for having a job (Fraser, 2001: 15).

［17］ For further discussion of the INS study, see Bjorhus (2002).

［18］ M. Courtney (personal communication, March 28, 2005).

［19］ WashTech obtained these slides from an anonymous Microsoft worker. For news coverage of Valentine's offshoring presentation, see Gongloff (2003) and Heim (2003). Contact author for slides.

## References

'A Survey of Information Technology Workers' (February 11, 2004) Seattle, WA: Evans & McDonough.

'Amazon.com to Begin Outsourcing Customer Service Operations to India' (September 7, 2000) *WashTech News*, URL (consulted January 1, 2001): http://www.washtech.org/amazon/090700_india.php3

Beckman, D. (January 24, 2003) 'The Great Tech Job Exodus', *Tech Worker News, TechsUnite*, URL (consulted April 3, 2006): http://www.washtech.org/news/industry/

display.php?ID_content=441

Beckman, D. (February 13, 2004) 'Survey Reflects U.S. Tech Worker Angst', *WashTech News*, URL (consulted February 13, 2006): http://www.techsunite.org/news/techind/040213_survey.cfm

Bishop, T. (July 29, 2004) 'Union: Work Going Offshore', *Seattle-Post Intelligencer*: E1, E2.

Bjorhus, J. (September 26, 2002) 'U.S. Workers Taking H-1B Issues to Court', *Mercury News*, URL (consulted 3 April, 2006): http://72.14.203.104/search?q=cache: kQk8muDOuoIJ:www.usbc.org/info/everything2002/0902h1btocourt.htm+ Workers+Taking+H-1B+Issues+to+Court+bjorhus&h1=en&lr+&strip=0

Braverman, H. (1974) *Labor and Monopoly Capital: The Degradation of Work in the Twentieth Century*. New York: Monthly Review Press.

Bronstein, M. (February 19, 2004) Testimony given to the Committees of Commerce and Labor, House State Government, and House Trade and Economic Development, Washington State Legislature, Olympia, Washington.

Castells, M. (2001) *Internet Galaxy: Reflections on the Internet, Business, and Society*. New York: Oxford University Press.

Cloud, D. (2001) 'Laboring Under the Sign of the New: Cultural Studies, Organizational Communication, and the Fallacy of the New Economy', *Management Communication Quarterly* 15(2): 268–278.

Cohn, J. (February 19, 2001) 'Amazon.com and the Return of the Old Economy', *The New Republic Online*, URL (consulted April 11, 2005): http://www.tnr.com

Compaine, B. (2001) 'Preface', in B. Compaine (ed.) *The Digital Divide: Facing a Crisis or Creating a Myth?*, pp. xi–xvi. Cambridge, MA: MIT Press.

Cook, J. (December 17, 2003) 'State Jobs Moving to Workers Overseas', *Seattle Post-Intelligencer*, URL (consulted April 3, 2006): http://seattlepi.nwsource.com/business/152829_outsource17.html.

Doussard, M. and S. Mastracci (2003) '*Uncertain Futures: The Real Impact of the High Tech Boom and Bust on Seattle's IT Workers*', Center for Urban Economic Development, University of Illinois at Chicago, URL (consulted April 1, 2006): http://www.washtech.org/reports/UncertainFutures/UncertainFutures.pdf

Fraser, A. (2001) *White Collar Sweatshop: The Deterioration of Work and Its Rewards in Corporate America*. New York: W.W. Norton & Company.

Frauenheim, E. (August 10, 2004) 'Statistician Defends his Outsourcing Figures', *CNET News.com*, URL (consulted April 3, 2006): http://insight.zdnet.co.uk/business/employment/0,39020484,39163028,00.htm

Gaudin, S. (November 19, 2002) 'Nearly 1 Million IT Jobs Moving Offshore', *Datamation*, URL (consulted April 3, 2006): http://itmanagement.earthweb.com/ career/article.php/1503461

Geary, L. (January 9, 2004) 'Structural Change in the Economy Means Many Jobs Are Never Going to Come Back', *CNN/Money*, URL (consulted April 3, 2006): http://money.cnn.

com/2003/ 12/17/pf/q_nomorework/

Gilson, D. (May–June, 2004) 'Left Behind', *Mother Jones:* 43.

Gongloff, M. (July 22, 2003) 'U.S. Jobs Jumping Ship', *CNN/Money*, URL (consulted April 3, 2006): http://money.cnn.com/2003/07/22/news/economy/jobless_offshore/

Gumpert, G. and S. Drucker (2002) 'Information Society: The Digital Divide, Redefining the Concept', *Intermedia* 30(4): 8–12.

Head, S. (2003) *The New Ruthless Economy: Work and Power in the Digital Age.* New York: Oxford University Press.

Heim, K. (January 25, 2003) 'Labor Group Protests Offshore Tech Hiring', *Mercury News*, URL (consulted April 3, 2006): http://72.14.203.104/search?q=cache:cr3r7IPHK7AJ:https://mail2,cni.org/Redirect/www.bayarea.com/mld/mercurynews/business/S029306.htm+heim+Labor+Group+Protests+Offshore+Tech+ Hiring&hl=en&gl=us&ct=clnk&cd=1

Henwood, D. (2003) *After the New Economy: The Binge ... And the Hangover That Won't Go Away.* New York: The New Press.

Hoffman, D., T. Novak and A. Schlosser (2001) 'The Evolution of the Digital Divide: Examining the Relationship of Race to Internet Access and Usage over Time', in B. Compaine (ed.) *The Digital Divide: Facing a Crisis or Creating a Myth?*, pp. 47–97. Cambridge, MA: MIT Press.

Jarboe, K. (2001) 'Inclusion in the Information Age: Reframing the Debate', Washington, DC: Athena Alliance. URL (consulted April 3, 2006): http://www.athenaaliance.org/inclusion.html

Jung, J., J. Qiu and Y. Kim (2001) 'Internet Connectedness and Inequality: Beyond the "Divide"', *Communication Research* 28(4): 507–535.

'Layoffs: One Click Away' (November/December, 2000) *Washington Free Press*, URL (consulted April 3, 2006): http://www.washingtonfreepress.org/48/layoffs.html

'Legislative Update' (2004) February 2004 ISTE Washington Notes, *International Society for Technology in Education*, URL (consulted April 3, 2006): http://www.iste.org/content/NavigationMenu/Advocacy/Policy/Washington_Notes/20046/Feb5/Feb.htm

Light, J. (2001) 'Rethinking the Digital Divide', *Harvard Educational Review* 71(4):709–733.

McChesney, R. (1997) 'Wither Communication?', *Journal of Broadcasting & Electronic Media* 41(4): 566–572.

Matloff, N. (2002) 'Debunking the Myth of a Desperate Software Labor Shortage', *Testimony to the U.S. House Judiciary Committee, Subcommittee on Immigration.* URL (consulted April 3, 2006): http://heather.cs.ucdavis.edu/itaa.others.html

Mattera, P. (2004) *Your Tax Dollars at Work...Offshore: How Foreign Outsourcing Firms Are Capturing State Government Contracts.* Washington, DC: Corporate Research Project of Good Jobs First.

Mossberger, K., C. Tolbert and M. Stansbury (2003) *Virtual Inequality: Beyond the Digital Divide.* Washington, DC: Georgetown University.

Nie, N. and L. Erbring (2001) 'Internet and Society: A Preliminary Report', in B. Compaine (ed.) *The Digital Divide: Facing a Crisis or Creating a Myth?*, pp. 269–271. Cambridge, MA: MIT Press.

Noble, D. (1984) *Forces of Production: A Social History of Industrial Automation*. New York: Oxford University Press.

Noble, D. (2001) *Digital Diploma Mills: The Automation of Higher Education*. New York: Monthly Review Press.

'Offshore Tracker' (April 3, 2006) URL (consulted April 3, 2006): http://www.techsunite.org/offshore/

Reich, R. (1992) *The Work of Nations: Preparing Ourselves for 21st Century Capitalism*. New York: Vintage.

Reich, R. (2000) *The Future of Success: Working and Living in the New Economy*. New York: Alfred A. Knopf.

Reingold, J. (April 1, 2004) 'Into Thin Air', *Fast Company*: 76–82.

Roach, R. (November 20, 2003) 'Report: Digital Divide Rooted in Home Computer Ownership', *Black Issues in Higher Education* 20: 50.

Schement, J. (2001) 'Of Gaps by Which Democracy We Measure', in B. Compaine (ed.) *The Digital Divide: Facing a Crisis or Creating a Myth?*, pp. 303–307. Cambridge, MA: MIT Press.

Sevron, L. (2002) *Bridging the Digital Divide: Technology, Community, and Public Policy*. Malden, MA: Blackwell.

Shapiro, S. (February 18, 1999) 'Temp's Rights', *The Stranger*: 9.

Silver, D. (2000) 'Looking Backwards, Looking Forwards: Cyberculture Studies 1990–2000', in D. Gauntlett (ed.) *Rewiring Media Studies for the Digital Age*, pp. 2–30. New York: Arnold.

Slack, J. (1984) 'Surveying the Impacts of Communication Technologies', in B. Dervin and M. Voigt (eds.) *Progress in Communication Sciences*, pp. 73–109. Norwood, NJ: Ablex.

Smith, P. (1997) *Millennial Dreams: Contemporary Culture and Capital in the North*. New York: Verso.

Sterne, J. (2000) 'The Computer Race Goes to Class: How Computers in Schools Helped Shape the Racial Topography of the Internet', in B. Kolko, L. Nakamura and G. Rodman (eds.) *Race in Cyberspace*, pp. 191–212. New York: Routledge.

Stewart, A. (2000) 'Social Inclusion: An Introduction', in P. Askonas and A. Stewart (eds.) *Social Inclusion: Possibilities and Tensions*, pp. 1–16. London: Macmillan.

Tonelson, A. (2000) *The Race to the Bottom: Why a Worldwide Worker Surplus and Uncontrolled Free Trade Are Sinking American Living Standards*. Boulder, CO: Westview Press.

U.S. Department of Commerce (1995) *Falling Through the Net: A Survey of the 'Have-Nots' in Rural and Urban America*. URL (consulted February 16, 2006): http://www.ntia.doc.gov/ntiahome/fallingthru.html

U.S. Department of Commerce (1999) *Falling Through the Net: Defining the Digital Divide*.

URL (consulted February 16, 2006): http://www.ntia.doc.gov/ntiahome/fttn99

U.S. Department of Commerce (2002) *A Nation Online: How Americans Are Expanding Their Use of the Internet*. URL (consulted February 16, 2006): http://www.ntia.doc.gov/ntiahome/

Warschauer, M. (2003) *Technology and Social Inclusion: Rethinking the Digital Divide*. Cambridge, MA: MIT Press.

Washington Higher Education Coordinating Board (January, 2002) *Washington Tuition Fee Report*, URL (consulted February 16, 2006): http://www.hecb.wa.gov/Docs/reports/TFWash01-02.pdf

Williams, R. (1992[1974]) *Television: Technology and Cultural Form*. Hanover, NH: Wesleyan University Press.

Worker Center (2001) Disparities Within the Digital World: Realities of the New Economy: A Report for the Washington Alliance of Technology Workers (WashTech), Communication Workers of America, Local 37083, URL (consulted April 3, 2006): http://washtech.org/reports/FordReport/ Ford_report.pdf

# Gendered Futures? Women, the ICT Workplace and Stories of the Future

Karenza Moore（卡伦娜·穆尔） Marie Griffiths（玛丽·格里菲思）
Helen Richardson（海伦·理查森） Alison Adam（艾莉森·亚当）[①]

[导读] 在英国的信息与通信技术领域,女性是一个素来不受关注的群体,而且这个趋势可能在未来也得不到改变。大约有 16% 的女性服务于这个领域,且主要集中于低收入的部门。在这篇论文中,作者们从信息与通信技术部门内职业女性的视角出发,通过社会性别、技术和未来之间的相互建构,在乌托邦和反乌托邦的二元分析框架内,勾勒出在女性日常生活中所发生的社会和技术的变化。

就技术对女性未来的影响,一直存在着乌托邦和反乌托邦之间的二元张力。一方面,乌托邦的观点认为,信息高度集中的服务部门的扩张意

---

① Karenza Moore, 现任教于英国兰卡斯特大学（Lancaster University）应用社会科学系。她的研究方向聚焦于软件工程伦理、传播技术的社会和犯罪问题,曾在《欧洲成瘾研究》（*European Addiction Research*）、《犯罪与刑事司法》（*Criminology & Criminal Justice*）、《当代毒品问题》（*Contemporary Drug Problems*）等期刊上发表学术论文多篇。

Marie Griffiths, 现任教于英国索尔福德大学（University of Salford）索尔福德商学院。她的研究方向聚焦于新媒体、商业中电子技术的作用、技术的社会影响,曾在《国际管理实践》（*International Journal of Management Practice*）、《技术管理与创新》（*Journal of Technology Management & Innovation*）、《传播与社会》（*Communication & Society*）等期刊上发表学术论文多篇。

Helen Richardson, 现任教于英国索尔福德大学信息系统学院。她的研究方向聚焦于科学技术研究、社会性别和科技,曾在《新技术、工作与就业》（*New Technology, Work & Employment*）、《工作、就业与社会》（*Work, Employment & Society*）、《信息系统前沿》（*Information Systems Frontiers*）等期刊上发表学术论文多篇。

Alison Adam, 现任教于英国谢菲尔德哈勒姆大学（Sheffield Hallam University）科学、技术与社会学院。她的研究方向聚焦于信息系统、社会性别研究和法医学历史,曾在《伦理与信息技术》（*Ethics and Information Technology*）、《信息、传播与社会》（*Information, Communication & Society*）等期刊上发表学术论文多篇。

味着女性可以从知识经济的终身学习模式中受益。在知识经济中,女性能够更好地发挥她们的交流和社会技能,以及"柔性"的管理方式。另一方面,反乌托邦的观点认为,随着未来的后工业资本主义社会仍依赖于廉价和短期的劳动力,女性仍是劳动力的重要组成部分;对于女性来说,她们不得不面对弹性雇佣制度,如在呼叫中心和快餐店打工。此外,随着在办公室和家庭中数字监控的日益泛滥,女性参与公共空间活动的可能性越来越小,同时加重了女性在家庭中的负担,更不用说与日俱增的外包,使得广大的女性——尤其是发展中国家的女性境况堪忧。总之,作者们认为,社会的未来是技术的未来,这一未来通过科学和技术、经济和政治等途径,脱胎于当代工业社会之中。当今社会越来越多地受到技术的影响,人类活动几乎已经离不开科技,而这种社会技术的未来同时具有性别性——未来社会是否可以成为一个更乌托邦的、更为解放的社会,我们不得而知。

在此基础上,作者们考量了与信息与通信技术相关的两种未来的趋势和可能性:信息与通信技术的外包实践和全球再定位、混合性/桥梁纽带成为信息与通信技术职业的核心特征,这为女性带来了更多的就业机会。通过对479位和12位女性信息与通信技术工作者的问卷调查和深度访谈,作者们指出,全世界的工作在社会性别关系方面可能会发生改变,但是"技术的男性化特征"却依旧顽固;而一种在社会性别、年龄、种族上多元化的劳动力组成才能消解"技术定时炸弹"(skills time bomb)。与此同时,混合性/桥梁纽带工作者将通过重新塑造科技和商业之间的关系,来推进信息与通信技术产业的发展,这种能力在一定程度上加强了不同群体间的交流(这些群体可能因为外包和全球再定位在地理上分离)。

网络技术在市场扩张、破除地理限制和消解组织方面发挥了重要的作用。外包实践为更多的女性进入劳动力市场提供了可能,但是在这个过程中,女性技能的价值被重新界定,同时她们可能也会因为不断贬值的技能,失去先前的地位和薪酬。在亚洲,随着越来越多的女性参与到信息与通信技术领域之中,她们的社会流动性增强和收入增多的同时,带来的却是地区性社会性别和科技关系的重塑。但是,考虑到基于性别的家庭劳动分工的固化,信息与通信技术领域的亚洲女性工作者在责任上的整体压力不断增加。而外包和全球再定位对于英国女性工作者的影响同样存在积极的和消极的方面。对于女性整体未来故事的描述是现代社会性别关系这个更宽泛的话语的一部分(往往由产业、跨国组织、政府和媒体共同构成),也是了解当代社会性别、工作、时间和科技话语中存在的问题的有效途径。同时,对于女性个体前景的分析需要将其放置在更广泛的未来话语之下,考察个体未来、社会技术未来和其他未来之间的关系,进而更细致和全面地理解这些要素是如何被性别化的,以及性别过程是如何发生的。

## INTRODUCTION

Women remain under-represented in the information and communications technology (ICT) profession in the UK and this seems likely to continue in the future. In terms of recruitment trends in the UK, it is estimated that the overall proportion of women working in ICT occupations is around 16 percent. In addition, women are concentrated in the lower paid ICT sectors (e-skills, 2006). Regarding retention, the Women in IT Champions Group (2003) report on achieving workforce diversity indicates that in recent years more women leave the ICT industry than are being recruited, so while 36 percent of new IT engagements in the UK (in the first quarter of 2002) were women, in the same period women accounted for 46 percent of all leavers. The low numbers of women in science, engineering and technology (SET) sectors more generally is of concern to liberal feminists[1] and 'technofeminists'[2] alike. From a latter perspective, Wajcman (2004: 111) writes:

> What has been missing from much of the debate about getting women into technoscience is that their under-representation profoundly affects how the world is made. Every aspect of our lives is touched by socio-technical systems, and unless women are in the engine rooms of technological production, we cannot get our hands on the levers of power.

Wajcman highlights the importance of imagining how different, if at all, our socio-technical world might be if women had a greater involvement in the shaping of technologies now and in the future, while stressing the important role that women's agency plays in transforming technologies. Those in industrial and educational sectors are concerned about the low numbers of women participating in computing and ICT precisely, because computer competence and engagement with ICTs has a broader impact on social life:

> The fact that women have practically no voice in the creation of major technological innovations that control our lives is surely to the detriment of the industry and society as a whole. (Selby et al., 1997: 6)

While there may be a highly problematic 'genderless' or 'gender-neutral' understanding of technological design and an absence of women at the design point (Henwood, 1993), gender reappears in full flow downstream, given that women are ubiquitous users of office and domestic technologies, for example, and shape their use (Wajcman, 2004).

Figures on female under-representation (e-skills, 2004a, 2006; Equal Opportunities Commission [EOC], 2005) and gender/age ICT workforce imbalances (Griffiths et al., 2007a, 2007b; Platman and Taylor, 2004) offer a contemporary picture of broad trends in the UK ICT sector, but do little to illuminate the future, as it is envisaged by professional women who are working in these often numerically and symbolically male-dominated ICT work environments. While it is laudable to focus on current female under-representation, this can leave largely unexplored the relationship between gender and ICTs, and the role the future plays in (re)producing gender relations. Looking at the co-construction of gender, technology, and the future through the eyes of professional women involved in the ICT sector means that we can challenge the assumptions embedded in these futures, and better reflect on the present state of play.

An explicit concern with the future, in the sense we present here is a relatively recent undertaking in the social sciences, although there are precedents, most notably, Wendell Bell and James Mau's (1971) *The Sociology of the Future: Theory, Cases and Annotated Bibliography* (for a discussion of early sociological approaches to the future, see Adam [2004b] and Moore [2003]). Shifts in thinking about time and the future are epitomized by the development of Barbara Adam's research interests (Adam, 1990, 1995, 1998, 2004a, 2004b, 2006) towards an explicit interest in the future. Looking at gendered futures is but one part of a wider academic remit of working towards a comprehensive, socially relevant theory of the future (Adam, 2004b; Moore, 2003) and a better understanding of relationships between technology and time (Wajcman, 2008).

The future is often depicted in terms of general (statistical) trends and taken as an abstract temporal entity that naturally follows on from the present moment. We suggest an alternative perspective on the future; not as a linear point in time that inevitably follows on from the past and present, but as a 'contested object of social and material action' (Brown et al., 2000: 3). Above all, futures are contested and complex (Urry, 2008). There remains disagreement about what the future will hold and should hold. Such contestations about future possibilities are at the very heart of what is defined as 'progress' and what actions are assumed to bring about or fail to bring about such progress. Rather than an abstract temporal entity, the future becomes something of interest to those attempting to understand the gendering of contemporary life. In keeping with this alternative, socially constructed view of the future, Brown et al. (2000: 3) suggest that:

> if actors are to secure successfully for themselves a specific kind of the future, then they must engage in a range of rhetorical, organizational and material activities through which the future might able to be colonised.

It has been suggested that the future can be thought of as an everyday mundane undertaking, engaged with by all groups of gendered social actants. In terms of gender and technology, much is at stake when these divergent groups produce the future. Subsequently, we must start fully engaging with those visions or stories of the future that shape and are shaped by gender and technology relations.

Writing on the relationship between feminism and technological advances, Wajcman (2004: 3) suggests that 'Feminism has long been conflicted [however] about the impact of technology on women, torn between utopian and dystopian visions of what the future may hold'. Utopian visions of the future[3] hold that the expansion of the information-intensive service sector means that women can benefit from the lifelong learning models of the knowledge economy as work becomes based on expertise, judgement and discretion. The (feminist) utopian view of this 'knowledge economy' is that women are best placed to capitalize on the growth in service work which utilizes 'feminine aptitudes for communication and social skills' (Wajcman, 2004: 5) and 'soft' styles of management (Wajcman, 1998). Alongside the (supposed) emancipatory potential of the Internet, where women can 'transcend' their corporeal 'limitations' to participate fully in the digital age (Turkle, 1995), one might be forgiven for thinking that the future of work (particularly in the ICT sector) is 'female' (Wajcman, 2004).

At the other extreme, dystopian visions of the future seen through the lens of various feminisms posit that technological advances will continue to subjugate women through the masculine project of dominating women and nature (see Henwood et al. [2000] for a critique of these polarized views of technologies and inequalities). From this view, for example, life becomes further biomedicalized and commodified through genetic and reproductive engineering.

In the world of work, the demands of post-industrial capitalist society for cheap and flexible labour will continue, with women remaining the pool from which the 'knowledge economy' draws to maintain and extend its capital gains. Writing about the dystopian flipside of 'emancipatory' socio-technical networks, Wajcman (2004: 5) notes that 'this future can also be depicted as a proliferation of flexible, temporary and contingent jobs for women ... typified by call centres and fast food establishments'. Increased capacity for digital surveillance of office and home-based employees (Whitty, 2004), tele/homeworking which undermines women's participation in the public sphere and can exacerbate women's domestic burden, and the growing practice of offshoring, or the global location of tasks to low-cost, often female labour in developing countries, all contribute to a dystopian view of the future in which women continue to be at a considerable disadvantage.

These contested futures need to be interrogated in relation to possibilities for the improvement of women's standing. We suggest that through research with female ICT professionals, it is possible to begin exploring the ways in which women's everyday lives intertwine with socio-technical change, for better and for worse, while steering a course between utopian and dystopian visions of the future. Before we move on to specifically placing female ICT professionals' futures in the context of the utopian/dystopian dichotomy apparent in gender and technology future-talk, we briefly summarize our theoretical approach to the study of the future in more general terms.

## PROBLEMATIZING THE FUTURE

The future is also something we all 'do'. Futures are created in our everyday lives, may or may not be acted on in the course of those everyday lives, and are profoundly shaped by our socioeconomic backgrounds and, as of interest to us here, our gender. It is in this sense that the inequities of contemporary times are profoundly implicated in the nature of the futures thought possible. In terms of gender and technology, we have noted the differential interpretation of present-day trends (of technology, of gender relations, of working patterns) in terms of their impact upon the future and women's standing in that future. Rather than thinking about the future as a moment in time that will bring change to our social world, which we may or may not be able to predict, we can interrogate the future as a domain made meaningful through people's mundane, yet politically charged accounts. Rather than looking into the future, we can look at contested futures (Brown et al., 2000) in terms of how people construct their own personal trajectories and how gender relations may shape the possibilities they see for themselves (and others).

The future as an abstract temporal entity is posited as the harbinger of change in itself. It is deemed to be an active force in the social sphere, a force that can impact upon what we know to be social life in the present. Further, notions of the 'natural', 'nature' and (technological/social) 'evolution' and 'revolution' are all enrolled to strengthen the stability and perceived viability of certain versions of the future. Without going so far as to maintain that (temporarily) accepted versions of the future wholly determine present and future-possible talk and action, we can consider the possibility that having 'ownership', however transitory, of a version of the future that is considered viable or even inevitable, may have implications for the talk and action that is deemed acceptable and feasible in the present. It is in this way that future-orientated discourses can be thought of as being implicated in producing the very 'reality' they anticipate, via the enrolment of significant people, material artefacts and discursive resources.

Personal futures are political futures, shaped as they are by the wider social and historical context. Social futures are also technological futures, produced in the context of contemporary industrial societies through scientific-technological, economic and political means (Adam, 2004b). As Wajcman (2004: 1) suggests, 'More and more of life is somehow mediated by technology, so that today there is hardly any human activity that occurs without it'. These socio-technical futures are also profoundly gendered in ways that may seem more or less utopian and emancipatory.

## ICT FUTURE DISCOURSES IN THE GLOBAL/LOCAL NEXUS

Wider discourses on the future of ICT circulate through material means. We can read reports on the future of the global ICT industry, predictions of skills shortages, forecasts of working practice trends in the sector and attempts to make ICT more attractive to women in the future (European Commission, 2004). In addition, scholars engage with the gendered impact of ICT and the social shaping and gendering of technology (Faulkner, 2001; MacKenzie and Wajcman, 1999; Wajcman, 2004). Such analyses are all part of the ways in which we imagine the future of ICTs.

Here we concentrate on two discourses concerned with ICTs that include speculation on future trends and possibilities. The first is the ICT industry practice of offshoring and global locating, notably the predicted impact of the practice upon women workers in the UK (Howcroft et al., 2008). The second is that of the 'hybrid/bridger[4] worker' as the future direction of working practices in the ICT profession. In the field of IT and computing, this latter discourse owes its origins, in part, to early work by a British Computer Society (BCS) Task

Force on 'hybrid managers'.[5] Through a brief examination of these two future-orientated discourses of ICT, we offer a context in which our female research participants' discussions about their own futures, and the future of the ICT industry, took place.

In 2004, the BCS published a report looking at offshoring as a challenge or opportunity for British ICT professionals. Offshoring and global locating is the transferring of professional IT activities to overseas workers. Within sweeping industrial analyses of offshoring and global locating, little mention is made of the localized gendered experiences of such globalized trends (Howcroft and Richardson, 2008). Nor is mention made of the localized and highly individual futures imagined by female ICT professionals in the face of global change. Woolgar (2002) alerts us to this form of sweeping analysis which tends to subsume the nuances of (here gendered) experience under summarizing descriptions and totalizing depictions. Woolgar makes the case for extreme academic caution when faced with 'cyberbole', that is, vastly exaggerated claims about the likely effects of new technologies and the advent of new technologically enabled leisure and working practices (Woolgar, 2002: 9). He calls instead for 'analytical scepticism' in the face of the bold depictions, and predictions, of deterministic technological 'impacts' upon social life (Woolgar, 1999).

Huws (2003) suggests that one of the most dangerous illusions of globalization being fostered is the notion that new ICTs mean that anything can now be done by anyone, anywhere. The entire population of the globe has supposedly become a potential virtual workforce, yet little is documented with regards to how the 'virtual economy' maps onto the physical surface of the globe we inhabit (Huws, 2003: 146). The 'anytime, anyplace, anywhere' thesis is constrained by spatial factors, including access to technology and infrastructure. In fact, not all human activities are 'delocalizable', and most jobs are likely to remain anchored in spots near raw materials or to be limited by transport or the delivery of physical services like health (Huws, 2003). However, the 'death of distance' is not only of dubious empirical merit. It can also be viewed as part of wider hyperbolic cybermythologies, or 'cyberbole' that both draw on and produce our supposed desire to transcend the bounds of materiality. Indeed, the 'anyone, anytime, anywhere' aspiration of perfect, 'always on' communication between various entities is a now standard part of versions of the future in relation to ICTs (Moore, 2003).

Alongside offshoring and global locating and the possible impact of globalization trends, mention was made by our female research participants of areas in ICT which are growing or changing in ways that may be beneficial to women (see, for example, e-skills Bulletin, 2004). This particular future-orientated discourse includes predictions made about the changing nature of computer science as a discipline. Wendy Hall, former President of the BCS, contends that, given predicted developments in the field of computer science and information technology, such as ubiquitous computing, smart technologies and biotechnology, women will, in the near future, be best placed to 'deal with this brave new world' (Hall, 2004). She maintains that:

> the sorts of skills required ... will be the ones women have in abundance, and the subjects that attract more women such as biology will be the ones that become more important.

Her story of the future envisages a time in which computing technologies are gendered as 'feminine' rather than 'masculine', as they are (assumed to be) in the present moment. It demonstrates the ways in which the future can be enrolled in contemporary times to enact the possibility of change, in this case the regendering of technologies and the positive transformation of gender relations.

Gender is a fundamental way of organizing and classifying our social experience, since, as Suchman (1994) points out, categories have politics. In particular, gender is a highly politically charged means of classification (Adam et al., 2001). What is classified as 'masculine' is often taken to be of higher status than what is regarded as 'feminine' (Evans, 1994). This point relates to the problematic of gender binaries involving the polarization of relations between the sexes through hierarchical distinctions between masculinity and femininity, male and female. Knights and Kerfoot (2004), drawing on the work of Hekman (1999), note how undermining gender binaries and the hierarchies of evaluation implicated, generally involves two strategies. The first is to deny, or at least downplay, gender difference and encourage women to 'play the male game' (Knights and Kerfoot, 2004: 432). The second involves seeking to reverse gender hierarchies by evaluating women's skills and attributes as already being, or becoming, superior to those of their male counterparts. The difficulty with both approaches is that 'in so far as they reinforce male domination or seek to usurp it by elevating "the feminine", both strategies reproduce a gender binary steeped in hierarchy' (ibid; see also Kelan, 2008).

Throughout history as certain occupations have shifted from 'masculine' work to 'feminine' (such as clerical or medical work), so has their perceived 'value' declined (Woodfield, 2000). However, future-orientated discourses – of changing disciplines (Hall, 2004) and of changing working environments and practices creating further demand for 'soft' skills – is generally presented as an opportunity for women, given their supposedly 'natural' attributes, such as empathy. Woodfield (2002) usefully charts the utopian elements of stories of

ICT futures and relates them to the real-time and real-world experiences of women in the computer industry. She notes how, confronted with a maturing IT user community whose relationship with providers was becoming more knowledgeable, critical and discerning, IT organizations recognized that

> what was needed was a major shift in the personnel profile of the industry, from workers who only held specialist technical skills to those who also possessed social and communication skills, or 'hybrid/bridger' workers. (Woodfield, 2002: 120)

This ideal type, the 'hybrid/bridger worker', was mentioned by several of our interview participants as the future of the ICT profession and a clear opportunity for women in ICT.

Woodfield (2002: 123) asserts that, in the organizations she studied positive discourses upheld the view that 'hybrids are best/women are the best hybrids'. However, she also notes two damaging counter discourses that circulate in ICT organizations. The first posits that women should 'naturally' have the 'soft' skills so integral to being a hybrid/bridger worker, and so they receive little or no recognition for their abilities in such areas (see also Kelan, 2008). The second posits that men are 'naturally' better technicians, a view in which technical ability and technical confidence being reassessed as ultimately more important than 'soft' skills since they 'get the deal closed' (Woodfield, 2002: 129). Hence, the relative merits of men and women are accessed and judged hierarchically, generally to the detriment of women, given that skill sets are filtered through gender stereotypes. Woodfield (2002) aptly demonstrates the caution with which we have to approach both utopian and dystopian visions of ICT futures that claim to be entirely beneficial or detrimental to women. Opportunities for some women may open up in the ICT field as offshoring and global locating practices grow, and if demand for hybrid/bridger workers develops, but the reverse is equally possible. Having described some of the previous work relevant to our concerns, we now turn to our empirical material to support our argument regarding the importance of problematizing the future in relation to gender, work and technologies.

## THE WOMEN IN IT (WINIT) PROJECT

The empirical material used in the remainder of this article is drawn from data generated by the WINIT research project funded by the European Social Fund, which is concerned with women in the ICT industry, and women working in ICT in non-ICT organizations, in England (WINIT, n.d.). The two key means of data generation for the project were an online questionnaire and in-depth interviews with women from public and private organizations of all sizes, as well as female returners and entrepreneurs working in ICT in some capacity.[6]

Given the importance of both problematizing and analysing the future in relation to women's (current) position in the ICT industry and women's (current and possible future) experiences of ICT work and ICT working environments, a number of questions regarding the future were included in the online questionnaire. These questions varied from asking whether respondents intended to change jobs in the coming year to asking whether they would encourage girls/women to enter the industry now and in the future. The online questionnaire, aimed at women over 16 years of age in the UK, was marketed to a broad range of ICT organizations in the public and private sectors and distributed predominately through women's Internet forums, BCS specialist groups, and ICT recruitment agencies. We base our questionnaire data in this article on data from 479 women who responded to the WINIT survey between October 2004 and October 2005 (Griffiths et al., 2007a).

This article also draws on 12 interviews with women working in ICT across various regions in England. Unstructured in-depth interviews were used, so the women were able to direct their own storytelling. Towards the end of each interview, we asked how they envisaged the future in personal, technological and industry-level terms. Such an open-ended approach builds on a long tradition of feminist research that aims to take women's stories and accounts of their gendered experiences seriously, using predominately qualitative and ethnographic methods to explore their thoughts and actions. In-depth interviews offer the space to explore the nuanced links between women's domestic situations, their public working lives, their perceptions of the ICT industry and their personal futures. All interviews were taped, transcribed and closely examined, using discursive analysis to draw out key themes, trends, links and disparities in female ICT professionals' accounts (for more information on WINIT methodology and methods, please see the archived WINIT website [n.d.]).

In the article, we chose to highlight the ways in which women talk about gender in the context of perceived wider changes in the ICT sector, towards a demand for hybrid workers and offshoring and global locating trends in ICT work. In our conclusions, however, we highlight the need to take the analysis of the future further by investigating more personal and domestic aspects of the futures, as imagined by female (ICT) professionals. The professional and personal aspects of the future are closely related, so as when women express concern about the long-hours culture in the ICT industry (particularly in client-facing and consultancy roles) and the implications this may have for their current or possible future caring responsibilities (Griffiths and Moore, 2006; Griffiths et al., 2007a).

## TELLING STORIES OF THE FUTURE

### 'It Could Be an Opportunity for Women': ICT, Gender and the Future

From our questionnaire, it was clear that female ICT professionals held a very mixed view of the future of the ICT industry, particularly in relation to the position of women within it. In Table 1, we see women imagining more or less dystopian and utopian futures. Most questionnaire respondents were relatively positive about the future reduction of female under-representation. However, they also presented the more pessimist view that the ICT industry's image was unlikely to become more female friendly in the future. The strength of the social construction of technology as masculine is clear from these results. While the world of work may be expected to change in terms of gender relations, the 'masculinization of technology' appears to be more obdurate (Lohan and Faulkner, 2004).

*Table 1   Online Responses to Selected Future-Orientated Questions*

| Future-orientated question posed | Extent of agreement |
| --- | --- |
| In the future, it is likely that the proportion of females [in ICT] will increase. | 63 percent indicated some level of agreement; 21 percent slightly, moderately or strongly disagreed and 16 percent did not know. |
| The IT industry [will have] a female friendly image in the future. | 2 percent strongly agreed; 8 percent moderately; 12 percent slightly and 16 percent agreed, 20 percent strongly disagreed; 10 percent moderately disagreed and 10 percent slightly disagreed with this statement. 22 percent selected 'don't know'. |
| I would encourage young women/girls to enter the IT industry. | 48 percent indicated that they would encourage other women/girls into IT. |

It has been suggested that the ICT sector, particularly in the western world, faces a predicted 'skills time bomb' unless a more diverse workforce in terms of gender, age and ethnicity is created (Platman and Taylor, 2004; e-skills, 2008). Within future-orientated discourses, it is posited that women will be the vital pool from which to draw candidates in order to diffuse this predicted ICT time bomb. Elements of this discourse were heard in the accounts of many of our female research participants, including Maya,[7] an ICT director:

> I mean, I have worked for male IT directors, they have just been generally strategists, but nowadays I don't think that works: they want someone who can do everything, especially as they are tightening up on their budgets – a hybrid ... You know, IT is never going to stand in isolation again, like in the 1990s. You could have this specialist and that is all they did. Now, you know, things are not going to happen that way any more. You are going to need more grounded, and all-round, skills. An all-rounder.

Hybrid/bridger workers are predicted to move the ICT industry forward, reshaping the relationship between technology and business. Ashton (2005: 16) argues that hybrids or 'bridgers'

> need the organisational and people skills to break down barriers between IT and business ... and help educate business about IT and IT about business. This means that they must have the confidence of both sides.

The ability to encourage communication between disparate groups that may also be geographically distant, given trends towards offshoring and global relocating, is highlighted as a key hybrid worker skill that will enhance the future productivity of businesses in the UK. This future-framing of a gendered skill (that is, communication) is reflected by Caroline, a senior ICT consultant and WINIT interviewee, who said:

> Communications? I think it's about ... communications is a very good opportunity for women, I think. Certainly in companies that need ... if they're going to outsource, have any of their operations, business operations, in India, Asia, wherever, communications is the most important item of any organization. Therefore, communications linked with web design or whatever, that's the area, I'd say, where women could work.

Another questionnaire respondent (a senior project manager) sees opportunities for women growing in the ICT sector as technologies increasingly, in her view, come to be seen more as business tools than ends in themselves:

> They [women] need to be made aware that not everyone in the industry is a 'backroom' techie, and that the way forwards is in the seamless integration of IT with business practices.

Many women saw ICT as becoming increasingly integrated with business needs and processes; an integration that would require both 'soft' and 'hard' skills from ICT professionals, forming this demand for the ideal gendered hybrid worker. One questionnaire respondent (a head of ICT), for example, speaks of her career satisfaction, linking it to her perceptions of changes to the ICT sector that may benefit women in the future:

> I had a good career in IT which I expect to continue! I would certainly encourage girls with an interest in IT to pursue a career in it – the general move to having closer links with other areas of an organization means that women's relationship skills are becoming more and more important.

Other women saw that, as some 20 million people in the UK use ICT for everyday work tasks (e-skills, 2004a, 2004b), there would be a growing need for ICT user support. This could be another opportunity for women in the UK, now and in the future. One questionnaire respondent (a web designer) said:

> I can understand why a lot of women are turned off by the IT sector ... the sad geekiness ... but it ain't all rocket science ... and can be a good career. Hell, as more and more people are pushed online, who's going to help them and who's going to bridge the gap between the technology and the user?

Here, by juxtaposing female ICT professionals with (male) 'sad geeks', a future is conceived in which women have a particular, positive role to play. The gender construction of women as 'naturally' better with people, and so more likely to be adept at managing the integration of ICT and business needs and processes, is problematic (Woodfield, 2000, 2002), due to its essentialist assumptions about naturalized gender roles (that is, women as caring and people-orientated, men as technical). However, in the face of the continued physical and symbolic under-representation of women in ICT careers and in SET fields in general, female professionals are able to draw on the future as a positive discursive resource to recast ICT as the natural domain of women, in which the hybrid/bridger worker discourse plays a part in the continuous reshaping of gendered experiences of technology.

The women in our study saw relatively positive futures for women in relation to ICT. However, some saw more negative futures, of further (essentialist) stereotyping of women's relationships with technology and of the need for a caring element to their ICT work before it could be 'natural'. As Kelkar and Nathan (2002: 440) suggest, we feel the shadow of the cultural ceiling [that] exhibits itself starkly in relation to women. The idea that technology is not for women, that women are not technologically-minded, is strongly embedded not only in Asian thinking, but also that of Europe and America.

As we move on to look at offshoring/global locating as a key 'future-possible', the cultural and historical specificities of assumptions about women, technology and the future become accentuated.

## 'It's the Management that Women Are Good at': Offshoring/Global Locating and the Future

The women in our study steered a course between utopian and dystopian accounts of the future by drawing on gendered experiences and perceptions of ICTs, highlighting the opportunities and barriers for women in an ever-changing socio-technical environment. Global employment trends indicate that the service sector is the largest provider of employment worldwide (International Labour Organization [ILO], 2008). Facilitated by continued developments in ICTs, this has contributed to the feminization of employment, with increasing numbers of women entering the global jobs market. International trends have been towards a rise in female labour force participation and a decline in male participation rates (Gillard et al., 2007; Standing, 2006). A common rhetorical theme suggests that ICTs are driving and enabling work transformations, with women as the likely benefactors (ILO, 2008).

Networking technologies are seen as enabling market expansion, removing geographical restrictions and allowing organizational diffusion (Ellis and Taylor, 2006). The shift from offshoring manufacturing to the increasing offshoring and outsourcing of ICT-enabled work is often seen as key to promoting development and offering opportunities for women to enter the labour market and become involved in enterprise (Arun et al., 2004). Yet, the global sourcing of ICT-enabled service work has benefited from the feminization of work as skills are revalued and devalued as women lose the pay and status they previously enjoyed (Howcroft and Richardson, 2008). There is also a persistent gap in the literature in the lack of recognition given to informal sector work (see, for example, Elson, 1999; Howcroft and Richardson, 2008). In India, women comprise 19 percent of the formal IT workforce and 37 percent of employees in ICT-enabled service work, yet 91 percent of the Indian labour force is said to be working outside the formally economy, which employs only 4 percent of India's working women (Hill, 2001). The formal and informal economies are integral (Breman, 2006; Howcroft and Richardson, 2008), and most women in the world work in two to three categories – paid labour in the formal sector, paid labour in the informal sector and unpaid work in the household (Howcroft and Richardson, 2008) aptly called the 'triple shift' (Hossfield, 1990).

In Asia, where much UK ICT work is outsourced (Economist Intelligence Unit, 2005), the participation of women in IT work is higher than in the workforce as a whole (NASSCOM, 2001). Such relatively high participation rates in the ICT sector among Asian women both consolidate and change existing gender and technology relations in the region. While their engagement with ICTs may enhance their social mobility and increase their income (Gothoskar, 2000; Mitter, 2000), the overall burden of responsibility of Asian female ICT workers also increases, particularly given the entrenchment of gender-based divisions of domestic labour (Kelkar and Nathan, 2002).

Just as engagement with ICTs and ICT work is perceived as both an opportunity and as problematic for women in Asian countries, the UK women in our study saw both positive and negative futures in relation to offshoring/global locating for themselves and others. Maya, a 38-year-old IT director of a large charity shared her in-depth knowledge of the ICT sector to create a story of where the industry is going in the future. She says:

> Well, IT affects everybody and it can only get bigger. I mean, IT is never going to be die away, where all computers get wiped out or something like that, but I think in terms of the ... in terms of the future, outsourcing, offshoring, is a big threat; and I think that for the people who want to remain in the industry, they need to go there and get a broader perspective of IT. It can't be any good being a networking specialist or just a programmer or developer: you will always need the management skills. Even when you become a manager, you need communication skills, you need interpersonal skills. You need HR skills.

Her measured account creates a vision where technology permeates all aspects of society, and in which outsourcing/offshoring is both a threat and an opportunity for women in the UK, particularly in relation to managing ICT projects and workers. Here the debate surrounding increasing demand in the future for 'soft' skills in ICT workplaces is interlinked by the interviewee, as it is more generally, with the perception of an increasingly globalized economy of offshore workers. The demands of managing such offshore workers and ICT work, it is argued by the following interviewee, are best suited to female UK ICT professionals. Caroline, a semi-retired ICT director and consultant suggests:

> Well, are you thinking of the future of IT as well? Are you looking at outsourcing, because that will make a big difference, you know, going forward? If you think, most companies are now looking at an 80/20 or a 90/10 percent outsourcing to mostly Asia,

India, somewhere like that, and I don't know whether you're considering it, but look at what's happening in India ... Is it equal opportunities for women? Which it's obviously not. I think it would be useful to put that in. That is pretty clear, you know there are things that are going forward, you know if you look at what's going to be left for IT opportunities that are in the UK.

Caroline frames her concern about the future in terms of the unevenness of opportunity for women across the world, and of shifts in the opportunities available to women in the UK ICT sector, given the possibility of further change in the future. Caroline continues by saying:

Yes, and if you look at the opportunities that will happen in the UK and you think about ... a lot of it will be quality control of what's happening; third party management, that sort of thing. So the link to the business needs, they putting pure IT work out to India, then I think the bits in the UK will be very suited to women, because women tend to more methodical, you know. They're not trying to be terribly creative necessarily. They're quite happy to follow, in my experience anyway, methods and best methods. It's the management, which I think women are very good at. The creative side would more likely be the offshore element, which is traditionally the male side.

Here we see the (re)construction of gender binaries of naturalized attributes, made sense of through talk about the future of ICT work and the ICT sector. From such extracts, the future and predicted future trends of work and technology are harnessed by women to imagine a change in gender, time, work and technology relations. However, again we see the presumption that women would 'naturally' benefit from a move away from 'pure' technical work towards business integration and offshore contract management. Such essentialized discourses, future-orientated or otherwise, serve to reinforce gendered assumptions about women's relationship with technology. Again, the future is produced through discourse as a realm in which disadvantageous gender relations are challenged and reinforced simultaneously.

## GENDERED TIMES, GENDERED FUTURES?

In this article, we have investigated some stories of the future in relation to women in the ICT sector. We began by outlining why looking at the future is important if we are to better understand the co-construction of gender, time, work and technology. To demonstrate the usefulness of problematizing the future in relation to utopian and dystopian visions of (working) women's changing relationships with ICT, we focused upon the discourse of the hybrid/bridger worker identified by Woodfield (2002) and on the discourse of the possible impact of offshoring and global locating on women. The inter-relations between individual women's accounts of their perceptions and experiences of ICT and wider talk of ongoing change in the UK ICT sector in a global knowledge economy have been explored.

WINIT research participants were keen to stress the possible positive impacts of future trends in ICT and the ICT industry, highlighting perceived opportunities for women given the (again perceived) future demand for 'soft' styles of management, for hybrid workers working with people as well as with technical skills, and for communication skills in ICT user support work. Problematically, within the often essentialist and binary nature of such future talk, women were seen as 'naturally' suited to what future ICT work is thought to increasingly involve. There are a number of dangers associated with such future-orientated assumptions. If, for example, female representation in ICT fails to improve, it becomes easier to blame women for not engaging in an industry that fits their 'natural' attributes, and for missing out a valuable and apparently rather obvious opportunity. Some stories about the future, of female hybrid workers flocking to join the skills-starved UK ICT industry, should be challenged.

The realities of the continuation of the gendered division of labour can be used as a check on gender-blind predictions in the UK and globally. We may also return to the issue of a future that does not engage women in the design and development of technologies (Henwood, 1993; Wajcman, 2004). It becomes possible to challenge some of the assumptions of gender-blind predictions and explore the possibility of futures gendered through discursive and material means. Finally, the role that women play downstream, as consumers and users, in shaping technologies should not be forgotten in talk of cutting-edge, futuristic innovations.

Examining stories of the future becomes a way of problematizing contemporary discourse about gender, time, work and technology. Notions of gendered futures or the gendering of the future, however, need to be further explored, in part through empirical work. Such empirical work is a small step towards answering how the futures that individuals imagine for themselves are shaped, if at all, by contemporary gender relations and norms. Can we investigate how futures are gendered? We may identify and analyse wider discourses of the future in relation to gender, time, work and technology, as produced by industry, transnational organizations, governments and the popular media. We may also explore with women their perceptions of their own personal futures, notably in terms of career and carer trajectories. An example from our empirical research is one interviewee's story of being bullied at work by a male colleague who continuously questioned her technical knowledge (Natasha, ICT support worker). Natasha felt that this experience had led her to the conclusion that ICT 'feeds my mind but not my soul'. Her personal, but clearly political, experience of the ICT workplace had led her to make future plans to retrain as a horticulturalist. She told a story of a past fascination with technology being diminished by her current ICT work-place situation, as she imagined a future for herself that involved less conflict and more 'time for me'.

By exploring individuals' personal futures, in the ICT sector and beyond, we can explore how gender relations shape what individuals think possible in the future, what they feel they should be doing in the future, what they wish they could be doing in the future and what plans are viable for them, given assumptions of contemporary gender (and technology) relations. Such personal concerns also need to be placed in the context of wider future-orientated discourses, with a focus on relationships between personal futures, socio-technical futures and other versions of the future, offering a more nuanced understanding of the ways in which these may come to be gendered and how this gendering process takes place.

## Notes

[1] The under-representation of women in the ICT sector has been the focus of various initiatives in the UK over the last 30 years. These initiatives predominately draw on liberal feminist approaches to the women in technology 'problem' (Faulkner, 2001). The liberal feminist approach to the 'problem' of women in computing, typified by women in science and engineering and SET discourses (Henwood, 1996) highlights the need to improve access to ICT, the need to encourage more women to take computing courses, and the need for better equal opportunities and managing diversity legislation.

[2] Briefly, technofeminism is characterized by a fusion of the visionary insights of cyberfeminism (or cyborg feminism) and feminist technoscience studies that draw on social shaping (or constructivist) theories of technology such as actor-network theory. The work of Donna Haraway (1991, 1997) and Judy Wajcman (1991, 2004) is significant in this area.

[3] See McBeath and Webb (2000) for a discussion of the relationship between utopias and future worlds. They argue that utopias and future worlds refer to possible worlds with varying degrees of plausibility, although utopias may be thought of as future worlds with 'explicit, inflexible, value commitments that either constrain or make demands upon a projected structure of the human world' (McBeath and Webb, 2000: 2).

[4] The term 'bridger' is used by Christine Ashton, chief information manager for BP Refining and Marketing. Ashton, co-founder of the BCS Business-IT Interface Specialist Group, uses the term to refer to ICT professionals who 'have a strategic role in helping businesses understand how IT fits and supports business strategy' (Ashton, 2005: 16).

[5] For a discussion of the BCS's position on hybrid managers, see Brackley (1996).

[6] For a detailed discussion of the difficulties of defining IT, ICT and the ICT industry, see Duerden-Comeau (2003).

[7] All names of respondents have been changed to preserve anonymity.

## References

Adam, A., Howcroft, D. and Richardson, H. (2001) Absent Friends? The Gender Dimension in IS Research. In Russo, N., Fitzgerald, B. and DeGross, J. (eds.) *Realigning Research and Practice in Information Systems Development: The Social and Organizational Perspective*, pp. 333–352. Boston, MA: Kluwer Academic Publishers.

Adam, B. (1990) *Time and Social Theory*. London: Polity Press.

Adam, B. (1995) *Timewatch: The Social Analysis of Time*. London: Polity Press.

Adam, B. (1998) *Timescapes of Modernity: The Environment and Invisible Hazards*. London: Routledge.

Adam, B. (2004a) Towards a New Sociology of the Future. Working paper 2. Available online at http://www.cf.ac.uk/socsi/futures/newsociologyofthefuture.pdf Last consulted September 2005.

Adam, B. (2004b) In Pursuit of the Future. Briefing paper 1. Available online at http://www.cf.ac.uk/socsi/futures/briefing1.pdf Last consulted September 2005.

Adam, B. (2006) Time. *Theory, Culture & Society*, 23, 2–3, 119–126.

Arun, S., Heeks, R. and Morgan, S. (2004) Researching ICT-Based Enterprise for Women in Developing Countries: A Gender Perspective. Institute for Development Policy and Management. Manchester, UK: University of Manchester.

Ashton, C. (2005) The Bulletin Interview: One of BP's Top IT Managers Has Firm Views on Melding Business and IT to Give Business an Edge – And Open New Career Options for IT Specialists, *ITNOW*, BCS Publishing, Swindon, UK, p. 16. Available online at http://archive.bcs.org/bulletin/may05/intervie.htm Last consulted June 10, 2008.

Bell, W. and Mau, J. (eds.) (1971) *The Sociology of the Future: Theory, Cases, and Annotated Bibliography*. New York: Russell Sage Foundation.

Brackley, A. (1996) Whatever Happened to Hybrid Managers? The Short History of the Hybrids, BCS Publishing, Swindon, UK, p. 16. Available online at http://archive.bcs.org/bulletin/dec96/what.htm Last consulted June 2008.

Breman, J. (2006) Informal Sector Employment. In Clark, D. (ed.) *The Elgar Companion to Development Studies*, pp. 281–285. Cheltenham, UK: Edward Elgar.

Brown, N., Rappert, B. and Webster, A. (eds.) (2000) *Contested Futures: A Sociology of Prospective Techno-Science*. Aldershot, UK: Ashgate.

Duerden-Comeau, T. (2003) Information Technology (IT) Employment: What Is IT? Workforce Ageing in the New Economy. Available online at http://www.wane.ca/PDF/WP1.pdf Last consulted June 2, 2008.

Economist Intelligence Unit (2005) CEO Briefing: Corporate Priorities for 2005. Available online at www.eiu.com/CEO_Briefing2005 Last consulted May 2005.

Ellis, V. and Taylor, P. (2006) You Don't Know What You've Got Till It's Gone: Re-contextualising the Origins, Development and Impact of the Call Centre. *New Technology, Work & Employment*, 21, 2, 107–122.

Elson, D. (1999) Labour Markets as Gendered Institutions: Equality, Efficiency and Empowerment Issues. *World Development*, 27, 3, 611–627.

Equal Opportunities Commission (EOC) (2005) Free to Choose: Tackling Gender Barriers to Better Jobs, *England Final Report – EOC's Investigation into Workplace Segregation and Apprenticeships*, TD/TNC. 81.513. Manchester, UK: EOC.

e-skills (2004a) IT Insights: Trends and UK Skills Implications Report. Available online at www.e-skills.com/register Last consulted November 2004.

e-skills (2004b) IT Insights: Drivers of Demand for Skill. Available online at www.e-skills.com/register Last consulted May 2005.

e-skills (2006) The Sector Skills Agreement for IT 2005–2008 – Summary. Available online from http://www.e-skills.com/ARCHIVES/Careers-Site-Archived/Careers/Case-Studies/Women/221 Last consulted March 2008.

e-skills (2008) Technology Counts: IT and Telecoms Insights. Available online at http://www.e-skills.com/Research-and-policy/Insights-2008/2179 Last consulted March 2008.

e-skills Bulletin (2004) *Quarterly Review of the ICT Labour Market*, 11, 4. Available online at http://www.e-skills.com/Research-and-policy/bulletin/1168 Last consulted June 2, 2008.

European Commission (2004) *WWW-ICT: Widening Women's Work in Information Communication Technology*. Namur, Belgium: Information Society Technologies.

Evans, M. (ed.) (1994) *The Woman Question*. London: Sage.

Faulkner, W. (2001) The Technology Question in Feminism: A View From Feminist Technology Studies. *Women's Studies International Forum*, 24, 1, 79–95.

Gillard, H., Howcroft, D., Mitev, N., Richardson, H. and Ferneley, E. (2007) Shaping the Global Economy, Gender ICTs and Development Research. Paper presented at the IFIP WG9.4 Conference, Sao Paolo, Brazil, May 2007.

Gothoskar, S. (2000) Teleworking and Gender. *Economic and Political Weekly*, 35, 26, 2293–2298.

Griffiths, M. and Moore, K. (2006) *Women in IT (WINIT)*. Final report. Manchester, UK: University of Salford.

Griffiths, M., Moore, K. and Richardson, H. (2007a) Celebrating Heterogeneity? A Survey of ICT Professionals in England. *Information, Communication & Society*, 10, 3, 338–357.

Griffiths, M., Moore, K., Burns, B. and Richardson, H. (2007b) *Disappearing Women*. Final report. Manchester, UK: University of Salford.

Hall, W. (2004) Women in Computing Professions: Will the Internet Make a Difference? Public lecture given to the Oxford Internet Institute, University of Oxford, UK, June 17.

Haraway, D. (1991) *Simians, Cyborgs, and Women: The Reinvention of Nature*. London: Free

Association Books.

Haraway, D. (1997) *Modest_Witness@Second_Millennium.FemaleMan©_Meets_Onco-Mouse™: Feminism and Technoscience*. London: Routledge.

Hekman, S. (1999) *The Future of Differences: Truth and Method in Feminist Theory*. Cambridge, UK: Polity Press.

Henwood, F. (1993) Establishing Gender Perspectives on Information Technology: Problems, Issues and Opportunities. In Green, E., Owen, J. and Pain, D. (eds.) *Gendered by Design? Information Technology and Office Systems*, pp. 31–49. London: Taylor and Francis.

Henwood, F. (1996) Wise Choices? Understanding Occupational Decision-making in a Climate of Equal Opportunities for Women in Science and Engineering. *Gender & Education*, 8, 2, 199–214.

Henwood, F., Wyatt, S., Miller, N. and Senker, P. (2000) Critical Perspectives on Technologies, Inequalities and the Information Society. In Wyatt, S., Henwood, F., Miller, N. and Senker, P. (eds.) *Technology and In/Equality: Questioning the Information Society*, pp. 1–18. London: Routledge.

Hill, E. (2001) Women in the Indian Informal Economy: Collective Strategies for Work Life Improvement and Development, *Work, Employment & Society*, 15, 3, 443–464.

Hossfield, K. (1990) Their Logic Against Them: Contradictions in Sex, Race And Class in Silicon Valley. In Ward, K. (ed.) *Women Workers and Global Restructuring*, pp. 149–178. Berkeley, CA: University of California Press.

Howcroft, D. and Richardson, H. (2008) Gender Invisibility and ICT-Enabled Service Work in the Global Economy. Paper delivered at the 26th International Labour Process Conference, 'Work Matters'. Dublin, Ireland, March 18–20.

Howcroft, D., Langer, S. and Westrup, C. (2008) *Women in North-West Shared Services*. Final project report. ESF Project number 061066NW3. Manchester, UK: University of Manchester and CRESC.

Huws, U. (2003) *The Making of a Cybertariat: Virtual Work in a Real World*. London: Merlin Press.

International Labour Organization (ILO) (2008) Global Employment Trends. *International Labour Organization*. Available online at http://www.ilo.org/public/English/employment/strat/global.htm Last consulted June 2, 2008.

Kelan, E. (2008) Emotions in a Rational Profession: The Gendering of Skills in ICT Work. *Gender, Work & Organization*, 15,1, 49–71.

Kelkar, G. and Nathan, D. (2002) Gender Relations and Technological Change in Asia. *Current Sociology*, 50, 3, 427–441.

Knights, D. and Kerfoot, D. (2004) Between Representations and Subjectivity: Gender Binaries and the Politics of Organizational Transformation. *Gender, Work & Organization*, 11, 4, 430–454.

Lohan, M. and Faulkner, W. (2004) Masculinities and Technologies: Some Introductory Remarks. *Men and Masculinities*, 6, 4, 319–329.

McBeath, G. and Webb, S. (2000) On the Nature of Future Worlds: Considerations of Virtuality and Utopias. *Information, Communication & Society*, 3, 1, 1–16.

MacKenzie, D. and Wajcman, J. (eds.) (1999) *The Social Shaping of Technology*. Buckingham, UK: Open University Press.

Mitter, S. (2000) Teleworking and Teletrade in India: Combining Diverse Perspectives and Visions. *Economic and Political Weekly*, 35, 26, 2241–2252.

Moore, K. (2003) *Versions of the Future in Relation to Mobile Communication Technologies*, Unpublished PhD thesis, Department of Sociology, School of Human Sciences, Guildford, UK: University of Surrey.

NASSCOM (2001) IT Industry in India, Delhi: NASSCOM. Available online at http://nasscom.org/it_industry/indic_statistics.asp Last consulted April 2005.

Platman, K. and Taylor, P. (2004) Workforce Ageing in the New Economy: A Comparative Study of Information Technology Employment. *Workforce Ageing in the New Economy* (WANE). Available online at http://www.wane.ca/PDF/Platman&TaylorSummaryReport2004.pdf Last consulted June 2008.

Selby, L., Young, A. and Fisher, D. (1997) Increasing the Participation of Women in Tertiary Level Computing Courses: What Works and Why. *Proceedings of ASCILITE 97*, 14th Annual Conference of the Australian Society for Computers in Tertiary Education. Perth, December 8–10. Available online at http://www.ascilite.org.au/conferences/perth97/papers/Selby/Selby.html Last consulted June 2, 2008.

Standing, G. (2006) Labour Markets. In Clark, D. (ed.) *The Elgar Companion to Development Studies*, pp. 323–328. Cheltenham UK: Edward Elgar.

Suchman, L. (1994) Do Categories Have Politics? The Language/Action Perspective Reconsidered. *Computer Supported Cooperative Work*, 2, 3, 177–190.

Turkle, S. (1995) *Life on the Screen: Identity in the Age of the Internet*. New York: Simon and Schuster.

Urry, J. (2008) Climate Change, Travel and Complex Futures. *British Journal of Sociology*, 59, 2, 261–279.

Wajcman, J. (1991) *Feminism Confronts Technology*. London: Polity Press.

Wajcman, J. (1998) *Managing Like a Man: Women and Men in Corporate Management*. Pennsylvania, PA: Pennsylvania State University Press.

Wajcman, J. (2004) *Technofeminism*. London: Polity Press.

Wajcman, J. (2008) Life in the Fast Lane? Towards a Sociology of Technology and Time. *British Journal of Sociology*, 59, 1, 59–77.

Whitty, M. (2004) Should Filtering Software Be Utilised in the Workplace? Australian Employees' Attitudes Towards Internet Usage and Surveillance of the Internet in the Workplace. *Surveillance & Society*, 2, 1, 39–54.

Women in IT (WINIT) (n.d.) Homepage. Available online at http://www.isi.salford.ac.uk/gris/winit/index.html Last consulted June 2, 2008.

Women in IT Champions Group (2003) Achieving Workforce Diversity in the E-Business in Demand Era. Available online at http://www.intellectuk.org/component/option,com_docman/task,cat_view/gid,291/?mosmsg=You+are+trying+to+access+from+a+non-authorized+domain.+%28www.google.co.uk%29 Last consulted July 2004.

Woodfield, R. (2000) *Women, Work and Computing*. Cambridge, UK: Cambridge University Press.

Woodfield, R. (2002) Women and Information Systems Development: Not Just a Pretty (Inter)face? *Information, Technology & People*, 15, 2, 119–138.

Woolgar, S. (1999) Analytic Scepticism. In Dutton, W. (ed.) *Society on the Line: Information Politics in the Digital Age*. pp. 335–339. Oxford, UK: Oxford University Press.

Woolgar, S. (2002) Five Rules of Virtuality. In Woolgar, S. (ed.) *Virtual Society? Technology, Cyberbole, Reality*, pp. 1–22. Oxford, UK: Oxford University Press.

# II

Digital Labour in the Manufacturing Industry

# Foxconned Labour as the Dark Side of the Information Age: Working Conditions at Apple's Contract Manufacturers in China

Marisol Sandoval(马里索尔·桑多瓦尔)[①]

[导读] 新自由主义的全球化、全球生产网络的转型以及中国的改革开放使得跨国企业在中国可以获得大量廉价的劳动力,而苹果公司大部分的利润就来自诸如 iPhone 和 iPad 在内的硬件产品的销售——这些硬件产品对于苹果公司来说是巨大的成功,但对于在与苹果公司签订合同的制造企业中工作的工人来说却是不幸的。也就是说,苹果公司是世界上最占支配地位和最令人向往的计算机企业,但是在苹果公司最先进电子产品"光鲜的"外表下,隐藏着一个"肮脏"的劳工世界。

这篇论文正是通过审视在中国与苹果公司签订合同的制造企业中工人的工作环境,揭示了信息时代"黑暗"的一面。在这篇论文中,作者首先提出了理解工人工作环境的系统性模式,这个模式同样可以被用来理解和比较不同国家中的工作。以马克思对资本循环的理论为出发点,该模式界定了在资本积累过程中,重塑工作环境的要素,这些要素包括:生产力、生产关系、生产过程、产品和劳动法。

在此基础上,作者将这样一种系统性模式运用到对电子制造业的分析之中。在这里,资本和劳动的关系以低工资、短期合同和零星的劳工抗争为

---

① 任教于英国伦敦城市大学(City University of London)文化和创意产业系。其研究方向主要聚焦于全球文化产业中的权力、商品化、剥削、意识形态和抵抗问题。研究成果包括《从企业到社交媒体:媒介和传播产业中的企业社会责任的批判视角》(*From Corporate to Social Media: Critical Perspectives on Corporate Social Responsibility in Media and Communication Industries*, 2014 )、《批判、社交媒体与信息社会》(*Critique, Social Media and the Information Society*, 2013 )、《网络与监控》(*Internet and Surveillance*, 2012 ) 等。

特点。生产过程中工人不仅工作和生活在工厂内,而且还遭受劳动时间的延长、重复且单调的体力劳动,以及严格的控制。大多数年轻"打工仔"的健康和安全都遭到威胁,并经历着异化、透支和绝望。他们正在生产着自己可能永远买不起的电子产品。劳动法经常被"漠视",为工人提供较少的保护。毋庸置疑,中国工厂中的劳动力正在为苹果公司创造利润,并为那些有能力购买的用户提供不可思议的科技产品,但对工人本身而言,他们经历的是单调、控制和绝望。

然而,信息与通信技术对于工人来说并非仅仅意味着不幸,它们同样可以对工人进行赋权。诚如邱林川教授指出的:工人阶级正在获取越来越多的网络和无线通讯手段,主要包括在市场上为"工人阶级"量身定制的廉价信息与通信设备(working-class ICTs),因此将中国低收入群体描述为"信息无产者"(information have-nots)是不准确的,至少应该将他们描述为"较少信息获得者"(information have-less)。包括手机在内的"工人阶级"的信息与通信设备使得他们考虑的问题可以被社会各阶层的人群所获知,且对社会产生直接的影响。关于劳动侵权和维权的信息也往往可以通过在线论坛或者自制的视频在网上传播。因此,工人阶级通过博客、诗歌和短信等途径来进行他们的文化表达和政治赋权,"工人阶级"的信息与通讯设备也日益成为21世纪新的阶级动力的物质载体。

这里还需要说明的是,作者所描述的在富士康发生的情况在整个电子产业和其他制造业(包括服装和玩具制造业)中也异常普遍。因此,富士康只是一个折射全球资本主义中结构性不平等和剥削的"普通"案例。为了解决这些结构性的难题,仅仅依靠企业的自律、行为规范和企业社会责任的培养是不够的。提高工人的工资、减少工人的工作时间,以及改善工人的健康和安全保护等措施都将加大企业的运营成本,进而削减企业的利润。没有国际法律和法规来强制要求企业执行一定的标准,工人的工作环境就不可能发生根本性的改变。

最后,作者强调对工厂中生产科技产品的产业工人进行研究的必要性,但这并不意味着忽视对工程师、设计师或是媒体从业人员工作和生活的研究。因为强调不同劳动形式之间的联系异常重要:今天的产业工人和知识劳工都需要面对新的信息与通信技术,他们同样面临着剥削、高强度的工作压力和"不稳定"的境况。与其使用"非物质劳动"（immaterial labour）这个强化体力和脑力劳动不同的概念,倒不如扩大知识劳工或数字劳工的外延：使之包括生产计算机技术、电子设备和新媒体技术的体力劳动者。因此,数字劳工的概念包括将信息与通信技术、数字技术等作为生产资料的脑力劳动者和体力劳动者,以及包括生产者和使用者。这为我们分析和理解数字劳工的全球分工提供了理论性的框架,对于数字劳工广义上的理解也成为全球价值链下劳工联合的起点,他们既包括制造信息与通讯设备的产业工人,又包括呼叫中心的工作人员、软件工程师,还包括"无酬"的"产消合一者"。

Information and Communication Technologies (ICTs) have played a double role in the restructuring of capitalism since the 1970s. On the one hand, they enable fast transnational communication that is needed for organising international markets and value chains. On the other hand, the production of these technologies is itself based on an international supply network (Dyer-Witheford, 2014; Hong, 2011: 9). Dyer-Witheford therefore describes the value chain as "the dirty secret of the digital revolution" (Dyer-Witheford, 2014). Part of this "dirty secret" is that "the global information economy is built in part on the backs of tens of millions Chinese industrial workers" (Zhao and Duffy, 2008: 229).

The clean, immaculate and advanced surface of modern computer products hides the dirty reality of their production process. Concepts such as "digital sublime" (Mosco, 2004) or "technological sublime" (Maxwell and Miller, 2012: 7) suggest that certain myths and utopian ideals are attached to media and communication technologies. Maxwell and Miller argue that this has as a consequence that the "way technology is experienced in daily life is far removed from the physical work and material resources that go into it" (ibid).

The tendency even of critical scholarship to focus on how the usage of ICTs as production technologies is transforming work, perpetuates the technological sublime rather than unmasking it. In this vein, Hardt and Negri (2004: 65) for example highlight that the "contemporary scene of labour and production [...] is being transformed under the hegemony of immaterial labor, that is labor that produces immaterial products, such as information, knowledge, ideas, images, relationships, and affects". Even if they recognize that the rise of "immaterial labour" does not lead to the disappearance of industrial labour, the term tends to mystify the actual impact of ICTs and digital technologies on work and workers on a global scale. Before and after ICTs serve as the instruments of the mental labour of software developers, journalists, designers, new media workers, prosumers, etc., their production and disposal is shaped by various forms of manual work, such as the extraction of minerals, the assembly of components into the final product and the waste work needed for their disposal. Conceptualizing digital labour only as mental and immaterial labour misrepresents the character of ICTs and digital technologies as it tends to downplay the physical and manual labour that goes into them.

The notion of immaterial labour only focuses on the bright side of the expansion of communication, interaction and knowledge, while leaving its dirty counterpart in the dark. What is rather needed is demystification by fostering "greater transparency in working conditions throughout the ICT/CE (consumer electronics) supply chain" in order to shed light on the work and life realities of "workers who disappear in the twilight zone of the technological sublime" (Maxwell and Miller, 2012: 108). As Mosco argues, only if computer technologies "cease to be sublime icons of mythology [...] they can become important forces for social and economic change" (Mosco, 2004: 6).

This paper contributes to this task of demystification as it looks at the working conditions in Chinese assembly plants of one of the world's most dominant and most admired computer companies: Apple Inc. Studying Apple is important because the company represents both the mental and the manual side of digital labour: for many years, Apple's products have been known as the preferred digital production technologies for the knowledge work of designers, journalists, artists and new media workers. iPhone, iPod and Co are symbols for technological progress that enables unprecedented levels of co-creation and sharing of knowledge, images and affects as well as interaction, communication, co-operation, etc. At the same time, during the past years, Apple has become an infamous example for the existence of hard manual labour under miserable conditions along the supply chain of consumer electronics. In this paper, I therefore use the example of Apple for highlighting that an adequate conceptualization of digital labour must not ignore its physical and manual aspects.

In the first part of this article, I give a brief overview of the developments that led to the rise of China as the "workshop of the world". Following this overview, I contrast Apple's business success with allegations from corporate watchdogs regarding poor working conditions in the company's supply chain. In order to examine these allegations in greater detail, I then introduce a systematic model of working conditions and apply it to Apple's contract manufacturers in China. Finally, I discuss Apple's response to labour rights violations and conclude with some reflections on solidarity along the global value chain.

## THE RISE OF CHINA AS "WORKSHOP OF THE WORLD"

The rise of neoliberal globalization and international value chains is generally considered as a reaction to the crisis of Fordist capitalism in the 1970s (Fröbel, Heinrichs and Kreye, 1981; Smith, 2012: 40; Harvey, 2005; Munck, 2002: 45). Part of the restructuring of capitalism was the gradual relocation of large parts of production activities from the industrialized core of the world economy to the former periphery. In this context, Fröbel, Heinrichs and Kreye coined the concept of the "new international division of labour" (NIDL). They argue that "the development of the world economy has increasingly created conditions (forcing the development of the new international division of labour) in which the survival of more and more companies can only be assured through the relocation of production to new industrial sites, where labour-power is cheap to buy, abundant and well-disciplined; in short, through the transnational reorganization of production" (Fröbel, Heinrichs and Kreye, 1981: 15). As a consequence, commodity production became "increasingly subdivided into fragments which can be assigned to whichever part of the world can provide the most profitable combination of capital and labour" (ibid). The result was the emergence of global value chains and production networks in various industries including the electronics sector.

This development had a substantial impact on labour relations and working conditions around the world. As the global labour force expanded (Munck, 2002: 109), the protection of labour rights was weakened. McGuigan (2005: 230) argues that neoliberal restructurings and the rise of post-Fordism led to "an attack on organized labour in older industrialised capitalist states and devolution of much manufacturing to much cheaper labour markets and poor working conditions of newly industrialising countries".

The rise of China as the "workshop of the world" needs to be seen in the context of these developments. Hung stresses that "China's labour-intensive takeoff coincided with the onset of an unprecedented expansion of global free trade since the 1980s" (Hung, 2009: 10). The integration of China into global capitalist production networks was made possible by a number of policy reforms pursued by the Chinese state. Harvey (2006) highlights that the Chinese economic reform programme initiated in the late 1970s coincided with the rise of neoliberalism in the US and the UK. This reform program included the encouragement of competition between state owned companies, the introduction of market pricing as well as a gradual turn towards foreign direct investment (ibid). The first Special Economic Zones (SEZs) in China were established in 1980. The first four SEZs were located in the coastal areas of south-east China: Shantou, Shenzhen and Zhuhai in Guangdong province, and Xiamen in Fujian Province. By 2002, Harvey argues, foreign direct investment accounted for more than 40 percent of China's GDP (ibid).

Hong (2011) highlights that China was particularly interested in entering the market for ICT production. In order to boost exports, tax refunds for the export of ICT commodities were set in place in the 1990s. In 2005, import tariffs for semiconductor, computer and telecommunication products were removed. These policies proved effective. Hong (2011: 2) argues that "in the global market, China has emerged as a leading ICT manufacturing powerhouse. In 2006, China became the world's second largest ICT manufacturer, and ICT products manufactured in China accounted for over 15 percent of the international trade of ICT products".

The fact that attracting foreign direct investment was made possible by granting tax exemptions means that foreign companies could make use of Chinese land area and exploit Chinese labour, while paying only little back to the Chinese public through taxes. Hong shows that by 2005, 40.4 percent of ICT companies in China were foreign enterprises, which controlled 71.1 percent of all profits from the industry, but due to tax benefits these foreign invested in ICT enterprises only made up 42.3 percent of the total tax contribution of the sector (Hong, 2011).

An effect of the shift towards pro-market policies and the privatization of state enterprises was the massive commodification of labour (Su, 2011: 346). The newly established market for labour power replaced the previous system in which workers were guaranteed employment as well as social welfare including medical care, education opportunities, pensions and housing (Friedman and Lee, 2010: 509). Zhao and Duffy (2008) point out that the adoption of a policy towards foreign direct investment in the ICT sector and the privatization of industries also meant a weakening of the power of the Chinese working class. Older industrial workers were replaced by young, often female migrant workers.

Low wages and cheap production costs made China attractive for companies in search for outsourcing opportunities. Hung (2009) argues that the prolonged stagnation of wages resulted from Chinese government policies that neglected and exploited the rural agricultural sector in order to spur urban industrial growth. This situation forced young people to leave the countryside in order to find work in the city, creating a "limitless supply of labour" while reinforcing "a rural social crisis" (Hung, 2009: 14). Among the companies that are taking advantage of the cheap labour supply in China is the computer giant, Apple.

## APPLE: CLEAN IMAGE VERSUS DIRTY REALITY

Steve Wozniak, Steve Jobs and Ronald Wayne founded Apple in 1976 (Linzmayer, 2004). However, it was not until the mid 2000s that Apple joined the elite of the most profitable companies in the world. In 2005, Apple's profits for the first time exceeded $1 billion, and during the following years continued to increase rapidly until they reached $41.7 billion in 2012 (Apple SEC-Filings, 2012), which made Apple the second most profitable company in the world[1]. Between 2000 and 2012, Apple's profits on average grew 39.2% each year[2] (ibid). See Figure 1 for more detail.

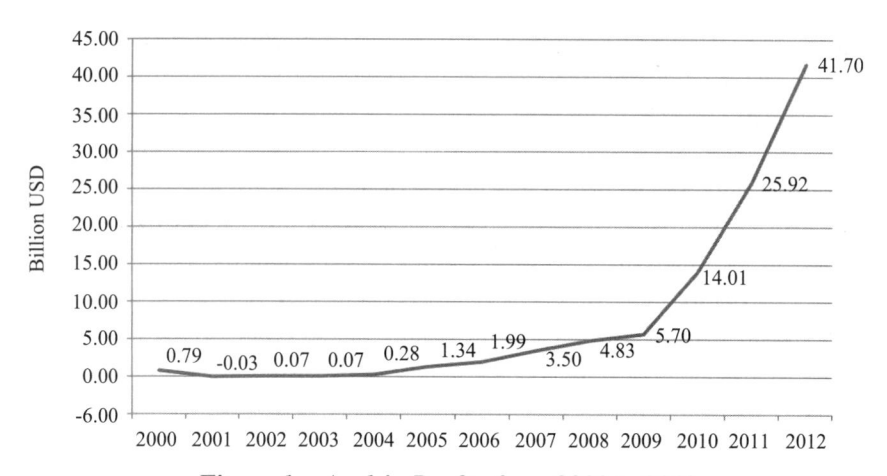

*Figure 1   Apple's Profits from 2000 to 2012*

In 2012, Apple's total net sales amounted to $156.51 billion. The largest share of it was derived from hardware, whereby the iPhone was Apple's most successful product (Figure 2).

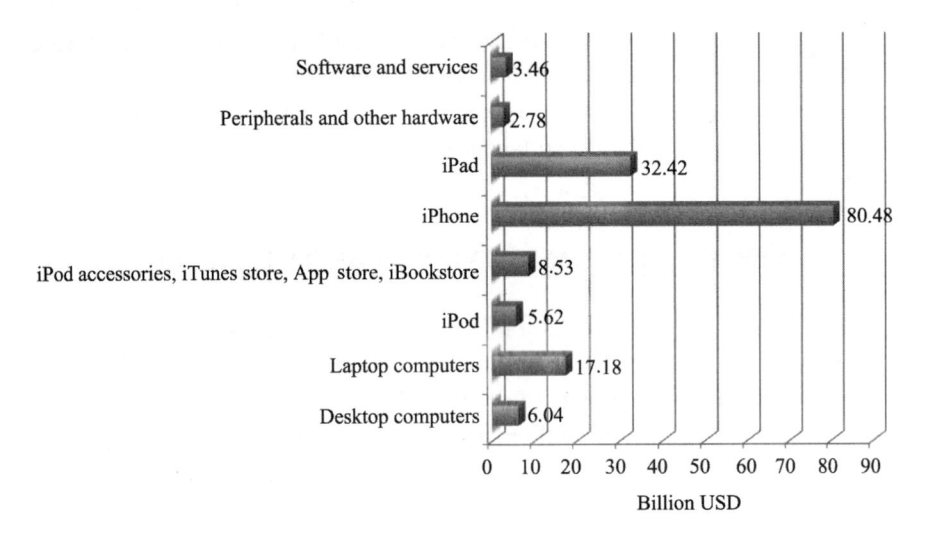

*Figure 2   Apple's Net Sales by Product 2012*

| Product | Billion USD |
|---|---|
| Software and services | 3.46 |
| Peripherals and other hardware | 2.78 |
| iPad | 32.42 |
| iPhone | 80.48 |
| iPod accessories, iTunes store, App store, iBookstore | 8.53 |
| iPod | 5.62 |
| Laptop computers | 17.18 |
| Desktop computers | 6.04 |

In addition to its economic success, Apple is also successful in building its reputation. Fortune Magazine, for six years in a row (2008-2013), has ranked Apple the most admired company in the world[3]. According to a survey among 47,000 people from 15 countries that was conducted by the consultancy firm Reputation Institute, Apple is the company with the 5th best Corporate Social Responsibility (CSR) reputation worldwide (Reputation Institute, 2012).

This image does not correspond to the company's actual business practices. The production of Apple's hardware products, on which its economic success is built (see Figure 1), is largely outsourced to contract manufacturers in China. In May and June 2010, many major Western media reported about a series of suicides at factory campuses in China. The factories, at which 17 young workers jumped to death between 2007 and May 2010[4] belong to the Taiwan-based company Hon Hai Precision Industry Co. Ltd, better known as Foxconn, which is a major supplier for computer giants such as Apple, Hewlett-Packard and Nokia (Finnwatch, SACOM and SOMO, 2011).

Hon Hai Precision is a profitable company itself. According to Forbes Magazine, it is the 113th biggest company in the world. In 2012, its profits amounted to $10.7 billion[5]. Nevertheless, the company strongly depends on orders from consumer brands such as Apple. Finnwatch, SACOM and SOMO (2009: 44) describe this situation as follows: "these companies often drive down the price they pay their suppliers, which then makes the suppliers less or no longer profitable. To get back in the game, suppliers reduce costs, often at the cost of workers, violating labour laws in the process." Competition between contract manufacturers such as Foxconn is also high, which is why profit rates can often only be achieved by keeping cost low (SOMO, 2005a). Although some Foxconn factories are exclusively producing for Apple, such as for example three plants in Zhengzhou, Henan (SACOM, 2012), Foxconn is not the only company that is manufacturing Apple products. Other Apple suppliers include Pegatron Corporation, Primax Electronics, Quanta Computers, Wintek or Foxlink[6]. Working conditions are similar throughout these factories (SACOM, 2010, 2012, 2013). SACOM (2012: 1) argues that "illegal long working hours, low wages and poor occupational health and safety are rooted in the unethical purchasing practices of Apple".

The losers in this corporate race for profit are the workers. When young Foxconn workers decided to end their lives by jumping from their employer's factory buildings, Western media for some weeks were looking behind the surface of bright and shiny computer products. For example, *The New York Times* published a story about *String of Suicides Continues at Electronics Supplier in China*[7]; the BBC reported on *Foxconn Suicides: Workers Feel Quite Lonely*[8]; *Time Magazine* published an article entitled *Chinese Factory Under Scrutiny As Suicides Mount*[9]; *The Guardian* headlined *Latest Foxconn Suicide Raises Concern Over Factory Life in China*[10], and CNN reported *Inside China Factory Hit By Suicides*[11].

However, these suicides are only the tip of the iceberg. For several years, NGOs have stressed that computers, mp3 players, game consoles, etc. are often produced under miserable working conditions (ICO, Finnwatch and ECA, 2005; SOMO, 2005b, 2007a). Far away from shopping centres and department stores, workers in factories in Asia or Latin America produce consumer electronics devices during 10 to 12 hour shifts, a minimum of 6 days a week for at best a minimum wage. Apple's suppliers are no exception. In the next sections, I develop a systematic account of working conditions, which I will subsequently apply to the situation in the workshops of Apple's contract manufactures in China.

## A SYSTEMATIC MODEL OF WORKING CONDITIONS

A suitable starting point for a systematic model of different dimensions of working conditions is the circuit of capital accumulation as it has been described by Karl Marx (1867/1976: 248-253; 1885/1992: 109). According to Marx, capital accumulation in a first stage requires the investment of capital in order to buy what is necessary for producing commodities, the productive forces: labour time of workers (L or variable capital) on the one hand, and working equipment like machines and raw materials (MoP or constant capital) on the other hand (Marx, 1885/1992: 110). Thus, money (M) is used in order to buy labour power as well as machines and resources as commodities (C) that then in a second stage enter the labour process and produce (P) a new commodity (C')

(Marx, 1885/1992: 118). This new commodity (C') contains more value than the sum of its parts, i.e. surplus value. This surplus value needs to be realized and turned into more money (M') by selling the commodity in the market (Marx, 1885/1992: 125). The circuit of capital accumulation can thus be described with the following formula: M → C ... P ... C' → M' (Marx, 1885/1992: 110).

According to Marx, surplus value can only be generated due to the specific qualities of labour-power as a commodity. Marx argued that labour power is the only commodity "whose use-value possesses the peculiar property of being a source of value, whose actual consumption is therefore itself an objectification of labour, hence a creation of value" (Marx, 1867/1976: 270).

Labour is thus essential to the process of capital accumulation. The model I constructed thus takes this process as its point of departure for identifying different dimensions that shape working conditions. The purpose of this model is to provide comprehensive guidelines that can be applied for systematically studying working conditions in different sectors.

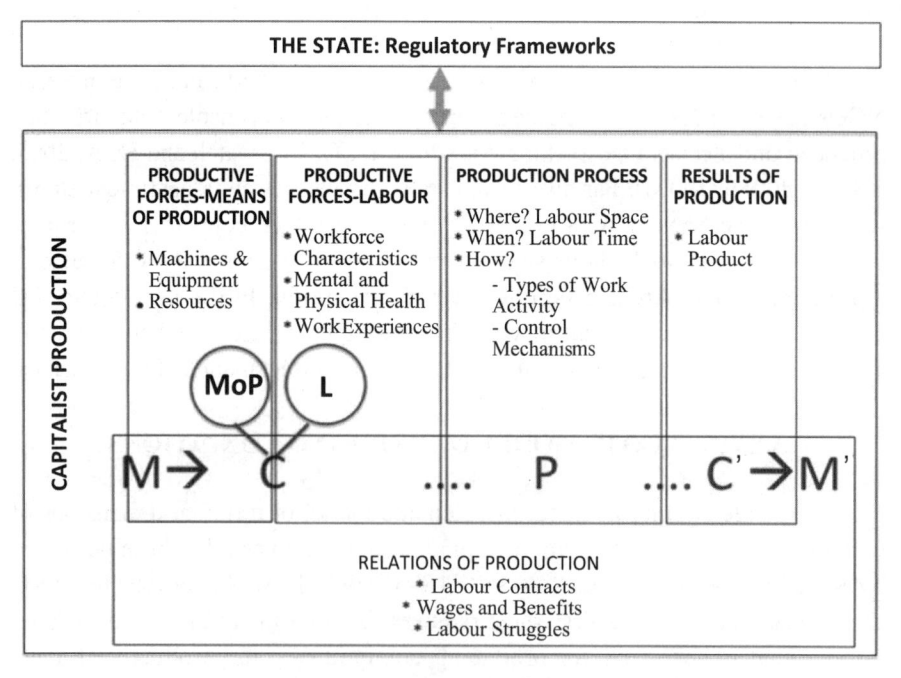

*Figure 3   Dimensions of Working Conditions*

The model pictured in Figure 3 identifies five areas that shape working conditions throughout the capital accumulation process: means of production, labour, relations of production, production process and results of production. Furthermore, this model

includes the state's impact on working conditions through labour legislation:
- **Productive forces – means of production:** Means of production include *machines and equipment* on the one hand and *resources* that are needed for production on the other hand. The question whether workers operate big machines, work at the assembly line, use mobile devices such as laptops, handle potentially hazardous substances, use high-tech equipment, traditional tools or no technology at all, etc. shapes the experience of work and has a strong impact on work processes and working conditions.
- **Productive forces – labour:** The subjects of the labour process are workers themselves. One dimension that impacts work in a certain sector is the question how the *workforce* is composed in terms of gender, ethnic background, age, education levels, etc. Another question concerns worker *health and safety* and how it is affected by the means of production, the relations of production, the labour process and labour law(s). Apart from outside impacts on the worker, an important factor is how workers themselves *experience* their working conditions.
- **Relations of production:** Within capitalist relations of production, capitalists buy labour power as a commodity. Thereby, a relation between capital and labour is established. The purchase of labour power is expressed through *wages*. Wages are the primary means of subsistence for workers and the reason why they enter a wage labour relation. The level of wages thus is a central element of working conditions. *Labour contracts* specify the conditions under which capital and labour enter this relation, including working hours, wages, work roles and responsibilities, etc. The content of this contract is subject to negotiations and often *struggles between capital and labour*. The relation between capital and labour is thus established through a *wage relation* and formally enacted by a *labour contract* that is subject to negotiations and *struggles*. These three dimensions of the relation between capital and labour set the framework for the capitalist labour process.
- **Production process:** Assessing working conditions furthermore requires looking at the specifics of the actual production process. A first factor in this context is its *spatial location*. Whether it is attached to a certain place or is location independent, whether it takes place in a factory, an office building, or outdoors, etc. are important questions. A second factor relates to the *temporal dimension of work*. Relevant questions concern the amount of regular working hours and overtime, work rhythms, the flexibility or rigidity of working hours, the relation between work time and free time, etc. Finally, working conditions are essentially shaped by how the production process is executed. It includes on the one hand the question which *types of work activity* are performed. The activities can range from intellectual work, to physical work, to service work, from skilled to unskilled work, from creative work to monotonous and standardized work tasks, etc. On the other hand, another aspect of the production process is how it

is *controlled and managed*. Different management styles can range from strict control of worker behaviour and the labour process to high degrees of autonomy, self-management or participatory management, etc. *Space, time, activity* and *control* are essential qualities of the production process and therefore need to be considered when studying working conditions.

- **Results of production:** Throughout the production process, workers put their time, effort and energy into producing a certain *product*. This actual outcome of production and how it relates back to the worker thus needs to be considered for understanding work in a certain sector.
- **The state:** Finally, the state has an impact on working conditions through enacting *labour laws* that regulate minimum wages, maximum working hours, social security, safety standards, etc. Table 1 summarizes the dimensions of working conditions aforementioned in full detail.

*Table 1   Dimensions of Working Conditions*

| | | |
|---|---|---|
| Productive forces - means of production | Machines and equipment | Which technology is being used during the production process? |
| | Resources | What resources are used during the production process? |
| Productive forces - labour | Workforce characteristics | What are important characteristics of the workforce for example in terms of age, gender, ethnic background, etc.? |
| | Mental and physical health | How do the employed means of production and the labour process impact mental and physical health of workers? |
| | Work experiences | How do workers experience their working conditions? |
| Relations of production | Labour contracts | Which type of contracts do workers receive, and what do they regulate? |
| | Wages and benefits | How high/low are wage levels and what are other material benefits for workers? |
| | Labour struggles | How do workers organize and engage in negotiations with capital and what is the role of worker protests? |

| Production process | Labour space | Where does the production process take place? |
|---|---|---|
| | Labour time | How many working hours are common within a certain sector, and how are they enforced and how is the relationship between work and free time? |
| | Work activity | Which type of mental and/or physical activity are workers performing? |
| | Control mechanisms | Which type of mechanisms are in place that control the behaviour of workers? |
| Results of production | Labour product | Which kinds of products or services are being produced? |
| The state | Labour law | Which regulations regarding minimum wages, maximum working hours, safety, social security, etc. are in place and how are they enforced? |

Based on research that has been conducted by corporate watchdogs, I will now take a closer look at all of the described dimensions in Apple's manufacturing factories in China.

## WORKING CONDITIONS AT APPLE'S CONTRACT MANUFACTURERS IN CHINA

Corporate watchdogs such as Students and Scholars Against Corporate Misbehaviour (SACOM), China Labour Watch (CLW) and the organisations involved in the European project makeITfair have collected comprehensive data about working conditions in Apple's supply chain. SACOM is a Hong-Kong based NGO that was founded in 2005. It brings together concerned labour rights activists, students, scholars and consumers in order to monitor working conditions throughout China and elsewhere[12]. SACOM's research is largely based on undercover investigations and anonymous interviews with workers, conducted outside of factory campuses. Its research results are documented in reports such as *iSlave behind the iPhone. Foxconn Workers in Central China* (SACOM, 2011b) or *New iPhone, Old Abuses. Have Working Conditions at*

*Foxconn in China Improved?* (SACOM, 2012) that are made available online. CLW is another independent NGO that was founded in 2000. Since then, it has collaborated with workers, unions, labour activists and the media in order to monitor working conditions in different industries in China. CLW's Shenzhen office works directly with local workers and factories, while CLW's New York based office produces investigation reports and makes them available to an international audience[13].

The project makeITfair[14], funded by the European Union (2006-2012), focuses on working conditions and environmental impacts throughout the live-cycles consumer electronics such as computers, mobile phones, photo cameras or mp3 players. The research that was conducted within the project is based on anonymous interviews with workers outside factory buildings and sometimes also includes interviews with management officials. Workers tend to be hesitant to answer questions about their working conditions as they depend on their jobs and are afraid of negative consequences, especially if the investigators are foreigners. Therefore, the European project partners such as Swedwatch, Germanwatch, SOMO, Finnwatch or Danwatch co-operate with local NGOs and researchers who approach and interview workers without the knowledge of factory managers. MakeITfair informs the electronics brand companies such as Apple, Dell or HP of its research results and invites them to comment on the findings. Based on its research, makeITfair aims at raising awareness among consumers, activists and policy makers about the work and life reality of workers in the manufacturing of consumer electronics and at pressuring electronics companies to improve working conditions in their supply chains.

I will in the following use data provided by these corporate watchdogs in order to shed light on the work reality of those who are manufacturing Apple's products in China.

**Productive Forces — Means of Production**

According to Marx, means of production consist of tools and instruments on the one hand and raw materials on the other hand (Marx 1867/1976). The fact that in capitalism means of production are privately owned lays the foundation for exploitation and the domination of man by man: "modern bourgeois property is the final and most complete expression of the system of producing and appropriating products, that is based on class antagonism, on the exploitation of the many by the few" (Marx and Engels, 1848/1991: 46). For the majority of people, private ownership of means of production in fact means non-ownership. Being deprived from the necessary capital to buy means of production that are needed to engage in a production process, workers have to sell their labour power in order to earn their means of subsistence. Private ownership of machines and equipment as well as resources is thus the starting point of the capitalist labour process. I will now consider which instruments and resources are needed for producing Apple's products.

*Machines and Equipment*

Compared to other manufacturing sectors such as apparel or toys, electronics manufacturing is relatively capital intensive and requires high-tech equipment (Plank and Staritz, 2013; Lüthje, 2006). This is even more the case as computer products are becoming more sophisticated, smaller in size and lower in weight (WTEC, 1997: 16). However, the consultancy firm McKinsey & Company classifies the final assembly of high-tech products as labour-intensive (McKinsey & Company 2012). One reason for this is that the fragmentation of the production process allows to separate "labour-intensive and more capital- and knowledge- intensive parts" so that "there is a considerable amount of low-value and thus low-skill and low-wage activity, which is often combined with advanced production technologies in this 'high-tech' sector" (Plank and Staritz, 2013: 9). Electronics manufacturing is thus characterized by both high-tech equipment and high demand for labour.

Electronics manufacturing is among those industries that account for the most robot purchases. According to McKinsey & Company (2012: 88), "in 2010, automotive and electronics manufacturing each accounted for more than 30,000 robot units sold globally, while industries such as food and beverage, rubber and plastics, and metal products each bought only 4,000 to 6,000 new robots".

A technology that Apple's contract manufacturers employ for the automated part of assembly is Surface Mount Technology (SMT) (WTEC, 1997; Lüthje, 2012). SMT uses programming to automatically solder electronics components such as chips or connectors onto circuit boards[15]. Lüthje (2012) argues that as labour costs in China are low, not the entire potential of automation is realized, thus the degree of automation in most factories in China and Asia is lower than it would be in Europe or the United States. This means that labour is sometimes cheaper than high-tech equipment. It also means that making use of the full range of automation technology available could eliminate parts of the repetitive and standardized work activities that are now part of electronics production.

*Resources*

Among the resources needed for the production of consumer electronics such as Apple's Mac's, iPads, iPhones and iPods are minerals such as tin, gallium, platinum, tantalum, indium, neodymium, ruthenium, palladium, lanthanum, and cobalt (SOMO, 2007b; Friends of the Earth, 2012). Often these minerals are sourced in conflict areas (SOMO, 2007b). The mining activities usually take place under extremely poor health and safety conditions. They are also extremely low paid, require the resettlement of local villages, and threaten the environment and the livelihood of local communities (SOMO, 2007b, 2011; Swedwatch 2007; Finnwatch 2007).

Cobalt for example is mainly extracted in the so-called copperbelt in Zambia and the Democratic Republic of Congo (DRC) (Swedwatch, 2007). It is needed for the production of rechargeable batteries for laptops, mobile phones, etc. as well as for speakers, headphones and the coatings of hard drives (ibid). Swedwatch in an investigation of mining activities in the Katanga province in DRC found that worker are risking their lives for an income of about $2-4 per day. Many of the miners are children: an estimated number of 50,000 children between the age of 7 and 18 are working in the mines of Katanga and thus form a large part of the total workforce of 10,000-14,000 miners.

The DRC is rich on mineral resources but has been shaped by poverty as well as colonial violence, civil war and armed conflict. A report by Free the Slaves shows that mines in DRC are often controlled by armed rebel groups that force local people into slavery (Free the Slaves, 2011). Many women and girls, who are often not allowed to work in the mines, are forced into sexual exploitation (ibid).

It is difficult to determine where exactly and under which conditions the minerals contained in a product of a certain electronics brand were sourced. However, sometimes watchdogs successfully trace the supply chain of a brand back to the point of mineral extraction. In 2012, Friends of the Earth published a report that traces the tin used in Apple's iPhones back to mines in Bangka, an island in Indonesia. The report reveals that Foxconn and Samsung, which are Apple's direct suppliers, buy their tin from the middle companies Shenmao, Chernan and PT Timah, which obtain their tin from Indonesia. 90% of Indonesian tin is mined at Bangka island (Friends of the Earth, 2012). The report shows how tin mining destroyed forests and farmlands, killed coral, seagrass and mangroves and led fish to disappear, and contaminated drinking water (ibid). The destruction of the ecosystem deprives local farmers and fishermen of their livelihood, forcing them to become tin miners themselves. Tin mining at Bangka island is dangerous and security standards are low. Friends of the Earth reports that that in 2011, on average, one miner per week was killed in an accident (ibid).

Conflict minerals are used for producing electronics parts such as researchable batteries (cobalt), magnets (cobalt), speakers (cobalt), power amplifiers (gallium), camera flashes (gallium), high efficiency transistors (indium), flat screens (indium, platinum), lead frames (palladium), plating connectors (palladium), chip resistors (ruthenium), capacitors (neodymium, lanthanum, tantalum) or circuit boards (tin) (Finnwatch, 2007).

Long before minerals enter the final assembly process of consumer electronics, they have passed through a process framed by destruction and exploitation. It is important to recognize this history of the components that are assembled in Apple's manufacturing factories. Threats to workers and the environment connected to these minerals, however, continue: due to the toxic qualities of many minerals, they can potentially harm workers in electronics manufacturing. Furthermore, the fact that toxic minerals are contained in electronics products can cause problems at the point of disposal. Toxic electronic waste often ends up in waste dumps in the global South where it contaminates the environment and threatens the health of waste worker (Danwatch, 2011).

**Productive Forces — Labour**

Focusing on the subjective side of the labour process, at workers themselves, shows that work on Apple's manufacturing sites is often performed by young female migrant workers, who are exposed to serious health hazards and experience their daily work life as alienating and exhausting.

*Workforce Characteristics*

The majority of production workers in China are young female migrant workers (Bread for All and SACOM, 2008; FinnWatch, SACOM and SOMO, 2009). Estimates show that in the Chinese Guangdong province, for example, migrant workers make up 65 percent of the workforce in the manufacturing sector (Finnwatch, SACOM and SOMO, 2009).

Migrant workers are a particularly vulnerable group of workers. Far away from their hometown, they lack social contacts and are therefore prone to isolation. Migrant workers also receive fewer social benefits. According to the FLA (Fair Labour Association) investigation, migrant workers at Shenzhen – which constitute 99% of the total workforce – are not covered by unemployment and maternity insurance systems because they do not have a Shenzhen residence card (FLA, 2012). Even if migrant workers have unemployment insurance, they often cannot claim benefits in their hometown due to lacking transfer agreements between provinces. They remain always dependent on their social networks in their hometowns, especially in times of unemployment, illness or pregnancy. This situation keeps many workers trapped as permanent migrants (Friedman and Lee, 2010).

Many workers in the electronics industry are young women, who leave their families on the countryside to find work in an industrial area and provide some financial assistance for their relatives. Often factories prefer to hire female workers because they are considered to be good at performing detail-oriented work and to be more obedient and less likely to engage in protests (Swedwatch, SACOM and SOMO, 2008).

Workers often have no other choice than to find employment in a factory in order to be able to earn enough money to support themselves and their families. This dependency increases the power of companies over workers. The lack of alternatives makes it likely that workers feel forced to accept bad working conditions.

### *Mental and Physical Health*

Threats to health and safety in electronics factories result from the usage of hazardous substances, insufficient information of workers about the substances they are using, a lack of protection equipment, and unsafe work routines. During the last couple of years, a number of serious incidents occurred at Apple's supplier factories.

For example, between July 2009 and early 2010, 47 workers at United Win, a subsidy of Wintek Corporation that produces Apple products, were hospitalized because of being poisoned with n-hexane (SACOM, 2010). If inhaled, n-hexane can cause nerve damage and paralysis of arms and legs. The poisoned workers were using n-hexane for cleaning iPhone touch screens. When the first poisoning occurred, workers organized a strike. As a result, United Win organized health examinations. However, no poisoning was diagnosed during these examinations. The affected workers therefore went to a hospital outside the factory, in which the poisoning was finally diagnosed. Similar health hazards were also found at Futaihua Precision Electronics, a Foxconn subsidiary in Zhengzhou, where around 52,500 workers are producing 100,000 iPhones per day. Workers were exposed to chemicals such as n-hexane without adequate protection equipment. Some workers suffered from allergies (SACOM, 2011b).

In 2011, SACOM monitored Foxconn's Chengdu factory that produces exclusively for Apple. The investigation revealed an alarming occupational health and safety situation. SACOM found poor ventilation, insufficient protection equipment, and noisy workplaces. Workers were using chemicals, without knowing whether they were harmful. At the milling and the polishing department — in which the iPads's aluminium cover is polished until it is untarnished and shiny — workers were constantly breathing in aluminium dust. Several workers were suffering from a skin allergy after working with glue like substances without wearing gloves (SACOM, 2011a). Shortly after SACOM's report was published, aluminium dust triggered an explosion at the polishing department at Chengdu that killed 3 workers and left 15 injured (SACOM, 2011b; Friends of Nature, IPE, Green Beagle, 2011). The Chengdu campus, which consists of 8 factory buildings, was built in only 76 days in order to meet growing demand from Apple. Furthermore, workers were insufficiently trained and not aware of the dangers connected to aluminium dust (ibid).

A similar incident occurred at the iPhone polishing department at a Pegatron factory in Shanghai in December 2011. 61 workers were injured (SACOM, 2013). SACOM furthermore reports that weak ventilations system at Pegatron's polishing department creates high levels of dust that cover worker's faces and penetrate their masks entering their noses and mouths (ibid).

Working conditions at electronics manufacturing factories are not only threatening workers' physical health but also creating psychological problems. Social life at Foxconn is deprived. Workers do not have time for any free time activities. Their life consists of working, eating and sleeping. Often they do not even find enough time to sleep. When asked what they would like to do on holiday, most interviewees said that they would like to sleep (SACOM, 2011a). Workers lack social contacts. SACOM's research shows that workers were not allowed to talk during work. They live in rooms with workers from different shifts, which they therefore hardly ever meet (SACOM, 2011a; FinnWatch, SACOM and SOMO, 2011).

Work and life at factory campuses have severe impacts on the bodies and minds of workers. The example of Apple's supplier factories in China illustrates that for many workers, selling their labour power also means selling their mental and physical health.

*Work Experiences*

During the past five years, corporate watchdogs have interviewed numerous workers at Apple's supplier factories. These interviews reveal that workers experience their work as exhausting and alienating. They feel stressed and under pressure in order to achieve production targets (FinnWatch, SACOM and SOMO, 2011) as well as exhausted due to extremely long working hours, long hours of standing, and stress during meal breaks (SACOM, 2011a).

One worker told SACOM that workers feel Apple's demand dictates their entire lives. Workers are torn between the need to increase their salary by working overtime and the need to rest:

> The daily production target is 6,400 pieces. I am worn out every day. I fall asleep immediately after returning to the dormitory. The demand from Apple determines our lives. On one hand, I hope I can have a higher wage. On the other hand, I cannot keep working every day without a day-off. (Foxconn worker quoted in SACOM, 2012)

Workers furthermore experience their work environment as unsafe and unpleasant. They are worried about their health due to a lack of protection equipment:

> In my department, the working conditions are unbearable. I'm a machine operator, producing the silver frame for the iPhone. We have to put some oil into the machines in the production. I don't know what kind of substance it is and the smell is irritating. The frontline management confided to us that we should not stay in the department for over a year because the oil could cause problems to our lungs. Although the shop floor has air conditioning, it is very hot and the ventilation is poor. For me, the installation of the air-conditioners is just a tactic to avoid paying high temperature subsidy to the workers. (Foxconn worker quoted in SACOM, 2011b)

Furthermore, workers describe the way they are controlled and managed as humiliating and exhausting:

> We have to queue up all the time. Queuing up for bus, toilet, card-punching, food, etc. During recess, we don't have a place to sit. We can only sit on the floor. We get up in early morning and can only return to the dorm in late evening. I am really worn out. (Foxconn worker quoted in SACOM, 2011a)

Workers are aware of the alienating characteristic of their work situation, which expressed by the fact that they are not able to own the products that they are themselves producing every day. One worker told SACOM that:

> Though we produce for iPhone, I haven't got a chance to use iPhone. I believe it is fascinating and has lots of function. However, I don't think I can own one by myself. (ibid)

These descriptions show that workers find themselves in a state of exhaustion and alienation. Marx described the alienation of worker as his/her labour becoming an external object that "exists outside him, independently, as something alien to him" (Marx, 1844/2007: 70). The more life the worker puts into his/her product, the more alienated s/he becomes: "the worker puts his life into the object; but now his life no longer belongs to him, but to the object. [...] The greater this product, the less is he himself" (ibid).

Workers in Apple's manufacturing factories have put their labour power into these products while producing them. Many workers left their families, gave up their free time and their health for producing products, which they will never be able to own. The finished products, although containing the workers' energy and labour, suddenly turn out of their reach. Workers are inside Apple's products, but at the same time insurmountably separated from them.

**Relations of Production**

The relation between capital and labour needs to be understood as a relation of domination. In capitalism, the only commodity workers possess is their labour power. In order to make a living, they thus have no other choice but to sell it by entering into a wage labour relationship (Marx, 1867/1976). Research conducted by corporate watchdogs shows that the relation between (mostly foreign) capital and labour in Apple's supplier factories in China is largely based on precarious labour contracts, characterized by low wages and occasionally contested through labour struggles.

*Labour Contracts*

Labour contracts that offer weak protection for workers are an expression of the unequal power relation between employers and workers. In 2004, the Institute for Contemporary Observation (ICO), FinnWatch and the Finnish Export Credit Agency (ECA) investigated the Shenzhen Foxconn campus. They found that workers could be dismissed anytime. If dismissed, employees had to leave immediately without any financial compensation. If workers decided to quit and to leave immediately, they would not receive their outstanding wage (ICO, Finnwatch and ECA, 2005).

Watchdogs found instances where workers in Apple supplier factories did not receive any contract at all (ICO, Finnwatch and ECA, 2005; Swedwatch, SACOM and SOMO, 2008; Bread for All and SACOM, 2008). Without a signed contract, workers are deprived of the possibility of taking legal steps in the case of labour law violations.

The majority of labour contracts in Apple's supplier factories are precarious. Short-term contracts allow supplier companies to remain flexible and to quickly respond to fluctuations of Apple's demand. Another measure Foxconn uses in order to cover sudden increases of labour demand is to recruit workers from labour agencies, or to relocate workers from other cities and provinces to another factory that has a heightened demand for workers

(SACOM, 2012). So-called dispatch or agency workers are hired by labour agencies rather than being employed directly by the contract manufacturer. According to SACOM, around 80% of the total workforce of the Apple supplier factories Foxlink in Guangdong, Pegatron in Shanghai and Wintek in Jiangsu are agency workers (SACOM, 2013).

New workers often have a 3-6 month probationary period during which their wages are lower than those of permanent workers. For example, the wage increases Foxconn implemented after the suicide tragedies were only granted to workers that had been working in the factory for more than 6 months (Finnwatch, SACOM and SOMO, 2011).

Another common practice among Apple's contract manufacturers is the employment of student interns. Especially during peak season, students are hired in order to cover the sudden labour demand (SACOM, 2012). Students are cheaper to employ since they do not receive regular social security benefits, and are not covered by labour law. They, however, have to work night shifts and overtime like regular workers. Student workers complain that the work they have to perform in Apple supplier factories is unskilled labour that is unrelated to the subject of their studies. Although students officially are not allowed to work more than 8 hours per day, they are treated like regular workers and have to work overtime as well as night shifts (SACOM, 2011a). They also feel forced to work at these factories, as they are afraid that they will not be able to graduate if they refuse to complete the internship (SACOM, 2013). Su argues that the internship programs led to the commodification of both student's labour and education (Su, 2011).

Finnwatch, SACOM and SOMO (2009) found that large numbers of 16- to 18-year old students were employed in Foxconn factories for periods between 4 and 6 months. SACOM (2011b) quotes reports from Chinese media according to which in 2010, 100,000 vocational school students from Henan province were sent to work at a Foxconn plant in Shenzhen to complete a 3-month internship. An investigation by the FLA, that Apple had requested, confirmed that Foxconn did not comply with the standards regarding maximum working hours for student interns (FLA, 2012).

Short-term precarious contracts and weak protection against dismissal increase factory management's power over workers. It makes workers vulnerable and serves as a means for controlling their behaviour by threat of dismissal. Because workers need to fear losing their jobs, they are more likely to agree to higher production targets or increased overtime. Precarious contracts make long-term life planning difficult. Short notice periods leave workers hardly any time to rearrange their lives after a dismissal. Furthermore, different types of contracts create divides between workers with fixed contracts, short-term contracts, agency contracts or internship contracts. The fact that different types of contracts confront workers with different kinds of problems makes it more difficult to formulate collective demands.

***Wages and Benefits***

Among the most pressing problems that occur throughout Apple's supplier factories is the low wage level. Already in 2007, the Dutch non-profit research centre SOMO (2007a) interviewed workers at five Apple supplier factories in China, the Philippines and Thailand: workers in all investigated factories reported that their wages were too low to cover their living expenses. Wages at the Chinese factory of Volex Cable Assembly Co. Ltd. were found to be below the legal minimum (ibid). However, even if wages comply with minimum wage regulations, they are often hardly enough to cover basic living expenses. In 2008, for example FinnWatch, SACOM and SOMO (2009) monitored buildings C03 and C04 of Foxconn's Shenzhen campus, in which 2,800 workers at 40 assembly lines are producing black and white models of the iPhone 8G and 16G. Wages corresponded to the legal minimum wage of around 980 *yuan*, which, however, is not an adequate living wage. A living wage should cover expenses for food, housing, clothes, education, social security and health care for a family, and allow for some savings[16].

After the suicide tragedies, Foxconn announced significant wage raises[17]. FinnWatch, SACOM and SOMO in 2010 did a follow up study at Apple's production line at Foxconn's Shenzhen campus in order to investigate how the promised wage raises[18] were implemented. 30 workers were interviewed. The investigation showed that Foxconn in June 2010 increased monthly wages from 900 *yuan* to 1,200 *yuan*. In October 2010, wages were further raised to 2,000 *yuan*, but only for workers who had been working at the factory for more than 6 months. However, only estimated 50% of the workforce actually worked longer than 6 months in this factory (FinnWatch, SACOM and SOMO, 2011). Furthermore, the wage increases only applied to Shenzhen and not to newly established upcountry factories to which Foxconn is increasingly relocating its production.

In 2011, SACOM conducted a similar investigation at three other Foxconn campuses in order to evaluate once more how effective the proposed changes really were and whether they improved working and living conditions of employees. SACOM visited Foxconn campuses at Shenzhen, Chengdu and Chongqing and found that Foxconn had increased wages, but at the same time cancelled food and housing subsidies. This means that despite Foxconn's claims, there was no actual wage increase (SACOM, 2011a). Foxconn was not paying a living wage. Figure 4 shows SACOM's estimations, regarding the gap between actual basic wages and living wages in April 2011.

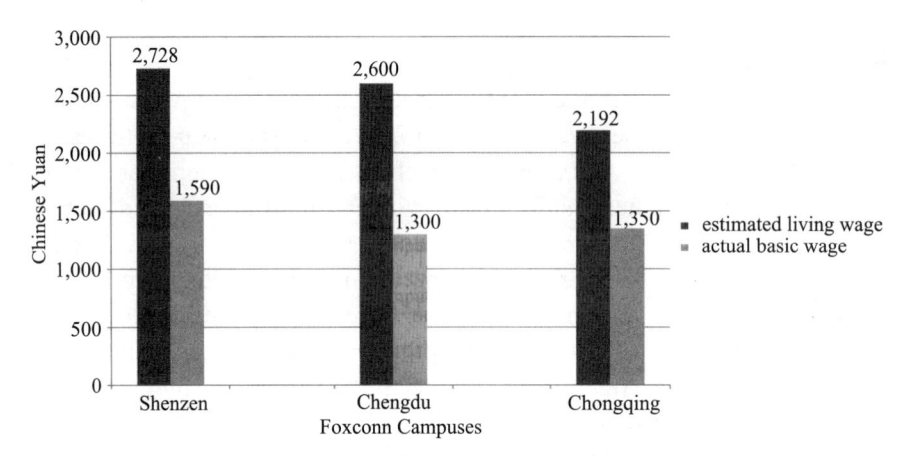

*Figure 4    Actual Basic Wages in Comparison to Estimated Living Wages at Foxconn Campuses in April 2011*

SACOM argues that one strategy Foxconn employs to avoid wage increases is to send workers away from cities with higher wage levels, such as Shenzhen, to ones with lower wages levels such as Chengdu (ibid).

The investigation conducted by the FLA confirms that workers at Apple suppliers perceive their wages as too low. In a survey that assessed the work satisfaction of 35,166 workers at two Foxconn campuses in Shenzhen and one Foxconn campus in Chengdu, 64.3% of all respondents and 72% of respondents working at Foxconn's Chengdu campus reported that their wages do not cover their basic needs (FLA, 2012).

Apple is the second most profitable company in the world. These high profits are made possible at the cost of workers. According to calculations made by Kraemer, Linden and Dedrick (2011), Apple kept 58.5% of the sales price of an iPhone, the costs of materials amounted to 21.9% of the sales price and only 1.8% were spent for the labour cost for final assembly in China in 2010. For the iPad, Chinese labour costs amount to 2%, input materials to 31% and Apple's profits to 30% of the sales price (ibid). The less Apple has to spend for paying wages, the higher are the company's profits. While Apple could certainly afford spending more money for the manufacturing of its products, this would have a negative impact on its profit goals.

Marx (1844/2007: 81) stressed that capitalism is based on a contradiction between capital and labour: "political economy starts from labour as the real soul of production; yet to labour, it gives nothing, and to private property everything". The example of Apple illustrates this fundamental injustice:

Apple's success would be impossible without the work performed in its supplier factories. This work allowed Apple to become profitable, while it left its workers impoverished.

*Labour Struggles*

The low wage level is only one of the reasons why workers engage in strikes and protests. For example, on November 15, 2011, several thousand workers of the Foxconn factory in Foshan were protesting against low wages[19]. In January 2013, over 1,000 workers protested at Foxconn facility in Fengcheng held demonstrations against low wages and poor working conditions[20].

Such protests are not without risks for factory workers. In 2011, during an investigation at Foxconn's Zhengzhou factory, some interviewees told SACOM about workers being dismissed after attempting to strike (SACOM, 2011b).

Labour unions only play a limited role in these protests. The only official trade union in China is the All China Federation of Trade Unions (ACFTU), which is subordinate to the Chinese Communist Party (Friedman and Lee, 2010). Friedman and Lee (2010) argue that the ACFTU acts like a government agency that represents workers in a top-down process, promotes the introduction of labour laws, and provides legal consultation to workers.

Often, workers either do not know what a union can do for them or do not even know that a union exists at their factory (Finnwatch, SACOM, SOMO, 2009, 2011). Similarly, the FLA in 2012 found that worker had very little knowledge about the function and activities of worker representatives. Furthermore, the FLA found that unions at Foxconn often consist of supervisors or mangers (FLA, 2012).

In response to the findings of the FLA, Foxconn in February 2013 announced that it will hold democratic union elections[21]. However, a study conducted by a corporate watchdog shows that in March and April 2013, 90.2% of 685 questioned Foxconn workers had not heard about any election plans (The New Generation Migrant Workers Concern Programme, 2013). The results show that more than 50% of the respondents did not know that union members can democratically elect their representatives and that they can themselves come forward as a candidate. 82.5% of the workers did not know who the leader of their union group was. 16.9% of the respondents reported that they are union members. Further 24.6% said that they think they are members of a union. These numbers show that actual union enrolment is much lower than 86.3%, the number given by Foxconn officials (ibid).

Despite these low levels of awareness regarding the existing union, the survey results show that workers nevertheless think that unions could potentially help to improve their situation. 45.8% of the interviewed Foxconn workers think that a union can play a "very important" role in achieving wage increases, while only 3.4% think that unions are "not important" in this context (ibid). Fostering awareness among workers regarding their rights and strengthening their right to choose union representatives thus seems crucial to support the struggle of workers over their working conditions.

There is the potential that Chinese workers become important agents of labour struggle in the 21$^{st}$ century. In this context, Zhao and Duffy (2008: 244) highlight that "the fact that tens of thousands of Chinese workers are engaging in daily struggles over hand-to-mouth issues must qualify any sweeping post-Marxist formulations by Western-centric scholars about the disappearance of the working class as historical agents of struggle in the information age". In this context, Time Magazine in March 2013 reported that "facing long hours, rising costs, indifferent managers and often late pay, workers are beginning to sound like true proletariat"[22]. Rather than regarding Chinese workers at Apple's suppliers and elsewhere as mere victims of capitalist exploitation, it is important to recognize that collectively organized, they can cause severe disruptions to the global value chain.

On several occasions, activists around the world have supported the struggle of Chinese workers. NGOs and labour rights activists have been protesting against Apple, tolerating unbearable working conditions in its supplier factories. For example, on May 7, 2011, an international day of action against unacceptable treatment of workers was held. MakeITfair, a project of a group of European corporate watchdog organizations, under the slogan "Time to bite into a fair Apple; Call for sustainable IT!" organized protest events throughout Europe[23, 24]. SACOM organized a protest in Hong Kong[25]. Such international solidarity from activists can support worker struggles by raising awareness within Western civil society, regarding the work and life reality of Chinese factory workers.

**Production Process**

In the production process, labour power and means of production are employed in order to produce a commodity (Marx, 1867/1976: 284). Taking a closer look at the production process in the factories of Apple's contract manufacturers reveals a predominance of unpleasant and unsafe labour spaces, long working hours, standardized and repetitive production steps, and strict and often humiliating control mechanisms.

***Labour Space***

Work at Apple's contract manufacturers takes place within the boundaries of the factory. Shopfloors often lack proper ventilation systems, which means that the work environment is hot, dusty and has a strong chemical smell (SCAOM, 2011b). The behaviour of workers within their workspace is strongly controlled: workers at Foxconn have to pass through security checks with metal detectors when entering or leaving the shopfloor as well as bathrooms (FinnWatch, SACOM and SOMO, 2011). Most of the life of electronics workers takes place on factory campuses. Many workers live in dormitories provided by their employer. Factory dormitories are often crowded and provide only little privacy. In 2009, Finnwatch, SACOM and SOMO, for example, reported that on Foxconn campuses in Shenzhen, the dormitory consists of a five storey building with 25 rooms per floor, each shared by 8 to 10 workers (Finnwatch, SACOM and SOMO, 2009). The strict discipline and control of the workshop also enters the dormitory. Pun (2012: 23) argues that "the dormitory labour system ensures that workers spend their off-hours just preparing for another round of production".

Most factory campuses are based within SEZs that that traditionally are located in urban coastal areas. A recent trend in China's manufacturing sector is the relocation of production to inland provinces where wage levels are still lower. Foxconn has been relocating parts of its production from coastal areas such as Shenzhen to inland provinces (SACOM, 2011b). Foxconn workers are forced to relocate to production factories even farther away from their hometowns (SACOM, 2012). Among the new inland campuses are Foxconn production sites in Zhengzhou, Henan province. Because of growing demand, new factories are often built and opened in a rush. SACOM reports that the new Zhengzhou factory was operating even before the construction work was finished. For workers, this means that basic facilities such as bathrooms or grocery stores are not available (SACOM, 2011b). At unfinished factory campuses, the environment is dusty on dry days and flooded on rainy days. Likewise, Friends of Nature, IPE, Green Beagle report that Foxconn's Chengdu campus was built in 76 days, which created a number of security risks (Friends of Nature, IPE, Green Beagle, 2011).

Labour spaces at Apple's supplier factories are unpleasant and dangerous. The fact that work takes place in centralized factory spaces makes it possible to exert strict control over working hours and behaviour of workers even in their "free" time.

### *Labour Time*

Workers are not only underpaid, but also overworked. SOMO in its 2005 investigation of the Foxconn campus in Shenzhen found: "on average, a worker that works 27 days a month and 10-11 hours a day will receive about 1,000 *yuan* a month, including all the subsidies and overtime compensation" (SOMO,

2005b). In 2005, 1,000 *yuan* was equivalent to about €100 or $120. Workers at Foxconn complained that during peak season, they would not receive a single day off in four months. Another investigation of five Apple supplier factories conducted in 2007 confirmed that overtime between 2.5 and 4 hours per day in addition to the regular working hours of 8 to 9.5 hours was common. In four out of five investigated factories, total working hours exceeded 60 weekly hours and at one factory, workers even had to work up to 80 hours per week (SOMO, 2007a). In 2008, Finnwatch, SACOM and SOMO found similar conditions at Apple's production line at Foxconn's Shenzhen campus. Employees had to work compulsory excessive overtime of up to 120 hours per month, which resulted in a total of 70 hours per week (FinnWatch, SACOM and SOMO, 2009).

After the suicides tragedies, Finnwatch, SACOM and SOMO conducted a follow up investigation of working conditions at Foxconn. The results showed that while at the beginning of 2010, excessive compulsory overtime was still the same as that of 2008, the situation changed after June 2010. From then on, workers were granted one day off per week and overtime was reduced from 120 hours to between 75 and 80 hours per month, with still exceeded the legal maximum of 36 hours (FinnWatch, SACOM and SOMO, 2011).

Low wage levels and the problem of long working hours are connected to each other. Low wages force workers to work overtime in order to earn enough money to be able to cover their living expenses. A 19-year-old worker who was producing iPhones at Guanlan, Shenzhen told SACOM: "We do not have much overtime work this month. Our department has three shifts a day now. I can only receive a basic salary at 1,600 *yuan* this month. It's really not enough for a living, but I believe the 8-hour shift is just a temporary measure for the low season" (Foxconn Worker quoted in SACOM, 2011a). SACOM's investigation of Foxconn campuses in Shenzhen, Chengdu and Chongqing furthermore showed that workers in Chengdu, where the gap between actual and living wage was highest (see Figure 4), also worked most overtime, between 80 and 100 hours per month (SACOM, 2011a). In 2012, the FLA found that at the three monitored Foxconn plants in Shenzhen and Chengdu, workers during peak season worked more than 60 hours per week. Despite these very long working hours, 48% of the interviewed workers stated that their working hours were reasonable, 33.8% said that they would like to work more in order to earn more money, and 17.7% reported that their working hours were too long (FLA, 2012). In September 2012, SACOM investigated three Foxconn plants in Zhengzhou, Henan that are only producing iPhones. The results show that working hours vary strongly depending on Apple's demand. During low season, overtime work was as low as 10 hours per month, while during peak season, 80-100 hours monthly overtime was common (SACOM, 2012). During low season, workers thus struggle to earn enough to cover their living expenses, while during high season, they are exhausted due to a lack of free time.

Even if overtime work is officially labelled voluntary, low wages often force workers into working excessive overtime. While companies comply with legal minimum wage standards, compliance with regulations for maximum working hours is often insufficient. The fact that minimum wage levels are too low makes compliance relatively easy for companies, while it creates the need for workers to work overtime to earn extra money. The relation between low wages and high overtime rates is a basic structural characteristic of contemporary electronics manufacturing. It allows companies to keep their payroll low at the expense of workers, and at the same time meet high production targets.

*Work Activity*

Work at Chinese contract manufacturers in the electronics sector in general is characterized by a strong segmentation of the labour process into small, standardized production steps (Lüthje, 2008). Low skilled assembly line labour and uniform work procedures therefore dominate work in electronics factories. Workflows are fragmented and repetitive. One worker told CLW: "We finish one step in every 7 seconds, which requires us to concentrate and keep working and working. We work faster even than the machines" (Foxconn Worker quoted in China Labour Watch, 2010). Reports from corporate watchdogs show that machine dictates work procedures: SACOM reports that machines at Foxconn's factories have to run 24/7, therefore some workers always have to remain at the shopfloor during meal breaks. These continuous shifts require workers to skip meals. One worker complained:

> The machines in our department are in operation 24/7. If some colleagues go out for dinner, then the workers who stay in the workshop have to take care of three machines at the same time. It is hard work but we do not have additional subsidy for that. Workers can only have dinner after the work shift ends. Continuous shift occurs every day. (Foxconn Worker quoted in SACOM, 2011a).

The work activities workers perform in Apple's supplier factories are monotonous, repetitive and dictated by machines. Their activity can therefore be described as an alienated labour process, as "an activity which is turned against" the worker (Marx, 1844/2007: 73). Marx argued that in capitalism, the production process turns against the worker, because "it is not the worker who employs the conditions of his work, but rather the reverse, the conditions of work employ the worker" (Marx, 1867/1976: 548).

Work in Apple's supplier factories is characterized by a separation between mental and manual labour as it is associated with Taylorist production methods. Each step of the labour process is defined and controlled by management, while executed by the worker: "the physical processes of production are now carried out more or less blindly [...] The production units operate like a hand, watched, corrected and controlled by a distant brain" (Braverman, 1974/1998: 86).

The computer industry furthermore illustrates the division between manual and mental labour on a global scale. While highly skilled engineers that design computer software and hardware tend to be located in the global North, the physical production and assembly of computer products largely takes place in the global South.

*Control Mechanisms*

Harsh and humiliating management styles are used to control the behaviour of workers at Apple's contract manufacturers. In 2009, Finnwatch, SACOM and SOMO reported about strict disciplinary measures in Apple's production line at Foxconn. No personal belongings were allowed in the factory, and procedures of how to start work and leaving the shopfloor were strictly regulated. Workers reported that if asked how they felt, they had to shout: "Fine! Very fine! Very, very fine!" Talking, giggling, and crossing legs was forbidden while sitting at the assembly line. Talking might be punished with shopfloor cleaning. Due to time-consuming security checks at toilets and short breaks, workers often had to choose between using the bathroom and having lunch (Finnwatch, SACOM and SOMO, 2009).

A follow-up investigation in 2011 showed that disciplinary measures at Foxconn were less strict, than they were in 2008. However, security checks at toilets still existed and workers still had to collectively reply "Fine! Very fine! Very, very fine!" when asked how they felt (Finnwatch, SACOM and SOMO, 2011). At a Foxconn plant in Chengdu, new workers for example had to participate in a 1-2 day long military training which only consisted of lining up and standing (SACOM, 2011a). During breaks, they were sitting on the floor often without talking to each other because they were too exhausted. If workers made mistakes, they had to write confession letters to their supervisors, and sometimes even read them loud in front of other workers. Supervisors were under pressure, too. If one of the workers they were supervising made a mistake, they had to face punishment themselves. The strict supervision and control mechanisms are a means for factory management to demonstrate its power over workers. It attempts to reduce human behaviour such as talking, eating or using the toilet, and to force machine-like qualities onto the workers.

**Labour Law**

Several laws are in place to regulate work and employment in China, including the Chinese Labour Law (1994), the Trade Union Law (1992, 2002), the Labour Contract Law (2007) and the Labour Dispute Mediation and Arbitration Law (2007) (Friedman and Lee, 2010). The Labour Contract Law, for example, entitles workers to a non-fixed term contract after their fixed term contract has been renewed twice and requires employers to pay higher severance payments in case of layoffs. However, a major problem is that these laws often remain unenforced. This is, for example, the case in regard to maximum overtime work hours. Chinese labour law limits maximum overtime to 36 hours per month (FinnWatch, SACOM and SOMO, 2011).

While Apple's contract manufacturers regularly exceed the legal maximum working hours, they mostly comply with minimum wage regulation. However, studies have shown that minimum wages in China are often too low (SACOM, 2011a), which provides an excuse for companies to pay wages that are below the living wage level.

Although a number of labour regulations are in place in China, they often are either too lax (for example, minimum wages) or not well enforced (for example, maximum working hours). China furthermore has not ratified the core conventions of the International Labour Organization (ILO) on Forced Labour[26] and Freedom of Association[27]. Without the ratification of these conventions, the legal obligation to protect these fundamental labour rights is weaker. Hong (2011: 6) argues that in order to stay competitive in global capitalism, the Chinese state "shares the interest with transnational capital to keep down the cost of production". Through tax benefits, China was successful in attracting foreign enterprises. The result of these policies is an economic dependency on multinational companies, exports and consumer markets in the global North. It is therefore important not to underestimate the power multinational corporations have on influencing government policies in China as well as elsewhere.

**Results of Production**

Apple's products are at the forefront of technological innovation. They are symbols for modern 21st century lifestyle and progress. The conditions under which these products are produced, on the contrary, resemble the early days of industrial capitalism. The fact that, for example, an iPhone costs often twice as much as the average monthly salary of a worker in electronics manufacturing, reveals a deep separation between workers and the fruits of their labour.

Computer technology has the potential to alleviate work, to increase productivity, and to reduce the amount of necessary labour time. It entails the potential that especially unqualified, monotonous, repetitive and mechanical assembly line labour, which reduces workers to extensions of machines without human intellect or creativity, could in the future increasingly be taken over by machines. The way computers are produced today contradicts this potential.

Apple's 2011 marketing campaign praised the design, premium materials, and high-quality manufacturing of Apple's products. Apple advertised the iPad as "amazingly thin and light"[28] as a "technology so advanced, and you'll forget it's even there"[29]. According to Apple's ads, "A Mac is as good as it looks. It's made from strong, beautiful materials like aluminium and glass"[30]. "Take MacBook Air, for example. Its unibody enclosure is machined from a solid block of aluminium. The result is a notebook that is thin and light, looks polished and refined, and feels strong and durable"[31]. This marketing strategy pictures Apple's products as trendy, clean, sophisticated, elegant and of high quality – a technology that is so advanced that it will expand the capacities of its users and fit their needs so neatly that they will "forget it's even there".

Apple's marketing slogans present its products as technological marvels without history. They divert attention away from the fact that underpaid Chinese workers are producing these products during 10 to 12 hour shifts at least 6 days a week, in exhausting and repetitive working procedures, while jeopardizing their health. Once displayed on posters, magazines and TV-spots, iPad, MacBook and Co have lost any trace of the conditions under which they were produced.

**Summary**

*Table 2  Working Conditions at Apple's Contract Manufacturers*

| Productive forces - means of production | Machines and equipment | High-tech equipment, e.g. Surface Mount Technology |
| --- | --- | --- |
|  | Resources | Minerals such as tin, gallium, platinum, tantalum, indium, neodymium, ruthenium, palladium, lanthanum, and cobalt; often sourced from conflict areas |

| | | |
|---|---|---|
| Productive forces - labour | Workforce characteristics | A majority of young, often female migrant workers |
| | Mental and physical health | Instances of injuries and deaths due to unsafe work environments, lack of protection equipment and insufficient information of workers<br>Psychological problems due to social isolation and exhaustion, instances of suicides |
| | Work experiences | Workers describe their experiences as exhausting, humiliating and alienated |
| Relations of production | Labour contracts | Dominance of precarious short-term contracts and agency labour |
| | Wages and benefits | Low wage levels despite compliance with minimum wage regulation, no living wage |
| | Labour struggles | Several instances of strikes and protests but low awareness of and support from unions |
| Production process | Labour space | Unpleasant and unsafe factory environments, crowded factory dormitories, instances of forced relocation of workers to production factories in other provinces |
| | Labour time | Long working hours of more than 60 hours per week during peak season<br>Working hours highly depend on shifts in demand |
| | Work activity | High workflow segmentation, uniform and repetitive production steps, separation of manual and mental work |
| | Control mechanisms | Harsh, military management styles and harassment of workers |
| Results of production | Labour product | High-tech computer products and consumer electronics: computers, mp3 players, mobile phones, and tablet computers |

| The state | Labour law | Insufficient enforcement of labour laws, low minimum wages and missing ratification of ILO core conventions on forced labour and freedom of association |

The results of the analysis provided here show that labour rights are systematically undermined in the factories of Apple's contract manufactures. The next section discusses Apple's response to the poor working conditions in the factories of its Chinese contract manufacturers.

## DEFENDING THE MYTH: APPLE'S RESPONSE TO LABOUR RIGHT VIOLATIONS

Apple's response to labour right violations in its supply chain is very reactive. The company published its first supplier responsibility document as a reaction to ongoing criticism of its supply chain management. It starts with the following sentence: "in the summer of 2006, we were concerned by reports in the press, alleging poor working and living conditions at one of our iPod final assembly suppliers in China" (Apple, 2006: 1). Since then, Apple published one Supplier Responsibility Report per year. These reports promise that Apple "is committed to the highest standard of social responsibility in everything we do. We are dedicated to ensuring that working conditions are safe, the environment is protected, and employees are treated with respect and dignity wherever Apple products are made" (Apple, 2006: 4).

Based on van Dijk's (2011) concept of the ideological square, I, in the following, analyse the arguments Apple puts forward in its Supplier Responsibility Reports in order to demonstrate its efforts to improve working conditions. The ideological square identifies four possible ideological strategies that describe different ways of how the relation between in-groups and out-groups, between "us" and "them" is represented in talk or text (van Dijk, 2011: 397). These strategies are: "Emphasize *Our* good things", "Emphasize *Their* bad things", "De-emphasize *Our* bad things", "De-emphasize *Their* good things" (van Dijk, 2011: 396). Three of these strategies are present in Apple's response to watchdog criticism: Apple is de-emphasizing its own wrongdoings by downplaying the extent of the problem of labour rights violations, while at the same time emphasizing its achievements by using a rhetoric of continuous improvement. The company furthermore emphasizes the wrongdoings of others by blaming Chinese managers and workers for the persistence of poor working conditions.

**De-Emphasize Our Bad Things: Downplaying the Extent of the Problem**

The strategy that is most dominant in Apple's response to labour rights allegations is to de-emphasize the extent of the problem. While watchdog reports document the persistence of serious labour rights issues, Apple's supplier responsibility reports suggest that the problems are much less severe.

In its reports, Apple defines "core violations" of its Code of Conduct, that require immediate improvements. These core violations include physical abuse, child labour, forced labour, false audits, severe threats to worker safety, and intimidation of workers that are interviewed during audits. Apple stresses that it considers core violations "as contrary to the core principles underlying Apple's Supplier Code of Conduct and require immediate corrective actions" (Apple, 2007: 7).

Apparently, it is not a "core principle" of Apple's business practices that workers who are producing the products that are the basis for Apple's profits, are paid for their work and have reasonable working hours. As neither underpayment nor overwork are considered a "core violation", no immediate solution needs to be found if these problems occur. Apple thus *de facto* tolerates that workers receive wages that hardly suffice for paying basic living expenses, while working up to a point of complete exhaustion. By not regarding these issues as "core violations", Apple downplays how severe these problems are for workers.

Apart from this general downplaying of the problem of low wages and long working hours, Apple's supplier responsibility reports furthermore hide the full extent of labour rights violations behind statistics and numbers, and describe the problem as the result of minor shortcomings while ignoring structural causes:

• **Fetishism of statistics:** Throughout Apple's supplier responsibility reports, hardly any descriptions about how working conditions in its supplier factories actually look like can be found. Apple only provides statistical data that actually tells little about the daily work and life experiences of workers. According to Apple's own audits, the non-compliance rate in regard to payment of at least minimum wages and transparent wage calculations was 46% in 2007, 41% in 2008, 35% in 2009, 30% in 2010, 31% in 2011, and 28% in 2012 (Apple, 2007-2012). Although these figures show an improvement, it still means that a large number of workers in Apple's supplier factories are paid below the legal minimum. Considering that even the legal minimum is often below a living wage, these numbers are even more troubling.

Apple's figures on working hours give a similar picture. Non-compliance with a maximum 60 hours per week was 82% in 2007, 59% in 2008, 54% in 2009, 68% in 2010, and 62% in 2011 before it suddenly dropped to 8% in 2012 (Apple, 2007-2012). As an explanation for this sudden decrease of non-compliance in regard to weekly working hours, Apple (2012: 29) states: "in 2012, we changed our measurement on working hours to one that is more meaningful and effective". This explanation suggests that the sudden decrease in working hours stems from changes in measurement rather than actual changes in working conditions. Furthermore, it is problematic that Apple considers a 60-hour working week as desirable. In fact, a 60-hour working week violates Chinese labour law. In China, a regular working week must not exceed 44 hours. In addition, maximum overtime, according to the law, is 9 hours per week. This means that including overtime, Chinese labour law limits working hours to 53 hours per week[32]. By calculating compliance with maximum working hours based on a 60-hour working week, which exceeds the legal maximum, Apple's audits misrepresent the extent to which workers are working excessive overtime. Without any descriptions of the work realities of workers, the statistics Apple presents furthermore remain abstract, and therefore hide how severe low wages, long working hours or the lack of health protection can be for the lives of individual workers and their families.

• **Ignoring root causes:** Apple has a strong business interest in keeping production costs low. In a 2012 financial statement, Apple highlights that it has to deal with strong price competition: "the markets for the company's products and services are highly competitive and the company is confronted by aggressive competition in all areas of its business. [...] The company's competitors who sell mobile devices and personal computers based on other operating systems have aggressively cut prices and lowered their product margins to gain or maintain market share" (Apple SEC-Filings, 2012: 6).

This structural contradiction between Apple's need to reduce labour costs in order to stay competitive, and low wages, low safety standards and long working hours is not addressed in Apple's supplier responsibility reports. Furthermore, Apple's response to the suicides tragedies ignores connections between bad working and living conditions and the suicide tragedies. In its 2010 report, Apple highlighted that it is "disturbed and deeply saddened to learn that factory workers were taking their own lives at the Shenzhen factory of Foxconn" (Apple, 2010: 18). Apple stressed that as a reaction to the suicides, it launched "an international search for the most knowledgeable suicide prevention specialists – particularly those with experience in China – and asked them to advise Apple and Foxconn" (ibid). A team of suicide prevention experts was formed, which conducted a questionnaire survey among 1,000 Foxconn workers, face to face interviews with workers and managers, investigated each suicide individually, and evaluated Foxconn's response to the suicides. The result of this evaluation was that Foxconn's reaction to the suicides was ideal: "most important, the investigation found that Foxconn's response had definitely saved lives" (Apple, 2010: 19). Suggestions for further improvement were only made, regarding the training of hotline and care centre stuff.

Both the measures taken by Apple and the improvement suggestions made by the "most knowledgeable suicide prevention specialists" seem rather limited. They do not include any improvement of working conditions, which according to different labour rights groups had been bad for many years (SOMO, 2005b; FinnWatch, SACOM and SOMO, 2009, 2011; SACOM, 2011a, 2011b, 2012, 2013). The anti-suicide team's findings suggested that the suicides had nothing to do with working conditions at Foxconn. A study conducted by CLW (2010) tells a different story. On May 17, 2010, CLW asked 25 Foxconn workers about what they believed were the reason for the suicides of Foxconn workers. 17 said that high pressure at work was the main reason. 5 workers argued that a lacking sense of community at Foxconn has led to the suicides, as even workers that were living in the same room would not know each other. 3 workers doubted that the reasons for the deaths actually were suicides.

Apple, by failing to discuss the connection between the suicides of workers and problems such as low wages, excessive working hours, humiliation, work pressure, social isolation, etc., de-emphasizes the extent to which workers are suffering from poor working conditions.

**Emphasize Our Good Things: A Rhetoric of Continuous Improvement**

Apple's supplier responsibility reports put forward a story of continuous improvement. They are officially labelled as "Progress Report". In the 2009 report, Apple (2009: 15) for example states: "in general, annual audits of final assembly manufacturers show continued performance improvements and better working conditions". The 2007 report states: "by aggressively auditing our suppliers and pursuing corrective actions, Apple has improved living and working conditions for tens of thousands of employees in our supply chain". Similarly, in the 2010 report, Apple (2010: 5) highlights that "our repeat audits showed continued performance improvements and better working conditions".

This rhetoric of improvement detracts from the fact that working conditions are bad, as independent research shows. Evidence for these alleged improvements is provided by reference to statistics from Apple's own audits. Apple claims that treatment of workers is "fair" in more than 90% of all monitored factories (Apple, 2007-2012). By pointing at improvements and stressing that workers are treated in a fair way in the majority of cases, Apple is putting forward a positive image about working conditions in its supply chain.

This focus on good things also characterized Steve Job's response to the suicide at the Foxconn factory campus. He stated that "Foxconn is not a sweatshop". "You go in this place and it's a factory but, my gosh, they've got restaurants, movie theatres, hospitals and swimming pools. For a factory, it's pretty nice." (Jobs, 2010) Considering the descriptions of unacceptable working realities at Foxconn campuses provided in watchdog reports as well as the low compliance rates according to Apple's own audits, this statement sounds overly euphemistic. The cynical character of Job's statement becomes evident when it is compared to a quote from a worker that appeared on a blog after the 12$^{th}$ suicide at Foxconn: "perhaps for the Foxconn employees and employees like us – we who are called *nongmingong*, rural migrant workers, in China – the use of death is simply to testify that we were ever alive at all, and that while we lived, we had only despair" (Foxconn worker quoted in Chan and Pun, 2010).

**Emphasizing Their Bad Things: Blaming Others**

Apple's supplier responsibility reports frame the problem of labour rights violation in a way that puts the entire blame on Chinese contract manufacturers. This rhetoric suggests that the existence of poor working conditions is solely due to a lack of management skills of suppliers, and has nothing to do with Apple. Apple presents itself as a benevolent saviour that is bringing knowledge to developing countries. According to its supplier responsibility reports, Apple seems to believe that its only responsibility consists in telling suppliers what they have to do. In the 2009 report, Apple (2009: 3) for example highlighted: "Apple's approach to supplier responsibility extends beyond monitoring compliance with our Code of Conduct. We help our suppliers meet Apple's expectations by supporting their efforts to provide training in workers' rights and occupational health and safety". At no point, Apple mentions how much money it is paying for the production of its products in these supplier factories and whether this amount is enough for ensuring adequate working conditions. By blaming its suppliers, Apple detracts attention away from the fact that these workers are in fact working for Apple, and Apple therefore is responsible for ensuring that at least their working environment is save, that they receive a wage which allows them to pay their living expenses, and that their working hours do not extend beyond certain limits. Blaming contract manufacturers detracts from the fact that Apple keeps almost 60% of the sales price of an iPhone as a profit while spending less than 2% for labour cost of final assembly in China (Kraemer, Linden and Dedrick, 2011).

Apple's response to labour rights allegations follows certain ideological patterns. It downplays the severity of the problem of low wages and long working hours, avoids descriptions of actual work and life realities of workers by only referring to statistics and numbers, and ignores structural causes of the labour rights problem (de-emphasizing Apple's wrongdoings). The company stresses that the situation is continuously improving although independent research shows that problems persist (emphasizing Apple's achievements). It also describes suppliers, rather than Apple itself, as the ones actually responsible for labour rights violations (emphasizing the wrongdoing of others).

Apple's rhetoric tends to downplay the scope of labour rights violations, mystify their relation to Apple's business interest in cheap labour, and attempt to deny the company's responsibility for poor working conditions in its supply chain. It defends Apple's business practices by detracting attention away from structural contradictions and social irresponsibilities that are connected to them.

## CONCLUSION

In this paper, I first showed that neoliberal globalization, the transformation of international production networks together with Chinese policy reforms allowed multinational corporations to gain access to millions of Chinese workers. Apple is an economically successful and admired company. Most of its profits are based on hardware products such as iPhone, iPad, iPod, laptops and desktop computers. While for Apple these products mean success, for the workers in the factories of Apple's contract manufacturers, they mean misery. Their labour and lives often remain invisible, hidden behind the shiny surface of modern high-tech products. In order to shed light on this dark side of computer products, I constructed a systematic model of working conditions based on the circuit of capital as it has been described by Karl Marx. This model starts with the productive forces including means of production on one hand, and the labour power of workers on the other hand. It then addresses the relations of production as they are expressed in a particular relation between capital and labour that determines both wages and labour contracts and is subject to struggles. In order to produce a commodity, labour and means of production enter the production processes, which is shaped by labour space, labour time, work activity and control mechanisms. The model also includes the produced commodity and the question how it relates back to the worker. Finally, it includes labour legislation and its impact on working conditions.

This model of working conditions can be applied to study and compare working conditions in a variety of different industries. In this paper, I used it for describing the "Foxconned labour" of workers in Chinese workshops of

Foxconn, Wintek, Pegatron and others where Apple's products are assembled. The results show that workers are partly dealing with high-tech equipment when assembling parts of computers that often contain conflict minerals. The relation between capital and labour is characterized by low wages, precarious contracts, and occasionally contested by labour struggles. The production process is shaped by work and life in the factory, long working hours, repetitive and monotonous manual work, and strict control. Mostly young migrant workers are risking their health and safety and experiencing alienation, exhaustion and despair. They are producing high-tech computer products that they are unlikely to ever own themselves. Labour laws often remain unenforced and therefore offer little protection for workers.

Finally, in discussing Apple's response to the problem of poor working conditions, I identified three ideological patterns that deflect attention away from the structural irresponsibility of Apple's business practices by using a rhetoric of improvement, hiding behind statistics, blaming others, looking at symptoms rather than root causes, or downplaying the problems.

The example of Apple illustrates that there is a wide gap between the qualities of the products workers are producing and the conditions under which they are produced. While working conditions resemble the early days of industrial capitalism, the produced-high tech computer products build the foundation for 21$^{st}$ century knowledge work. Apple thus represents progress and regression at the same time. Marx described this contradictory quality of capitalism when he stressed:

> It is true that labour produces for the rich wonderful things – but for the worker, it produces privation. It produces palaces – but for the worker hovels. It produces beauty – but for the worker, deformity. It replaces labour by machines – but some of the workers it throws back to a barbarous type of labour, and the other workers it turns into machines. It produces intelligence – but for the worker idiocy, cretinism. (Marx 1844/2007: 71)

The labour performed in Chinese workshops produces profits for Apple and marvellous computer products for those who can afford them, while for workers, it produces monotony and despair.

However, ICTs at the same time do not only mean misery for workers, but can also be a means of empowerment. Qiu (2009) points out that the internet and wireless communication is increasingly available to members of the Chinese working class. He stresses that rather than describing Chinese low-income groups as "information have-nots", they should be regarded as "information have-less" as they increasingly have access to the internet and to inexpensive "working-class ICTs" that are produced for the Chinese market (Qiu, 2009: 243). These "working class ICTs" such as mobile phones or computers can be used "in order for the concerns of the have-less to reach across social divisions and have a general impact on society" (ibid). Information about labour rights violations or protest can sometimes reach the mass media via online forums or self-made videos. Qiu highlights that in the context of the spread of working-class ICTs, there are "important instances of working-class cultural expression and political empowerment, using tools as blogs, poetry, and mobile phones, which serve as the substance of new class dynamics in the twenty-first century" (Qiu, 2009: 232). ICTs can thus be used as tools to support struggles for worker rights.

Although this paper focuses on Apple, it is important to be aware that similar working conditions as described here can be found throughout the electronics industry as well as other manufacturing sectors such as garment or toy production. Apple thus is more than a "bad apple". It is an example of structures of inequality and exploitation that characterize global capitalism. In order to confront these structural problems, it is not enough to rely on corporate self-regulation, Codes of Conduct and promises of Corporate Social Responsibility. It is important to recognize that cheap production costs that result in poor working conditions are an important competitive advantage for companies. Raising wages, reducing working hours, improving health and safety protection, etc. would increase expenditures and thus negatively impact profit goals. Without international laws and regulations that force companies to meet certain standards, it is unlikely that working conditions will improve.

However desirable stricter regulation might be, rather than waiting for top-down changes to occur, workers need to organize and struggle for their rights. In times of international value chains, increasing pressure on governments and corporations requires international solidarity.

Pointing at the need to study the industrial labour of those who produce computer technologies in factories does not mean to idealize the working life of engineers, designers or media professionals. It rather seems important to highlight connections between these different forms of labour: what unites them is not only that they all, in different ways, deal with new ICTs, but also that they are all subject to exploitation, high work pressure and often precariousness. Rather than using concepts such as "immaterial labour" (Hardt and Negri, 2004) that reinforce the separation of manual and mental work, it seems more useful to extend concepts such as knowledge work or digital labour to include the manual work of those who are producing computer technologies, electronic equipment and media technologies. I therefore agree with Hong who argues that "in the context of information and communications, we actually need to extend the concept of the 'knowledge worker' to include manual and industrial workers who are also essential to this industry" (Hong, 2011: 11). Digital labour likewise includes both the manual and mental labour of workers who use ICTs and digital technologies as means of production and of those who produce and dispose them. Such extended notions can provide a conceptual framework for analysing the international division of digital labour. Broad understandings of digital labour can furthermore be a starting point for building connections and moments of solidarity along the global value chain of computer technologies from mineral miners and production workers to call centre agents, software engineers, and the labour of unpaid prosumers, back to waste workers in electronics dumping grounds.

## Notes

［1］ Forbes Magazine. The World's Biggest Public Companies. Retrieved from http://www.forbes.com/global2000/#page:1_sort:4_direction:desc_search:_filter:All%20industries_filter:All%20countries_filter:All%20states on April 24, 2013.

［2］ Compound Annual Growth Rate, CAGR.

［3］ Fortune Magazine. 2013. World's Most Admired Companies. Retrieved from http://money.cnn.com/magazines/fortune/most-admired/ on April 24, 2013.

［4］ Wired. 2011. 1 Million Workers. 90 Million iPhones. 17 Suicides. Who's to Blame? By Joel Johnson on Februar 28, 2011. Retrieved from http://www.wired.com/magazine/2011/02/ff_joelinchina/all/1 on October 23, 2011.

［5］ Forbes Magazine. The World's Biggest Public Companies. Retrieved from http://www.forbes.com/global2000/list/#page:1_sort:0_direction:asc_search:_filter:Electronics_filter:All%20countries_filter:All%20states on May 1, 2013.

［6］ Apple. List of Suppliers. Retrieved from http://www.apple.com/supplierresponsibility/our-suppliers.html on May 1, 2013.

［7］ The New York Times. 2010. String of Suicides Continues at Electronics Supplier in China. By David Barboza on May 25, 2010. Retrieved from http://www.nytimes.com/2010/05/26/technology/26suicide.html on October 24, 2011.

［8］ BBC. 2010. Foxconn Suicides: Workers Feel Quite Lonely. On May 28, 2010. Retrieved from http://www.bbc.co.uk/news/10182824 on October 24, 2011.

［9］ Time Magazine. 2010. Chinese Factory Under Scrutiny As Suicides Mount. On May 26, 2010. Retrieved from http://www.time.com/time/world/article/0,8599,1991620,00.html on October 24, 2011.

［10］ The Guardian. 2010. Latest Foxconn Suicide Raises Concern Over Factory Life in China. By Tania Branigan on May 17, 2010. Retrieved from http://www.guardian.co.uk/world/2010/may/17/foxconn-suicide-china-factory-life on October 24, 2011.

［11］ CNN. 2010. Inside China Factory Hit By Suicides. By John Vause on June 1, 2010. Retrieved from http://articles.cnn.com/2010-06-01/world/china.foxconn.inside.

factory_1_foxconn-suicides-china-labor-bulletin?_s=PM:WORLD on October 24, 2011.

［12］ SACOM. About Us. Retrieved from http://sacom.hk/about-us on July 22, 2013.

［13］ China Labour Watch. Who We Are. Retrieved from http://www.chinalaborwatch.org/aboutus.html on July 22, 2013.

［14］ MakeITfair: http://makeitfair.org/en?set_language=en

［15］ Surface Mount Technology Association. Glossary of Acronyms Relevant to Electronics Manufacturing. Retrieved from http://www.smta.org/files/acronym_glossary.pdf on May 18, 2013.

［16］ The Asia Floor Wage Campaign suggested a method for calculating the living wage. According to this calculation, a living wage needs to cover the costs for food, equivalent of 3,000 calories per adult family member multiplied by two, in order to cover also other basic need such as clothing, housing, education, healthcare, and savings. The living wage should provide for a family of two adults and two children. It thus should cover the cost for food worth 3,000 calories for three consumption units (two adults and two children) multiplied by two. It is thus calculated as followings: price for food worth 3,000 calories x 3 x 2. A worker should be able to earn a living wage within a working week of a maximum of 48 hours. This calculation of a living wage was developed with specific regard to the garment sector, but is also applicable for other sectors such as electronics manufacturing.

［17］ Reuters. 2010. Foxconn to Raise Wages Again at China Plant. Retrieved from http://www.reuters.com/article/2010/10/01/us-foxconn-idUSTRE6902GD20101001 on April 28, 2013.

［18］ Ibid.

［19］ M.I.C. Gadget. 2010. More Problems With Foxconn: Workers Protest Against Their Wages. Retrieved from http://micgadget.com/9620/more-problems-with-foxconn-workers-protest-against-their-wages/ on October 27, 2011.

［20］ SACOM. 2013. Strike Erupted Over Dire Working Conditions at Foxconn. Retrieved from http://sacom.hk/archives/971 on May 14, 2013.

［21］ The Financial Times. 2013. Foxconn Plans Chinese Union Vote. Retrieved from http://www.ft.com/cms/s/0/48091254-6c3e-11e2-b774-00144feab49a.html#axzz2TFz9DeNG on May 14, 2013.

［22］ Time Magazine. Karl Marx's Revenge.

［23］ SOMO. 2011. Time to Bite Into a Fair Apple; Call for Sustainable IT! Join Action Day on May 7th. Retrieved from http://somo.nl/events-en/time-to-bite-into-a-fair-apple-call-for-sustainable-it-join-action-day-on-may-7th on October 27, 2011.

［24］ A video that docments one camaign activitiy can be watched here: http://www.youtube.com/watch?v=kaiXni3h2Ug&feature=player_embedded Retrieved on October 27, 2011.

［25］ ChinaWorkers. 2011. "Rotten Apple: Worldwide Protests Against IT Giant's Labour Abuses. Retrieved from http://chinaworker.info/en/content/news/1451/ on October 27, 2011.

［26］ Forced Labour Convention (CO29) and the Abolition of Forced Labour Convention (CO105). 2013. Source: ILO. Retrieved from http://www.ilo.org/dyn/normlex/en/f?p=1000:11210:0::NO:11210:P11210_COUNTRY_ID:103404 on May 14, 2013.

［27］ Freedom of Organisation and Protection of the Right to Organise Convention (CO87) and the Right to Organise and Collective Bargaining Convention (CO98). 2013. Source: ILO. Retrieved from http://www.ilo.org/dyn/normlex/en/f?p=1000:11210:0::NO:11210:P11210_COUNTRY_ID:103404 on May 14, 2013.

［28］ Apple. 2011. Retrieved from http://www.apple.com/ipad/ on October 25, 2011.

［29］ Apple. 2011. Retrieved from http://www.apple.com/ipad/features/ on October 25, 2011.

［30］ Apple. 2011. Retrieved from http://www.apple.com/why-mac/better-hardware/on October 25, 2011.

［31］ Ibid.

［32］ China.org. Labour Law of the People's Republic of China. Retrieved from http://www.china.org.cn/living_in_china/abc/2009-07/15/content_18140508.htm on May 15, 2013.

## References

Apple. 2006-2012. *Supplier Responsibility. Progress Report.* Accessed May 2013. http://www.apple.com/supplierresponsibility/reports.html

Apple SEC-Filings. 2012. Form 10-k. In *Edgar Database.* Accessed May 20, 2013. http://www.sec.gov/cgi-bin/browse-edgar?action=getcompany&CIK=0000320193&type=10-k&dateb=&owner=exclude&count=40

Braverman, Harry. 1974/1998. *Labor and Monopoly Capital: The Degradation of Work in the Twentieth Century.* New York: Monthly Review Press.

Bread for All and SACOM. 2008. *High Tech – No Rights?* Accessed May 13, 2013. http://sacom.hk/wp-content/uploads/2008/07/report-high-tech-no-rights-may2008.pdf

Chan, Jenny and Ngai Pun. 2010. Suicide as Protest for the New Generation of Chinese Migrant Workers: Foxconn, Global Capital, and the State. *The Asia-Pacific Journal* 37(2): 1-33.

China Labour Watch (CLW). 2010. *"We Are Extremely Tired, With Tremendous Pressure" A Follow-up Investigation of Foxconn.* Accessed October 20, 2011. http://www.chinalaborwatch.org/pro/proshow-100.html

Danwatch. 2011. *What a Waste.* Accessed May 16, 2013. http://makeitfair.org/en/the-facts/reports/reports/2011

Dyer-Whiteford, Nick. 2014. The Global Worker and the Digital Front. In *Critique, Social Media and the Information Society*, edited by Christian Fuchs and Marisol Sandoval. New York: Routledge.

Finnwatch. 2007. *Connecting Components, Dividing Communities: Tin Production for*

*Consumer Electronics in DR Congo and Indonesia.* Accessed May 14, 2013. http://makeitfair.org/en/the-facts/reports/2007-2009/reports-from-2009/Connecting-Components-Dividing-Communities.pdf/at_download/file

Finnwatch, SACOM and SOMO. 2009. *Playing with Labour Rights: Music Player and Game Console Manufacturing in China.* Accessed October 19, 2011. http://makeitfair.org/the-facts/reports/playing-with-labour-rights/at_download/file

FinnWatch, SACOM and SOMO. 2011. *Game Console and Music Player Production in China.* Accessed October 19, 2011. http://makeitfair.org/the-facts/reports/game-console-and-music-player-production-in-china

FLA. 2012. *Independent Investigation of Apple Supplier, Foxconn.* Accessed April 10, 2012. http://www.fairlabor.org/sites/default/files/documents/reports/foxconn_investigation_report.pdf

Free the Slaves. 2011. *The Congo Report: Slavery in Conflict Minerals.* Accessed May 13, 2013. http://www.freetheslaves.net/Document.Doc?id=243

Friedman, Eli and Ching Kwan Lee. 2010. Remaking the World of Chinese Labour: A 30-Year Retrospective. *British Journal of Industrial Relations* 48(3): 507-533.

Friends of Nature, IPE, Green Beagle. 2011. *The Other Side of Apple II: Pollution Spreads Through Apple's Supply Chain.* Accessed October 23, 2011. http://www.ipe.org.cn/En/about/notice_de_1.aspx?id=10281

Friends of the Earth. 2012. *Mining for Smartphones. The True Cost of Tin.* Accessed April 12, 2013. http://www.foe.co.uk/resource/reports/tin_mining.pdf

Fröbel, Folker, Jürgen Heinrichs and Otto Kreye. 1981. *The New International Division of Labour: Structural Unemployment in Industrialised Countries and Industralization in Developing Countries.* Caubridge, UK: Cambridge University Press.

Hardt, Michael and Antonio Negri. 2004. *Multitude: War and Democracy in the Age of Empire.* New York: Penguin

Harvey, David. 2005. *A Brief History of Neoliberalism.* New York: Oxford University Press.

Harvey, David. 2006. *Spaces of Global Capitalism: A Theory of Uneven Geographical Development.* London: Verso.

Hong, Yu. 2011. *Labor, Class Formation, and China's Informationized Policy and Economic Development.* Lanham, MD: Rowman & Littlefield.

Hung, Ho-Fu. 2009. America's Head Servant? The PRC's Dilemma in the Global Crisis. *New Left Review* 60: 5-25.

ICO, FinnWatch and ECA. 2005. *Day and Night at the Factory.* Accessed October 19, 2011. http://www.corporatejustice.org/IMG/pdf/en_kiina-raportti.pdf

Jobs, Steve. 2010. *Interview at the 2010 D8 Conference.* Accessed May 10, 2013. http://www.youtube.com/watch?v=KEQEV6r2l2c

Kraemer, Kenneth, Greg Linden and Jason Dedrick. 2011. *Capturing Value in Global Networks: Apple's iPad and iPhone.* Accessed May 14, 2013. http://pcic.merage.uci.edu/papers/2011/Value_iPad_iPhone.pdf

Linzmayer, Owen. 2004. *Apple Confidential 2.0: The Definitive History of the World's Most Colourful Company*. San Francisco, CA: No Starch Press.

Lüthje, Boy. 2006. The Changing Map of Global Electronics: Networks of Mass Production in the New Economy. In *Challenging the Chip: Labour Rights and Environmental Justice in the Global Electronics Industry*, edited by Ted Smith, David Sonnenfeld and David Pellow, 17-30. Philadelphia, PA: Temple University Press.

Lüthje, Boy. 2008. *Arbeitspolitik in der Chinesischen IT Industrie – neue Perspektiven in der Diskussion um internationale Arbeitsstandards*. Accessed May 13, 2013. http://www.boeckler.de/pdf_fof/S-2007-14-1-1.pdf

Lüthje, Boy. 2012. Interview. Accessed May 20, 2013. http://www.cultofmac.com/153784/heres-what-working-conditions-at-chinese-electronics-plants-are-really-like-exclusive-interview/

Marx, Karl. 1844/2007. *Economic Philosophic Manuscripts of 1844*. New York: Dover Publications.

Marx, Karl. 1867/1976. *Capital*, vol 1. London: Penguin.

Marx, Karl. 1885/1992. *Capital*, vol 2. London: Penguin.

Maxwell, Richard and Toby Miller. 2012. *Greening the Media*. New York: Oxford University Press.

McGuigan, Jim. 2005. Neoliberalism, Cultural and Policy. *International Journal of Cultural Policy* 11(3): 229-241.

McKinsey & Company. 2012. *Manufacturing in the Future: The Next Era of Global Growth and Innovation*. Accessed May 18, 2013. http://www.mckinsey.com/insights/manufacturing/the_future_of_manufacturing

Mosco, Vincent. 2004. *The Digital Sublime*. Cambridge, MA: MIT Press.

Munck, Ronaldo. 2002. *Globalisation and Labour: The New "Treat Transformation"*. New York: Palgrave.

Pun, Ngai. 2012. *Apple's Dream, Foxconn's Nightmare and the Struggle of the Chinese Worker*. Accessed May 15, 2013. http://burawoy.berkeley.edu/Public%20Sociology,%20Live/Pun%20Ngai/PunNgai.Suicide%20or%20Muder.pdf

Plank, Leonhard and Cornelia Staritz. 2013. *Precarious Upgrading in Electronics Global Production Networks in Central and Eastern Europe: The Cases of Hungary and Romania*. Accessed May 18, 2013. http://www.capturingthegains.org/pdf/ctg-wp-2013-31.pdf

Qiu, Jack. 2009. *Working-Class Network Society*. Cambridge, MA: MIT Press.

Reputation Institute. 2012. *Is CSR Dead or Just Mismanaged*. Accessed February 14, 2013. http://www.reputationinstitute.com/thought-leadership/complimentary-reports-2012

SACOM. 2010. *Apple Owes Workers and Public a Response over the Poisoning*. Accessed October 16, 2011. http://sacom.hk/wp-content/uploads/2010/05/apple-owes-workers-and-public-a-response-over-the-poisonings.pdf

SACOM. 2011a. *Foxconn and Apple Fail to Fulfil Promises: Predicaments of Workers after the Suicides*. Accessed October 20, 2011. http://sacom.hk/wp-content/

uploads/2011/05/2011-05-06_foxconn-and-apple-fail-to-fulfill-promises1.pdf

SACOM. 2011b. *iSlave Behind the iPhone. Foxconn Workers in Central China.* Accessed October 20, 2011. http://sacom.hk/wp-content/uploads/ 2011/09/20110924-islave-behind-the-iphone.pdf

SACOM. 2012. *New iPhone, Old Abuses. Have Working Conditions at Foxconn in China Improved?* Accessed May 13, 2013. http://www.waronwant.org/attachments/SACOM%20-%20%20New%20iPhone,%20Old%20Abuses%20-%2020-09-12.pdf

SACOM. 2013. *Apple Fails in Its Responsibility to Monitor Suppliers.* Accessed May 13, 2013. http://makeitfair.org/en/the-facts/reports/apple-fails-in-its-responsibility-to-monitor-suppliers/at_download/file

Smith, John. 2012. Outsourcing, Financialization and the Crisis. *International Journal of Management Concepts and Philosophy* 6(1/2): 19-44.

SOMO. 2005a. *CSR Issues in the ICT Hardware Manufacturing Sector.* By Irene Schipper and Esther de Haan. Accessed October 17, 2011. http://somo.nl/publications-nl/Publication_476-nl/at_download/fullfile

SOMO. 2005b. *ICT Hardware Sector in China and Corporate Social Responsibility Issues.* By Monina Wong. Accessed October 16, 2011. http://somo.nl/publications-en/Publication_624/at_download/fullfile

SOMO. 2007a. *Apple: CSR Company Profile.* By Michiel van Dijk and Irene Schipper. Accessed October 17, 2011. http://somo.nl/publications-en/Publication_1963/at_download/fullfile

SOMO. 2007b. *Capacitating Electronics: The Corrosive Effects of Platinum and Palladium Mining on Labour Rights and Communities.* Accessed May 13, 2013. http://makeitfair.org/en/the-facts/reports/2007-2009/reports-from-2009/Capacitating-Electronics-november-2007.pdf/at_download/file

SOMO. 2011. *Unheard Voices: Mining Activities in the Katanga Province and Impact on Local Communities.* Accessed May 13, 2013. http://makeitfair.org/en/the-facts/reports/unheard-voices/at_download/file

Su, Yihui. 2011. Student Workers in the Foxconn Empire: The Commodification of Education and Labour in China. *Journal of Workplace Rights* 15(3-4): 341-362.

Swedwatch. 2007. *Powering the Mobile World: A Report on Cobalt Production for Batteries in the DR Congo and Zambia.* Accessed May 13, 2013. http://makeitfair.org/en/the-facts/reports/2007-2009/reports-from-2009/Powering-the-Mobile-World-Swedwatch-November-2007.pdf/at_download/file

Swedwatch, SACOM and SOMO. 2008. *Silenced to Deliver: Mobile Phone Manufacturing in China and the Philippines.* Accessed May 13, 2013. http://makeitfair.org/en/the-facts/reports/2007-2009/reports-from-2009/silenced-to-deliver/at_download/file

The New Generation Migrant Workers Concern Programme. 2013. *The Report on Foxconn Trade Union Research.* Accessed May 13, 2013. https://www.dropbox.com/s/qzwo85nzly5u8wh/2013.05.01%20-%20English%20excerpt%20on%20Foxconn%20

union%20research%20report.pdf
WTEC (World Technology Evaluation Center). 1997. *Electronics Manufacturing in the Pacific Rim.* Accessed May 18, 2013. http://www.wtec.org/loyola/pdf/em.pdf
van Dijk, Teun. 2011. Discourse and Ideology. In *Discourse Studies: A Multidisciplinary Approach*, edited by Teun van Dijk, 379-407. London: Sage.
Zhao, Yuezhi and Robert Duffy. 2008. Short-Circuited? The Communication and Labor in China, In *Knowledge Workers in the Information Society*, edited by Catherine McKercher and Vincent Mosco, 229-248. Lanham, MD: Lexington Books.

# 'The Future's Bright, the Future's Mobile': A Study of Apple and Google Mobile Application Developers

Birgitta Bergvall-Kåreborn(碧吉塔·伯格维尔-卡里伯恩)
Debra Howcroft(德布拉·霍克洛夫特)[①]

[**导读**] 软件行业总是被冠以"朝阳产业"的称谓,从事软件行业的知识劳工也经常与"拥有稳定的职业生涯"画上等号。但随着分包(subcontracting)和外包(outsourcing)的出现,在软件行业,标准劳动合同不断减少、自主创业不断增加,以及与之伴随的是软件行业工作者不安全感的与日俱增。在这篇论文中,作者们分析了目前作为市场领导者的苹果和谷歌公司给移动应用程序开发和发行(mobile application development and distribution, MADD)领域带来的主要变化,以及变革中的市场结构如何塑造和控制移动应用软件开发者的工作经历,进而填补了学术界对于移动应用软件开发者研究的"空白"——这篇论文对于了解移动应用软件开发者如何应对产业变化以及技术的发展如何影响流动的劳动力市场至关重要。

具体来说,信息技术部门以"众包"(crowdsourcing)为代表的结构性变革引发了软件开发工作的偶然性和不安全性——"众包"的出现使得企业获得巨额利润成为可能。这些利润一方面来自于企业避免与软件开发者签订直接劳务合同而节约的成本,一方面来自于企业用近乎于志愿者的人力成本在市场中获得劳动生产力,因此"众包"日益成为企业雇佣软件开发者最具吸引力和可行的方式。这些变化在作者们对瑞典、英国和美国工作的 60

---

[①] Birgitta Bergvall-Kåreborn, 现任教于瑞典吕勒奥理工大学(Luleå University of Technology)计算机科学、电子和工程系。她的研究方向聚焦于计算机科学。
Debra Howcroft, 现任教于曼彻斯特大学(University of Manchester)曼彻斯特商学院。她的研究方向聚焦于社会文化变迁、全球化背景下社会和经济的重构。

位移动应用软件开发者的访谈和对 12 位移动应用软件开发者实验对比的结果中体现得"淋漓尽致"。

自我控制。自我控制要求个体独立地安排、控制和监督自己的工作活动。移动应用软件开发者需要根据市场的变化不断重新培养自己新的能力,"所有的一切都在变化,落后意味着致命性的打击"。不断更新自身知识结构和提升自身能力的压力成为了移动应用软件开发者焦虑的"源泉",同时他们用大部分的非工作时间来更新这些知识和提高相应的技能,以获得行业内的知名度,为将来的工作打下"坚实"的基础。但是因为苹果和谷歌公司控制了移动应用软件的开发和发行,并对于哪些移动应用软件可以进入市场具有决定权——这对于独立应用软件开发者的影响是致命的,因此在现行的市场结构下,自我控制的局限性被"无限放大"。即使那些被苹果和谷歌公司使用的移动应用软件,他们的开发者也并不具有产品的定价能力。

自我商品化。自我商品化要求移动应用软件开发者不仅在公司内,而且在更广阔的劳动力市场,将自己的活动变为积极的生产,同时将自己的能力不断商品化。移动应用软件开发者需要创造力、专业技术能力和好的构想;但如何使自己的产品能在苹果和谷歌公司控制的电子化市场上占据"前100"的地位,进而被用户了解,要求他们对于消费者的兴趣有准确的把握,同时培养忠实的用户。同时,随着在这个行业中,个人的地位和社会关系变得越来越重要,移动应用软件开发者会用大量的时间构建自己的"网络社会"(network sociality),这也是自我商品化的重要环节。

自我理性化。自我理性化要求移动应用软件开发者将自己的日常生活和长期的计划自主地以工作为中心。长时间的工作、工作中的起伏对于生活不可预见性的影响、对工作缺乏控制都成为移动应用软件开发者的"日常"。对于他们来说,利润最大化成为了在这个充满"不确定性"的市场中生存下去的唯一方法——但是很多时候他们不得不为了鼓励用户的下载和为将来潜在的好处而免费提供他们的移动应用软件。不得不承认部分的移动应用软件开发者享受着原创性的产品给他们带来的精神上的愉悦和满足,但这同时进一步模糊了工作和家庭之间的边界,鞭笞他们在工作中更好地表现。

毋庸置疑,变革中的市场结构导致了劳动者令人堪忧的工作环境和不稳定的劳动力市场。通过将汉斯·蓬格拉茨（Hans Pongratz）和君特·沃斯（Günter Voß）教授"企业家雇员"（entreployee）的概念引入对于移动应用软件开发者自我控制、自我商品化和自我理性化的分析之中，我们不难发现，当苹果和谷歌公司在这样一个权力不平等的市场中通过对平台的控制而获取巨额利润的时候，提供智力支持的移动应用软件开发者获得的报酬远远小于他们实际应得的——他们共同承担了苹果和谷歌公司对于产品开发和市场营销的成本，对于这些企业来说，"压榨"数字劳工成为了规避风险最好的方法，这同时也是为什么"众包"倍受青睐的缘由。

## INTRODUCTION

IT work is frequently portrayed as a 'sunrise occupation' (Kraft and Dubnoff, 1986) with 'new economy' writers projecting the benefits of a self-managed and 'boundaryless' career (Baldry et al., 2007). Yet, broader changes in work and employment, such as subcontracting or outsourcing (Taylor, 2010), the decline of standard labour contracts (Baldry et al., 2007), rising self-employment (Smeaton, 2003) and mounting insecurity (Green, 2009; Thompson, 2010) appear particularly pronounced in software work. While a small body of research reports on the labour process within the IT industry (Barrett, 2001; Beirne et al., 1998; Kennedy, 2010; Marks and Scholarios, 2008), there is limited knowledge regarding what software developers do, how they react to changes within the industry and how technology developments impact upon shifting labour markets (Barrett, 2001; Gill, 2007; Pratt, 2009). Therefore, this study investigates these broader changes within the area of mobile application development and distribution (MADD), based on platforms owned by current market leaders: Apple and Google. The focus lies in understanding how changing market structures shape and control developers' working experiences.

Employing software developers is costly to firms and controlling their productivity is notoriously difficult (Barrett, 2001). With mobile development, the coming together of new technology platforms with a changing market environment has enabled Apple and Google to outsource development to a global base of developers; this business model, which harnesses the creativity of a distributed network of individuals, has been termed 'crowdsourcing' (Brabham, 2008: 76). Structural changes in the IT sector have resulted in increasing casualization and insecurity (McDowell and Christopherson, 2009), which has triggered crowdsourcing as an attractive and viable form of employment for developers; at the same time, products designed by the crowd enable companies to generate substantial profits. Crowdsourcing mobile applications entails a move away from salaried forms of exchange within an internal labour market to an external market of competing contractors, thus allowing large firms to avoid the incurred costs of the direct employment contract while profiting from the productivity of what is effectively a volunteer workforce. This broader context is relevant to understanding the dynamics shaping the working environment of software developers.

The purpose of the article is to analyse the experiences of MADD developers and the coping strategies they adopt in the context of wider environmental changes and an intensification of market relations. The authors' interest lies in the commonalities experienced by developers that cut across employment categories, rather than exploring distinctions. Drawing on compelling evidence, the research details how software workers react and respond to increasingly precarious employment and insecure prospects. Before presenting the evidence from developers, the broader context of the IT sector and mobile application platforms is established, followed by an explication of the research approach.

## SETTING THE SCENE: IT WORK, ENTREPRENEURISM AND MOBILE APPLICATIONS DEVELOPMENT

While software development is frequently portrayed as an exemplar of knowledge work (Castells, 2000), the more critical literature has described it as 'white collar manufacturing' (Marks and Baldry, 2009: 61) and 'a scientific management of mind work' (Kraft and Dubnoff, 1986: 194). Over the last decade or so, the IT workforce has been confronted with considerable turmoil including the burst of the dot.com bubble, the offshoring of software work, and a more general thinning out of the industry. Although regulatory contexts differ, sectoral transformation has resulted in a bifurcation with large firms consolidating their position as the proportion of small firms increases, confirmed by studies in Australia (Barrett, 2001), Holland (Gill, 2007), Sweden (Movitz and Sandberg, 2009), the UK (Marks and Huzzard, 2010) and the US (Batt et al., 2001).

For IT workers, the archetype of a stable career begins to waver as firms change size, location, projects and organizational structures, with a modification from full- to part-time work and from employees to freelancers (Lash and Wittel, 2002). Even when hopes were high for the 'new economy', the IT workforce experienced an increase in casual contracts, self-employment, multiple job holding and low paid work (McDowell and Christopherson, 2009). These trends are coupled with the 'projectification' of work (Maylor et al., 2006) which has seen project-based working patterns becoming the norm (Kennedy, 2010). Workers move rapidly between different types of employment – freelancing, working for a company, setting up their own business – not necessarily sequentially and often in parallel (Gill, 2007). While new media workers may be celebrated as 'model entrepreneurs' (Florida, 2002), often the reality is the disintegration of stable careers and discontinuous employment. Entrepreneurism is frequently presented as offering new opportunities, but the erosion of salaried employment sees a reduction in security (Christopherson, 2004) and is market dependent. Precariousness can be a typical concomitant, often associated with self-exploitation (Ross, 2003).

Changes in the IT sector echo trends of casualization and insecurity, which have become increasingly relevant to high paid, high skilled workers (Gill and Pratt, 2008). Pongratz and Voß (2003) argue these changes have contributed towards a fundamental transformation of work, which they conceptualize in terms of the 'entreployee' or self-employed employee. This concept is used to explain the response to highly flexible forms of capitalism with an increasing lack of distinction between employee and employer, as employees redefine their capacity both within the firm and the wider labour market. The quasi-entrepreneurial nature of working life sees the promotion of employee responsibility as employees are tasked with transforming their labour power into concrete performance. The conceptualization of 'entreployee' refers primarily to individuals working within firms and is typified by the rise of performance metrics, profit centres, project/team work, and increasing flexibility. Between firms, the 'autonomization' of work sees the growth of outsourcing and increasing cooperation with freelancers.

The research was further developed by Pongratz (2008) who theorized a 'society of entrepreneurs' as one in which entrepreneurial functions are relegated commonplace, and everyone potentially faces the prospect or acts as an entrepreneur at some point throughout his/her working life – either selectively or permanently, self- or other-directed, partially or comprehensively, successfully or not. In contrast to the conventional definition of the capitalist entrepreneur as social elite, Pongratz (2008) provides a more encompassing classification which broadens out the category to include the self-employed (more commonly referring to a single person business or freelancer) and the 'entreployee'. Faced with changing market structures, the category covers overlapping forms of entrepreneurial action. In this regard, enterprise is not simply an organizational form, but a certain mode of activity that could be applied to organizations, and individuals within organizations and to their everyday existence (Miller and Rose, 1995: 455). Depending on the particularities of given markets, workers will occupy different positions and perform various entrepreneurial functions;

this could be within the roles of formal employment, self-employment and freelancing. Fluidity is key, so that while workers may sit in a particular category at any given career point, they are inclined (and often forced) to adapt. In this market reorientation, workers as entrepreneurs become 'profit-seeking sellers of commodities' (Pongratz, 2008: 3) as they channel their individual labour power into producing and marketing goods or services to maintain their economic existence, which allows for a reconceptualization of work so that productivity is maximized, innovation is assured, and worker commitment is guaranteed. The political vocabulary of enterprise offers a means for improving employee capacity *and* enhancing self-fulfilment and responsibility (Miller and Rose, 1995).

The critical lens on emerging forms of entrepreneurism and entrepreneurial behaviour in the context of changing market structures will be drawn upon to analyse mobile applications developers and their experiences. Management faces numerous challenges when managing software workers as they nurture creativity while maintaining a semblance of control. The crowdsourcing of MADD by Apple and Google facilitates access to a mass of labour while placing responsibility for productivity firmly at the door of developers themselves, allowing capital to reap the financial benefits while sidestepping the costs of recruiting, training and sustaining labour.

**Apple and Google**

Understanding IT work requires an appreciation of how wider socio-economic trends and developments in product and technology markets frame working practices. Until recently, the mobile phone market was one of maturity and sophistication, with five manufacturers covering 75 percent of the world market (Nokia, Motorola, Samsung, Siemens and Sony Ericsson) (Hess and Coe, 2006). This changed significantly in 2007 when Apple launched the iPhone and entered the mobile phone market with a product equipped for internet access. Apple is renowned in the industry for the extreme secrecy surrounding product launches, which enhances the anticipation. The unveiling of the iPhone was marketed with staged launches outside retail stores, as queues of young film extras were paid by Apple to generate interest among passers-by (Goggin, 2009). Apple artefacts are embedded into a digital ecosystem that seamlessly links products with the electronic marketplace (iTunes, the App Store). As the lead firm in the supply chain, Apple enhances control using multiple sourcing and working closely with even the suppliers' suppliers (Dedrick et al., 2009).

In March 2008, Apple released the iPhone Software Development Kit (SDK) which enables third-party developers to create applications for the iPhone, iPod touch and iPad. In keeping with their centralized strategy, Apple commandeers the distribution and sales channel for mobile applications via the App Store. Developers set their own price for the application and Apple top-slice 30 percent of sales revenues. The process is mediated by Apple who may halt the release of applications if they are deemed inappropriate or unsuitable; their control is underlined with 113 guidelines outlining acceptance criteria.

Turning to Google, their entry into new markets includes mobile technology and in 2008, they announced their open source Android platform for mobile phone development. Open source is perceived by many as anti-corporate, which ostensibly links neatly with Google's image, exemplified in their mission statement: 'Don't be evil'. At the same time Android was released, Google founded the Open Handset Alliance (OHA). This business consortium consists of around 50 technology and mobile firms (such as Samsung, Motorola, LG, Vodafone and Intel) that are committed to open standards for mobile devices. In contradistinction to its name, membership of the OHA is based on personal invitation from Google (Grotnes, 2009), which suggests that Android is far from an open source project.

By using the OHA to assemble together mobile phone handset makers and carriers, Google has managed to mobilize a range of manufacturers to develop products for the Android platform. The founding of the OHA supports Google's endeavour to have Android available across a range of devices and the OHA's declaration that 'building a better mobile phone would enrich the lives of countless people across the globe' (Open Handset Alliance, 2009) suggests that their strategy is geared towards the global distribution of Android handsets. This is of particular interest given the United Nations report on the information economy (United Nations, 2010) which points to mobiles emerging as the preferred ICT tool, with rapid increases in the numbers of subscriptions, particularly within developing economies.

Although variations exist between Apple and Google platforms, common to both are the provision of the SDK to enable the creation of applications and the distribution channel, which, crucially, provides the link between developers and consumers. In opening up the platform, Apple and Google have outsourced mobile applications development to a global base of freelancers, thereby minimizing risk, while developers create and market applications that may or may not be successful. This form of crowdsourcing has been described by *Business Week* (Hempel, 2006) as a novel way of 'milking the masses for inspiration'.

## RESEARCH APPROACH

In 2009, a qualitative study of developers' experiences of MADD was undertaken. The research focuses on how market relations (and significant institutions such as Apple and Google) interact with, shape and control developers' experiences and expectations. The study covered Sweden, the UK and the US since they have significant levels of maturity in the mobile marketplace. The aim was to capture the everyday working experiences of developers with varying expertise and a mixture of employment contracts. Topics discussed included: working practices, reasons for developing for mobile devices, attraction to and experience of particular platforms, the development process, and marketing strategies. The study was piloted using two focus groups, each consisting of 6 Android/iPhone developers, a strategy which provided a vantage point from which to launch the broader study. In total, 60 developers were recruited using social media channels, including online forums and blogs, as well as sending personal messages via email and Facebook. A mixture of face-to-face, co-located interviews, synchronous Skype interviews and asynchronous online discussion forums was adopted, depending on preferences and geographical location (Table 1). Interviews lasted 1-2 hours; all were recorded and transcribed.

*Table 1 Number and Type of Interviews*

| ID no. | Developers | Date | Residence | Format |
| --- | --- | --- | --- | --- |
| 1–2 | 2 Android | May 2009 | Sweden | Skype focus group |
| 3–4 | 2 Android | May 2009 | Sweden | Face-to-face interviews |
| 5 | 1 Android | May 2009 | Sweden | Face-to-face interview |
| 6 | 1 Android | May 2009 | Sweden | Skype interview |
| 7 | 1 Android | June 2009 | UK | Skype interview |
| 8 | 1 Android | June 2009 | UK | Skype interview |
| 9 | 1 iPhone | June 2009 | UK | Skype interview |
| 10 | 1 Android | June 2009 | UK | Skype interview |
| 11 | 1 Android | June 2009 | UK | Skype interview |
| 12 | 1 Android | June 2009 | Sweden | Skype interview |
| 13–14 | 1 Android and 1 iPhone | June 2009 | UK | Face-to-face focus group |
| 15–16 | 2 Android | June 2009 | UK | Skype focus group |
| 17–23 | 7 iPhone | Sept. 2009 | USA | Online forum |
| 24–41 | 18 Android | Sept. 2009 | USA | Online forum |
| 41–43 | 2 iPhone | Sept. 2009 | USA | Online forum |

| ID no. | Developers | Date | Residence | Format |
|---|---|---|---|---|
| 44–45 | 2 Android | | | |
| 46–47 | 2 iPhone | Aug. 2010 | Sweden | Face-to-face focus group |
| 48–49 | 2 Android | | | |
| 50–51 | 2 Android | Sept. 2009 | UK | Face-to-face focus group |
| 52 | 1 Apple | Sept. 2009 | UK | Face-to-face interview |
| 53 | 1 Apple | Sept. 2009 | UK | Face-to-face interview |
| 54–55 | 2 Apple | Sept. 2009 | UK | Face-to-face focus group |
| 56 | 1 Apple | Sept. 2009 | UK | Face-to-face interview |
| 57 | 1 Apple | Sept. 2009 | UK | Face-to-face interview |
| 58–59 | 2 Apple | Sept. 2009 | UK | Face-to-face focus group |
| 60 | 1 Apple | Sept. 2009 | UK | Skype interview |

Three online forums were created, which lasted for 10 days with a question posted daily. This was not perceived as onerous and so the response rate was excellent (100%). Every participant answered each question and often commented on each other's answers, thereby generating debate in a similar way to a focus group. Given the IT sector is characterized by a multitude of firm types, no one organization was studied and in this respect, the research is neither organizationally nor spatially bounded.

The process of data collection and analysis occurred dynamically and interactively as the data was input into a data analysis tool (NVivo). The method of analysis was based on an ongoing iterative process of reflection to help identify concepts and themes (Miles and Huberman, 1984). As the data collection progressed, the predominance of precarious work became apparent and the boundaries between different employment structures appeared permeable. A mapping of the relationships between data and emerging themes was created, guided by the literature, with the work of Pongratz and Voß (2003) seemingly apposite. Initial findings were shared with participants and their comments confirmed and elaborated the themes. The quotes have been selected from the full range of participants to highlight the multiplicity of views.

## The Developers' Profile

The developers represented a fairly homogeneous grouping with extensive experience and platform knowledge. In total, 60 developers participated in the study. Given the IT industry is notorious for the under-representation of women (Adam et al., 2006), effort was placed into recruiting developers from 'Girl Geeks', resulting in 5 female participants. Overall, publishing experience spanned from 1 to 45 applications, with around half of the developers having published between 10 and 40. The development process varied and could range from half a day (e.g. a new ringtone) to several months (e.g. the Edinburgh Festival app). Some developers and firms specialized in developing one main product (e.g. a self-employed developer spent 18 months creating an e-book reader), investing time in updates and user support, while others released numerous apps and offered limited support, quickly moving on to the next development project.

Most of the developers opted for single platform development to focus their expertise and their preference was largely pragmatic as opposed to evangelical. Many began using the iPhone platform because it preceded Android and provided a digital infrastructure supported by strong branding. Conversely, other developers chose Android because its open source features enabled them to share code. Android developers Stressed their reasons for *not* developing for Apple: the iPhone is 'too controlled' with numerous conformance rules and applications risk rejection from the App Store. Some developers worked on outsourced applications, but the majority 'owned' the product they were developing. For those developing outsourced applications, platform choice was dictated by the terms of the contract. There were differences in levels of success as the number of downloads for their *most successful* application ranged from over 1m to just over 10,000, but there were examples of some applications receiving zero downloads. While this was relatively uncommon, more widespread was the level of unpredictability (either positive or negative) which points to the unstable nature of app development. The amount of revenue generated also varied widely – from $150,000 from one application to just $50 for a developer with six applications.

The developers represented a diversity of employment types (see Table 2), a fact which reflects market structures, the nature of the commodities and the competitive environment. The employment categories are derived from Pongratz and Voß (2003) and are fluid as developers move between categories. Our interviewees often experienced multiple types of employment simultaneously, such as formal employment and freelancing in their leisure time, or freelancing and sub-contracting for a specific project. As Pongratz (2008: 9) notes: 'An actor is not *per se* an entrepreneur or non-entrepreneur, but is one or the other with regard to a certain market.' Almost 60 percent of the participants were self-employed, either working as contractors or managing their own start-up.

Of interest is the small proportion of developers that are formally employed to develop apps as compared with those that are formally employed, yet developing apps as a sideline, outside of the boundaries of the firm. Even for those developers that are formally employed, the sector predominantly consists of micro firms with self-starting individuals (Barrett, 2005) and an expectation of 'enterprising' behaviour.

*Table 2   Employment Categories*

| | Category | Number of developers | | |
|---|---|---|---|---|
| | | Sweden | UK | US |
| 1 | Formally employed, either solely developing apps or developing apps/other IT commodities | 5 | 2 | 5 |
| 2 | Self-employed (includes establishing own company and contract work), either developing apps or developing apps/other IT commodities | 13 | 16 | 17 |
| 3 | Formally employed and only developing apps as a sideline | 5 | 2 | 5 |
| 4 | Unemployed/student and only developing apps as a sideline | | | 2 |

In the three geographical locations selected for the research, different regulatory frameworks govern employment conditions and may result in variations (Christopherson, 2004). In the US, there was a predominance of entrepreneurial contractors (Batt et al., 2001). In Sweden, work is predominantly based on an employment-based professional model, with studies in the early 2000s demonstrating a prevalence of full-time, permanent employees (Movitz and Sandberg, 2009). However, there is an adjustment towards self-employment and micro firms, with 98 percent of Swedish IT companies having less than 20 employees (Statistics Sweden, 2008). The UK sits midway between these extremes with increasing emphasis being placed upon the growth of small firms and self-employment. Despite regional distinctions, there are also common patterns across these economies, such as urban orientation, the tension between creativity and control, continuous re-skilling, and gender segmentation.

## FINDINGS FROM THE STUDY

The data has been analysed according to Pongratz and Voß's (2003) ideal type of the 'entreployee'; this analysis is used to illustrate the increasingly entrepreneurial and precarious nature of software work. The categories derived from Pongratz and Voß (2003) are those of self-control, self-commercialization and self-rationalization. These will be discussed next.

**Self-control**

Integral to the concept of 'entreployee' is the manner in which individuals have to independently plan, control and monitor their work activities (Pongratz and Voß, 2003: 8). In the context of MADD, of relevance are the restrictions created by Apple and Google, as they consolidate their position while the remainder operate predominantly as small firms, freelancers and sub-contractors.

Exercising self-control in a sector reliant on continuous innovation requires developers to redefine their capabilities in response to changing markets. The mobile market was typically described by interviewees as 'where everything is moving' and lagging behind is viewed as detrimental: 'If you are developing for an outdated or dying device, then you're wasting your time' (ID no. 36; category 2)[1]. The desire to work on leading-edge technology and become enriched motivates many developers, given socio-economic mobility is seen as more accessible as compared with traditional professions (Marks and Baldry, 2009). Yet, entering emerging markets represents new risk. A couple of developers described how their enterprises had changed from web to iPhone development within a six-month period: 'Essentially, we have no other income than our iPhone applications. So we have kind of jumped into it with both feet' (ID no. 9; category 2).

Many developers focus on continuous competence development (Adams and Demaiter, 2008) which is key to self-control, enabling them to keep pace while remaining attractive in the jobs market. Indeed, studies show career and remuneration distinctions between those working with advanced technology and those working with older systems (Marks and Scholarios, 2008). Yet, the pressure of 'keeping up' (Ross, 2003) could be a source of anxiety and allocating time for up-skilling frequently occurred outside of office hours:

> For personal development, I wanted to try a new [programming] language. I mean, how hard can it be? But it turned out to be quite hard! The opportunity to earn some money has crossed my mind, but I did it more for my own sake than to get crazy rich. (ID no. 7; category 3)

Many of the developers displayed intense self-motivation and commitment, so receiving a positive response to their labour was highly desired. Peer group recognition enhanced self-control as it could lead to lucrative contracts in the future: 'My motivation to create games is to get recognition within the community. You're the guy that has done this' (ID no. 44; category 3). Success was equated with getting noticed, described as having 'celebrity status', which could become self-fulfilling as publicity often correlated with product downloads and higher commercial value. In this respect, reputation among peers was crucial since future employment was dependent on past performance, yet peer group response was difficult to direct, which could heighten the lack of control.

Self-control remained limited given that Apple and Google owned the development and distribution platform. Although developers had considerable discretion over how they organized their work and participated in the market, this market was shaped by business models determined by Apple and Google. Prior to Apple and Google's incursion into the MADD market, there were limited opportunities for developers to access this marketplace and so many viewed crowdsourcing as opening up opportunities. However, criticism frequently surfaced regarding lack of control. Particularly problematic for iPhone developers was that Apple ultimately decided whether or not applications were permitted on the App Store: 'Occasionally, we have had apps refused for no reason. You have heard all the horror stories and they apply to us' (ID no. 13; category 2). One developer was irritated by the lack of consistency:

> [Apple] rejected us for a feature that wasn't functional apparently. But we can actually see from their server logs that they had tested it and it worked, but they said that it didn't work because they were doing it so quickly. They didn't give it their full attention. We know countless people that have been rejected for crazy reasons. (ID no. 9; category 2)

The digital infrastructure created by Apple pointed to diminishing control by developers, but criticism of Google also emerged regarding restrictions which limited developers' ability to function effectively in the market:

> There are significant barriers to me as an independent developer. The Android market has very limited searching capabilities. That's especially disturbing since this is an application created by Google. The payment system is still not available to all countries. In fact, I was reading the other day that even Canada is still not accepting payments. Incredible! So, let's assume the customers are in a country where they can make a payment and even if they enjoy your app, they can return it within 24 hours.

> Insane! ... Google is not interested in selling apps; they are interested in the advertising carried by the platform. (ID no. 27; category 2)

The cost of developing mobile applications was front-loaded as they were digitally reproduced, with more copies sold yielding a greater return. However, products often had a short shelf-life within a highly competitive marketplace: 'There are so many apps now that it's hard to be noticed' (ID no. 41; category 2). Consequently, price cutting occurs:

> The top 50 list is just flooded with 99-cent applications. Some individual developers say that those prices are too low to get any money, real money. But that's not really Apple's problem – it is the developers' problem. (ID no. 48; category 1)

While developers had the freedom to determine pricing, this was seldom applied. They were constrained by the market as well as pricing categories recommended by Apple and Google, which imposed normative control to the extent that the majority of applications sat within predefined (low-price) categories. Furthermore, top-slicing 30 percent by Apple caused resentment:

> I find it very unfair that 30 percent of my application bill goes to a company that had nothing to do with it. Apple gets the money from the actual hardware [iPhone] and even the software [SDK] they created. When you develop apps, this makes the phone better, so Apple shouldn't then be making money out of developers as well. (ID no. 14; category 2)

Developers tried to maximize self-control with competency development, by adopting strategies for enhancing recognition and the generation of future work. However, self-control was hampered considerably by market structures within which they operated, which were directed by Apple and Google.

**Self-commercialization**

The concept of self-commercialization is central to 'entreployees' whose activities are directed towards active production and commercialization of one's own capacities, both within the firm and in the wider labour market (Pongratz and Voß, 2003). The very nature of mobile applications means that there is strong individual association with the product, and therefore the commercialization of applications is intimately linked to the commercialization of oneself. The relationship is symbiotic in that product success feeds off worker success and *vice versa*.

IT development weaves together multiple skills, with MADD requiring creativity and ideation, along with technical skills. Yet, market structures mean that generating interest from consumers is also crucial to success. Given that Apple and Google's e-marketplaces offer limited showcasing beyond the 'top 100 lists' (in a market consisting of hundreds of thousands), the volume of applications means that high visibility is a challenge. Therefore, developers invest time in commercializing their capacities and drawing attention to products, using social network sites like YouTube, Twitter and blogs.

Ostensibly, the purchase of predominantly low-cost applications appears to represent a clear separation of production from consumption, but how products are received by the user community can strongly influence sales and reputation. Therefore, many developers put effort into fostering loyalty from users. One developer maintained an electronic list with around 10,000 users, informing them of product updates, while other developers cultivated user contact via blogs. A common theme was the importance of responding positively to users: 'I think the only way is to listen to the feedback and really try to deliver exactly what the user wants. You have to keep the updates coming which have noticeable new features' (ID no. 32; category 2). The ease with which users could digitally review products meant that negative feedback could enter the public domain with ease:

> I don't like the ratings system on the market. If you have a couple of people who give your app 1 star for no good reason, while the predominant score is 4 or 5, you're still affected by those 1-star reviews – it's not an accurate measure, in my opinion. (ID no. 34; category 1)

Another element of self-commercialization concerns how people generate work based on respect and recognition from the occupational communities of which they are part. As the 'job for life' diminishes, future prospects become reliant on contacts, as well as information on past achievements. In one study of IT professionals, only 2 percent of work was secured through formal means (Gill, 2007), which signifies that personal standing and social relations are crucial. A developer explained that the value of social networks centred on 'awareness inwards and outwards' (ID no. 50; category 2). These networks enhanced awareness of 'who you are and what you're doing' as well as providing access to future employees. A CEO of a small firm commented, 'I pay a lot of attention and try to stay involved in different communities and that's how we've managed to find our staff' (ID no. 53; category 2). A freelance culture requires an active and effective network, both in terms of finding work and workers, becoming a key conduit of knowledge about job opportunities.

Many developers participated in numerous social networks and while this could be time consuming, it was essential for self-commercialization. The types of networking described by interviewees were a form of 'network sociality' (Wittel, 2001) whereby social relations were primarily informational, based on transient encounters, reflective of the project-based nature of the work. While developers simply existed as the 'crowd' to Apple/Google, they relied upon their own occupational communities for support in surviving crowdsourcing. These networks create a form of voluntary collegiality and enable developers to cope with highly fragmented labour markets while being leveraged as a mechanism for work distribution (Kennedy, 2010). Given the low levels of unionization among the IT workforce, networks can provide developers with a sense of control (Beirne et al., 1998). Those who do not participate can suffer serious disadvantages as networks operate increasingly as informal labour markets, as individuals self-market their capacities and potential. Given the IT industry is notoriously gendered (Adam et al., 2006), working in an industry centred around personal recommendation and informal meetings means that gender discrimination may be enhanced (Christopherson, 2008; Pratt, 2002). Inequalities are exacerbated as traditional terms and conditions are rendered irrelevant in an environment of crowdsourcing as opposed to one centred on an employment contract.

**Self-rationalization**

Another characteristic of 'entreployees' concerns the self-determined organization of daily life and long-term plans, often willingly accepting the centrality of work (Pongratz and Voß, 2003: 8) and the blurring of boundaries between work and home life. Common among respondents was the intensity of working life, typified by long hours. One CEO described his circumstances over the past three years: 'I work too many hours. It's somewhere over 80 ... it's far too many' (ID no. 56; category 2). Although long hours were prevalent, equally challenging was how life was organized around accommodating unpredictability and the peaks and troughs of projects. Even when projects were completed, the pressure to acquire the next contract was unrelenting: 'I very rarely turn down an opportunity to sell an application, which lumps more pressure on me' (ID no. 54; category 2). While the apparent flexibility seemed appealing, many developers had limited power over either the quantity of work or the conditions under which it was undertaken, and the level of control was less substantial than assumed. The consequences of being forever present were commented on by a female developer: 'The one thing I don't think you can do in this profession is to take maternity leave. For that you would have to take a year off and then you'd never get back in' (ID no. 59; category 3).

When working in an uncertain market where the future direction of Apple and Google is undisclosed, maximizing revenue is key to survival. However, some developers offered their application for free ('freemiums') to encourage downloads and stimulate interest. The data analysis identified a repertoire of practices which entailed sacrificing pay in anticipation of forthcoming rewards. The CEO of a start-up explained: 'There are more shareholders than myself. But they are all sort of employees – or past employees – who've worked below the market rate and so taken some of the risk of getting involved' (ID no. 57; category 2). A recurring theme was a willingness to accept intensive working conditions in the hope that success lay just around the corner. For some, this involved developing their small firm to a level that required less input: 'I'm trying to get the company to a stage where I can work less' (ID no. 19; category 2). For others, future success rested on the expectation of funding from elsewhere, with some optimistically anticipating being bought out by a large firm such as Google: 'My strategy for growth is finding someone who'll pay for it. Doing software development well is expensive' (ID no. 60; category 2).

While economic factors predominantly dictated the prevalence of working life, other motivations were apparent. Frequently mentioned was the fun element of work as developers described the pleasure associated with creating an innovative product: 'Most people watch TV, I programme' (ID no. 11; category 1). Enjoyment arose not simply from developing 'fun' products such as games, but from the intrinsic satisfaction associated with mastering a technical conundrum. For software developers, occupational identity is closely aligned with gratification derived from interesting work (Barrett, 2001):

> I didn't start out doing this for money. I've had a lifelong fascination with gadgets and I like the idea that new technologies make it possible to create applications that simply didn't exist three years ago. (ID no. 17; category 3)

Yet, this playful attitude enhances the centrality of work, weakening the distinction between work and private life which yields higher performance (Wittel, 2001). A female developer who was formally employed but hoped to move into self-employment explained: 'I want to prioritize this [app development], but I have three kids and I'm a single parent so I've quite a busy life at home. It's a case of sorting out the family and then spending a couple of hours at night on it' (ID no. 58; category 3). The informal extensions of work into the domestic sphere were also captured by a developer who worked with her partner: 'I don't think we would have started the company if it wasn't for my husband. We actually came up with the idea on our honeymoon' (ID no. 55; category 4). She went on to explain how working with her partner enabled her to justify paying reduced attention to domestic duties.

The predominant economic logic of work also permeated social activities with a blurring of demarcations:

> There's not much time for a social life, but I do love what I do. A lot of it is work-related. I don't count the networking as work; there is a social element to it ... definitely. But I would like more of a social life. (ID no. 51; category 2)

Profession-driven communities centred on 'talking shop' to cement occupational cohesiveness yet also closely integrated work and non-work activities, accentuating the relative importance of work. While this might foster deep attachment to careers, those with families might well resent the negative spillover into domestic life.

Common among interviewees were the ways in which the enhanced centrality of work was largely accommodated without question, creating distance from other significant aspects of living. Their professional circumstances heightened their acceptance of the relative importance of work for a number of reasons. Firstly, socioeconomic trends and changing market structures meant software workers had to adapt to greater instability and insecurity. Secondly, the IT industry was predominantly masculinized (this seemed especially pronounced with MADD) and so IT workers were more likely to exercise some measure of control over work-domestic boundaries. Thirdly, the technical nature of the job suggested an appropriate domestic infrastructure, enabling virtual work and thereby further allowing the public sphere of work to encroach upon the private sphere of home.

## DISCUSSION AND CONCLUSIONS

This study aims to provide a counterpoint to the hyperbole that characterizes IT work as a 'sunrise occupation' and an exemplar of 'new economy' working practices. Software developers are often portrayed as being driven by love of the job, rather than shaped by their environment. This article offers an examination of the everyday practices of mobile developers within the backdrop of socioeconomic changes and considers how the wider context influences working lives.

As a comparatively new arena of employment, social commentators had high hopes for IT work. Optimism was quickly dashed as research highlighted the replication of traditional control and command structures (Kraft and Dubnoff, 1986) and an ageist and gendered profession (Adam et al., 2006). Persistent IT failures intensified management control, resulting in routinization, fragmentation and the imposition of rationalistic models (Beirne et al., 1998). Yet, enhanced control failed to deliver significant improvements in a sector faced with labour shortages while requiring high levels of productivity. Consequently, the industry is deemed ripe for commodification, as market pressures are leveraged to enhance efficiency, reduce costs and engender enterprising traits among workers.

Broader workplace trends indicate the cultivation of 'enterprising subjects' as a 'commercially compelling' project that responds to the problems of productivity and control (Miller and Rose, 1995: 453). Pongratz and Voß's (2003) conceptualization of 'entreployee' and rising entrepreneurism illuminates increasing market orientation, as workers strive for economic survival. This reorientation appeals to capital as it generates improved productivity while neutralizing the problem of control; it also entices labour with the promise of self-fulfilment, self-discipline, responsibility and flexibility. As the study of MADD developers revealed, the facade of self-control is restricted by market conditions and power asymmetries. Self-commercialization obscures the hidden pressures associated with developing 'successful' products and generating a reputation in an environment that is dependent upon 'who you know'. The process of self-rationalization reveals the centrality of the economic logic of working life as developers are regularly exposed to project-based work, excessive working hours and discontinuous employment. Survival necessitates the development of entrepreneurial behaviour and it is in this context that crowdsourcing is able to thrive.

In the context of MADD, the power base within the mobile industry has adjusted over a relatively short period of time as Apple and Google have risen to prominence. This duopoly control centralized digital platforms for development and distribution, constructing a circuit of production whereby micro companies and individual developers create products and market them in vertically disintegrated systems. The success of Apple and Google can be attributed to various inter-related elements: the adaptation of mobile phones into internet-enabled devices; enhanced content-driven functionality arising from a multitude of applications; Apple's and Google's brand reputation and infrastructure; and the success of the crowdsourcing business model. While these changes are aided by technology platforms, it is not pre-determined that technology *per se* will influence direction in any one specific way. It is the combination of technology, firm strategies and regulatory context which enable technology to steer change along a particular course. The distinctive aspect of this buyer-seller network is the centralization of control via the platforms, providing the gateway to consumers, while leveraging the crowd to boost capital. Developers provide intellectual labour, which, when aggregated, has a combined value that is far higher than revenue generated. However, developers shoulder the burden of costs while Apple and Google circumvent the investment and resources required for in-house product development and marketing. This is the essence of crowdsourcing as corporations are able to harness creative labour at little or no cost, while minimizing risk.

Given dominating market structures, it is tempting to depict MADD as simply exploitative, yet unique to this setting is how crowdsourcing *potentially* enables developers to craft a viable career. This does not appear to be replicated in other crowdsourcing environments, where the emphasis is purely (low) cost-driven (e.g. Amazon's MechanicalTurk.com, where 'requesters' post tasks for a fixed monetary payment). The reasons why MADD seemingly promises an alternative career path may be explained by contextual changes such as: the move to a more enterprising model; increasing projectification; the normalization of outsourcing/freelancing; and the connotation of formal employment status as 'corporate, staid, and boring' (Pratt, 2002: 16). Barriers to entry are comparatively low and the 'myth of success', epitomized in exceptional cases such as Angry Birds[2], bolsters the crowdsourcing model. However, there are significant drawbacks with crowdsourcing, since there is no guarantee of success and income is both variable and unpredictable. Indeed, the downside of working on emerging technologies is that their contemporaneousness is characterized by uncertainty and impermanence. Unless developers can secure a third-party contract, revenue generation is difficult to predict. The higher status accrued from working on leading-edge technologies, combined with a strong sense of personal identity, means that job satisfaction can further impinge on private life. Elements of self-control exist, but it would be folly to overplay the level of influence MADD developers are able to exert. Boundaries are set and controlled by Apple and Google, and the relationship is uni-directional, with glaring power asymmetries as the workforce contends with minimal influence over platform owners and their future strategic direction.

In relation to careers, Baldry et al. (2007) argue that diversity in the IT industry is reflected in various career paths with 'organizational careerists' as well as 'horizontal-boundaryless careerists'. The former category often relates to those deemed less employable in the external market, while the latter proactively pursue wider opportunities in the profession with high levels of autonomy and market value. Crucial to careers is whether preferences arise as an active choice or emerge in response to workplace conditions and the constraints of market structures. As the IT industry is confronted with permanent restructuring and reorganization, organizational careers shrink and boundaryless entrepreneurism looks like a good option. Market relations take prominence, workplace conditions alter and project-based workers assume responsibility for productivity. The changing nature of IT working practices provides the groundwork that complements the crowdsourcing business model. Almost three decades ago, Kraft and Dubnoff's (1986) study showed how IT occupations replicate rather than revolutionize existing patterns of work and employment; our findings confirm the continuation of this tendency. MADD, as the archetype of 'new economy' work, accentuates persistent trends and further enhances precarity and uncertainty.

Finally, the MADD arena is dynamic and has not yet achieved stabilization. Although prediction is futile, it appears that the dominance of Apple/Google looks set to continue, especially given the limited emergence of strong competitors. However, although the crowdsourcing model may seem to be in extremes, the triumph of Apple and Google has seen other firms wishing to emulate their success with the adoption of comparable business models and platforms (e.g. Nokia, Microsoft and Blackberry). None of which bodes well for software developers.

## Notes

[1] Each quote has a unique identifier in the form of (participant number from Table 1; category number from Table 2).

[2] A gaming application developed by a small Finnish firm which has maintained top-10 status in over 30 countries.

## References

Adam, A., Richardson, H., Griffiths, M., Keogh, C., Moore, K. and Tattersall, A. (2006). Being an 'It' in IT: Gendered Identities in the IT Workplace. *European Journal of Information Systems* 15(4): 368–378.

Adams, T. and Demaiter, E. (2008). Skill, Education and Credentials in the New Economy: The Case of IT Workers. *Work, Employment & Society* 22(2): 351–362.

Baldry, C., Bain, P., Taylor, P., Hyman, J., Scholarios, D., Marks, A., et al. (2007). *The Meaning of Work in the New Economy*. London: Palgrave Macmillan.

Barrett, R. (2001). Labouring Under an Illusion? The Labour Process of Software Development in the Australian Information Industry. *New Technology, Work & Employment* 16(1): 18–34.

Barrett, R. (2005) Working at Webboyz: An Analysis of Control over the Software Development Labour Process. *Sociology* 38(4): 777–794.

Batt, R., Christopherson, S., Rightor, N. and van Jaarsvald, D. (2001). *Networking: Work Patterns and Workforce Policies for the New Media Industry*. Washington D.C.: Economic Policy Institute.

Beirne, M., Ramsay, H. and Panteli, A. (1998). *Developments in Computing Work: Control and Contradiction in the Software Labour Process*. In: Thompson, P. and Warhurst, C. (eds.)

*Workplaces of the Future*. London: Palgrave Macmillan, 142–162.

Brabham, D. (2008). Crowdsourcing as a Model for Problem Solving. *Convergence* 14(1): 75–90.

Castells, M. (2000). *The Rise of the Network Society*. Cambridge, MA: Blackwell.

Christopherson, S. (2004). The Divergent Worlds of New Media: How Policy Shapes Work in the Creative Economy. *Review of Policy Research* 21(4): 543–558.

Christopherson, S. (2008). Beyond the Self-Expressive Creative Worker: An Industry Perspective on Entertainment Media. *Theory, Culture & Society* 25(7/8): 73–95.

Dedrick, J., Kraemer, K. and Linden, G. (2009). Who Profits from Innovation in Global Value Chains? A Study of the iPod and Notebook PCs. *Industrial & Corporate Change* 19(1): 81–116.

Florida, R. (2002). *The Rise of the Creative Class: And How It's Transforming Work, Leisure, Community, and Everyday Life*. New York: Basic Books.

Gill, R. (2007). *Techno-Bohemians or the New Cybertariat?* Amsterdam, the Netherlands: Institute of Network Cultures.

Gill, R. and Pratt, A. (2008). In the Social Factory? Immaterial Labour, Precariousness and Cultural Work. *Theory, Culture & Society* 25(7/8): 1–30.

Goggin, G. (2009). Adapting the Mobile Phone: The iPhone and Its Consumption. *Continuum* 23(2): 231–244.

Green, F. (2009). Subjective Employment Insecurity Around the World. *Cambridge Journal of Regions, Economy & Society* 2(3): 343–363.

Grotnes, E. (2009). Standardization as Open Innovation: Two Cases from the Mobile Industry. *Information Technology & People* 22(4): 367–381.

Hempel, J. (2006). Crowdsourcing: Milk the Masses for Inspiration. *Business Week*, September 25, pp. 38–39.

Hess, M. and Coe, N. (2006). Making Connections: Global Production Networks, Standards, and Embeddedness in the Mobile-Telecommunications Industry. *Environment & Planning A* 38(7): 1205–1227.

Kennedy, H. (2010). Net Work: The Professionalization of Web Design. *Media, Culture & Society* 32(2): 187–203.

Kraft, P. and Dubnoff, S. (1986). Job Control, Fragmentation, and Control in Computer Software Work. *Industrial Relations* 25(2): 184–196.

Lash, S. and Wittel, A. (2002). Shifting New Media: From Content to Consultancy, from Heterarchy to Hierarchy. *Environment & Planning A* 34(11): 1985–2001.

Marks, A. and Baldry, C. (2009). Stuck in the Middle with Who? The Class Identity of Knowledge Workers. *Work, Employment & Society* 23(1): 49–65.

Marks, A. and Huzzard, T. (2010). Employability and the ICT Worker: A Study of Employees in Scottish Small Businesses. *New Technology, Work & Employment* 25(2): 167–181.

Marks, A. and Scholarios, D. (2008). Choreographing a System: Skill and Employability in Software Work. *Economic & Industrial Democracy* 29(1): 96–124.

Maylor, H., Brady, T., Cooke-Davies, T. and Hodgson, D. (2006). From Projectification to Programmification. *International Journal of Project Management* 24(8): 663–674.

McDowell, L. and Christopherson, S. (2009). Transforming Work: New Forms of Employment and Their Regulation. *Cambridge Journal of Regions, Economy & Society* 2(3): 1–8.

Miles, M. and Huberman, A. (1984). *Qualitative Data Analysis: An Expanded Sourcebook*. Beverley Hills, CA: Sage.

Miller, P. and Rose, N. (1995). Production, Identity and Democracy. *Theory & Society* 24(3): 427–467.

Movitz, F. and Sandberg, Å. (2009). The Organisation of Creativity: Content, Contracts and Control in Swedish Interactive Media Production. In: McKinlay, A. and Smith, C. (eds.) *Creative Labour: Working in the Creative Industries*. London: Palgrave Macmillan, 234–260.

Open Handset Alliance. (2009). *Overview*. Available (consulted June 30, 2012) at: http://www.openhandsetalliance.com/oha_overview.html

Pongratz, H. (2008). Eine Gesellschaft von Unternehmern Expansion und Profanierung 'Schöpferischer Zerstörung' in Kapitalistischen Ökonomien. *Berliner Journal für Soziologie* 18(3): 457–475.

Pongratz, H. and Voß, G. (2003). From 'Employee' to 'Entreployee': Towards a 'Self-Entrepreneurial' Work Force. *Concepts & Transformation* 8(3): 239–254.

Pratt, A. (2002). Hot Jobs in Cool Places. The Material Cultures of New Media Product Spaces: The Case of South of the Market, San Francisco. *Information, Communication & Society* 5(1): 27–50.

Pratt, A. (2009). Situating the Production of New Media: the Case of San Francisco. In: McKinlay, A. and Smith, C. (eds.) *Creative Labour: Working in the Creative Industries*. London: Palgrave Macmillan, 195–209.

Ross, A. (2003). *No Collar: The Humane Workplace and Its Hidden Costs*. New York: Basic Books.

Smeaton, D. (2003). Self-Employed Workers: Calling the Shots or Hesitant Independents? A Consideration of the Trends. *Work, Employment & Society* 17(2): 379–391.

Statistics Sweden. (2008). *Labour Force Survey*. Stockholm. Available (consulted January 7, 2010) at http://www.scb.se/Pages/Product_23276.aspx

Taylor, P. (2010). The Globalization of Service Work: Analysing the Transnational Call Centre Value Chain. In: Thompson, P. and Smith, C. (eds.) *Working Life: Renewing Labour Process Analysis*. Basinstoke, UK: Palgrave Macmillan, 244–268.

Thompson, P. (2010). The Capitalist Labour Process: Concepts and Connections. *Capital & Class* 34(1): 7–14.

United Nations. (2010). *The Information Economy Report*. Available (consulted May 1, 2012) at: www.unctad.org

Wittel, A. (2001). Towards a Network Sociality. *Theory, Culture & Society* 18(6): 51–76.

# III

Digital Labour in the Services Industry

# The Subterranean Stream: Communicative Capitalism and Call Centre Labour

Enda Brophy（恩达·布罗菲）[1]

[导读] 在这篇论文中，作者聚焦了呼叫中心的劳工，他们饱受低薪、高强度工作压力、不稳定的雇佣关系、僵化的管理体制、冷漠的工作环境以及无处不在的电子监控等问题的"折磨"。呼叫中心劳工的研究对于21世纪劳工的重新构成具有重大的启示意义，因为它是信息社会中关于工作的、更广阔的社会转型的具体表现，这些转型包括大型企业的重构、企业提供更多的服务、外包的普遍化、工作中传播形式的强化，以及弹性雇佣实践的加强——因此，呼叫中心成为了对劳工在数字经济中适应和重组能力的重要试验田。

作者将对呼叫中心劳工的研究放置在乔迪·迪恩（Jodi Dean）提出的"传播资本主义"（communicative capitalism）的研究框架之下。一方面，随着信息技术成本在过去的10年间大幅度地降低，以及人们在不同程度上成为信息技术的消费者，20世纪90年代以来，对于在"信息享有者"和"信息无产者"之间日益加剧的"数字鸿沟"的忧虑越来越显得"不合时宜"。另一方面，日常生活中传播的无处不在并未带来很多媒介理论家所期待出现的对社会不平等的削弱。在信息交换"纽带"的呼叫中心，这些在传播资本主义及其不同主体之间持续的传播"数据流"被重新组织和精简，最大限度地为利润的最大化服务。也就是说，呼叫中心作为传播生产隐蔽场所的存在是

---

[1] 现任教于加拿大西门菲莎大学（Simon Fraser University）传播学院。他的研究方向聚焦于传播政治经济学、传播和社会变化、媒介和传播产业的劳工组织，以及自治马克思主义。研究成果包括：《张嘴来钱：全球呼叫中心劳动力的形成》（*Language Put to Work: The Making of the Global Call Centre Workforce*, 2017）、《质问实习：无偿劳动、创意产业与高等教育》（*Interrogating Internships: Unpaid Work, Creative Industries, and Higher Education*, 2015）等。

20世纪最后10年间资本追逐利润最集中体现之一。离开了传播劳工,传播资本主义也就不复存在。

  作者从自治马克思主义理论出发,对呼叫中心人员的工作进行研究,并用自治理论对"非物质劳动"(immaterial labour)进行界定——强调从抗争和集体组织的视角考察新兴的雇佣形式。和劳动过程理论家一样,自治马克思主义理论研究者将劳动和资本之间的关系视为具有本质性的冲突,强调劳工的抵制和寻求更多的自主性,进而期待或引发资本主义的重构。在呼叫中心,对于"不可容忍"的工作环境,每年大约有35%的离职率;但离职只是劳工抗争众多形式中的一种,在全球范围内,其他更有组织性的抵抗形式还包括:协作(包括集体式的幽默,如对领导和经理的公开嘲笑;集体请愿,抗议过分的监控)、孕育中的工会(通过现有工会或创建新工会来组织劳工)、罢工等。

  通过对21世纪最初10年内呼叫中心员工集体组织最典型的三个案例(爱尔兰、加拿大、意大利)的分析,我们不难发现:在呼叫中心,虽然来自劳工的抵抗从未消失,但其作为信息经济中数字"血汗工厂"的称谓却依旧"恰如其分"。传播资本主义中充满着新的形式的不公平,而呼叫中心正见证了它如何对这些不公平进行延续和再生产。对于当代劳工抗争和集体组织的研究有助于我们认识一个不一样的"数字鸿沟",它不断地疏离雇主和他们所依赖的雇佣劳动力——愈发具有情感性、具有传播力和语言能力的"数字劳工"。

## INTRODUCTION

  'Workers should not be expected to be the eyes and ears of corporate capitalism while working on poverty wages with no job security in a call centre that often has its carpet infested by fleas', thus labour organiser Omar Hamed explained some of the conditions that triggered a 24-hour hunger strike by employees at the New Zealand market research firm Synovate in 2009. Their action was a part of the Calling for Change campaign, organized through the 11,000-member UNITE! Union and aimed at achieving better wages and working conditions at seven research companies in Auckland. Tele-researchers at these firms, many of them teenagers, have organized strikes and community pickets outside company headquarters in recent years as a response to inadequate breaks, job insecurity, and low pay compared to employees at their Australian parent companies, and they have won collective agreements and raises (New Zealand Press Association, 2009). As Hamed's words underscore, their daily production of information about the public is of profound importance in a digital market, but their labour is systematically devalued and exploited. The situation of employees at one of the targeted companies, SurveyTalk, illustrates the tech-saturated power relations unfolding within global call centres today: as the New Zealander employees carry out market research on behalf of Australian corporations such as the telecommunications firm Telstra, management demands they lie and tell Australian survey participants they are calling from Australia. Incidentally, this is where they are monitored via a video camera affixed to the call centre's wall.

This paper introduces an international research project into emergent forms of labour resistance and collective organization in call centres. While call centre work has been one of the fastest-growing sources of employment in the twenty-first century, it has not exactly lived up to the rosy portraits of rewarding 'knowledge work' that have been served up for almost 50 years now by economists, sociologists, futurists and management gurus. To begin with, working in a call centre tends to include a well-established mix of low wages, high stress, precarious employment, rigid management, draining emotional labour and pervasive electronic surveillance. They have been called digital sweatshops and compared to battery farms and Roman slave galleons. But the intent of the inquiries tying together this research project, however, is not to dwell on the ways in which employment in call centres tends toward exploitative and disciplinary relations. Rather, its goal is to offer a portrait of this emblematic form of informational labour in which language, culture and communication are put to work that begins with the resistance and collective organization produced within its ranks. Such an approach has implications that resonate well beyond the world of call centres. Call centres are a quintessential product of processes that have characterized the broader transformation of work in the information society, including the restructuring of large companies, a shift toward the provision of services, the growth of outsourcing, the intensification of communicative forms of work, and the imposition of flexible employment practices. As such, call centres are a vital testing ground for labour's ability to adapt and reorganize in a digital economy (Guard, Steedman and Garcia Orgales, 2007).

This paper situates the global explosion of call centres over the last two decades by adopting and extending political theorist Jodi Dean's (2009) concept of 'communicative capitalism'. Second, it surveys the dominant research perspectives on the labour performed by call centre workers and proposes the autonomist Marxist concept of immaterial labour, one which encourages us to approach emergent forms of employment from the perspective of the struggles and the collective organization they produce. Third, it offers an overview of the forms of labour resistance emerging out of call centres globally, and concludes by offering a sketch of the research project's primary case studies in Italy, Ireland and Canada.

## COMMUNICATIVE CAPITALISM AND THE CALL CENTRE

Academic research on call centres has tended to neglect the broader political and economic processes that have shaped these new workspaces and propelled their remarkable growth (Ellis and Taylor, 2006). In a bid to limit such a tendency, this article adopts and extends Jodi Dean's concept of communicative capitalism in order to frame the call centre within the contemporary political-economic landscape. Dean's term names the way our economy has, over recent decades, incorporated and become increasingly dependent upon the 'proliferation, distribution, acceleration and intensification of communicative access and opportunity' (Dean, 2009: 17). The tremendous investments in telecommunications infrastructure made throughout much of the world in recent decades have brought about a situation in which, as political economist Dan Schiller (2007: 81) suggests, communicative scarcity has begun to recede. Fears during the 1990s over a growing digital divide between information 'haves' and 'have-nots' now appear to have been slightly off-track, as IT costs have dropped dramatically over the last decade and the differential inclusion of populations as IT consumers – rather than their outright exclusion from the market – has become the norm in an economy that derives increasing value from communication, information and knowledge. Examples of such differential inclusion abound. In China, migrant workers keep in touch with their extended social networks by texting. Disposable cell phones are offered for sale at corner stores in otherwise devastated American cities. Cyber-cafes around the world offer refuge to gamers with insufficient download speeds at home. Connecting with others at a distance has never been quite as easy as it is today.

But Jodi Dean's concept is polemical, not celebratory. The profusion of communication in daily life has not eroded social inequalities as some media theorists hoped it would, as Hamed's words underscore, it has merely fuelled an informational economy that is the scene of new power asymmetries. Different sectors of industry reap major profits from our newfound communicative possibilities, from telecommunications to high-tech, from new media companies to electronics manufacturers and to e-waste 'recyclers'. But communicative capitalism, Dean maintains, is especially formidable in the ideological domain. Offering us expanded possibility to express ourselves has become a central plank of neoliberalism's alluring communicative promise, one that both reinforces its legitimacy and buffers it from democratic social change. We can all have our say on whether Iraq should be invaded, but then it happens anyway. Never mind whether or not our messages ever reach their target, register, or provoke a response from those in power – what counts is the ability to send them. For Dean, this emerging relationship between networked digital media and the global market has only led to the strengthening of neoliberalism, a reduction of meaningful political discourse, and a creeping marginalization of progressive social movements, who may know how to twitter in the infosphere but have forgotten how to organize in the real world. More communication has led to more inequality, not less.

Our political-economic system has become 'communicative' in other domains as well. Most strikingly, recent decades have witnessed the extension of 'communicative access and opportunity' (Dean, 2009: 17) to billions of consumers who are now engaged in regular and ongoing interactions with the corporations in their lives. Once famously characterized by rigidity and a lack of responsiveness in the post-War, Fordist economy, from the 1980s on firms increasingly encouraged the development of a permanent, intense and vital flow of informational exchange between themselves and their lifeblood, consumers. At the centre of this informational flow lies the call centre, a vital product of communicative capitalism that both reflects the political-economic formation and plays a key role in its daily reproduction. In everything from providing tech support for web hosting to gauging the effectiveness of advertising campaigns, call centres have become a vital means for mediating the relationship between the institutions and the subjects of communicative capitalism in what has been described as a 'paradigmatic shift in the reordering of the customer interface across the entire economy' (Bain et al., 2002: 184). If for some companies, communicating with their customers remotely now delivers the lion's share of sales, for most there is an increasingly widespread expectation that consumers will be offered the opportunity to get or keep in touch, customize their deal, get help using the product, check the status of their account, report failures, offer feedback, threaten to break their contract, and so on. If this accommodation of the 'diversity, multiplicity, and the agency of consumers' (Dean, 2009: 9) sounds utopian, it is worth remembering that this vortex of informational exchange, the ceaselessly-circulating 'data stream' (Dean, 2009: 26) between communicative capitalism and its subjects must be organized and compressed so as to ensure it costs capital as little as possible. The birth of the call centre during the last decades of the twentieth century represents the dominant corporate response to this necessity, its rationalization of these functions, and its hidden abode of communicative production.

As part of what Huws (2009) calls the new 'interface' that has been installed between communicative capitalism and the rest of us, call centres therefore stand in for the promises of accessibility, responsiveness, and personalized attention that it would otherwise be much more expensive for institutions to make. The interface itself is of course renowned for being alienating and impersonal, frequently exasperating, and often designed to extract something from us while offering little or nothing in return – a first-rate example of how in the digital economy, as Dean (2009: 26) puts it, communication 'produces its own negation'. But it is when one begins to examine the labour relations within the call centre that our era's real digital divide, the one separating employers and workers, becomes apparent. Indeed, the discussion of the relationship between the call centre and the broader political economy of communicative capitalism, like Dean's concept itself, risks losing sight of the fact that these customer relations factories are fuelled not by savvy entrepreneurs or Wall Street liquidity, but by a diverse, global and communicative workforce. Communicative capitalism could not exist were it not for communicative labour.

## WORKING IN THE CALL FACTORY

For millions around the world, the experience of the call centre is much more immediate than fielding the infamous consumer research calls around dinnertime or being routed to another country in order to figure out what might be wrong with the printer. It is their way of making a living as frontline workers in the digital economy. As a result of the steady meshing of call centres into the quotidian circuits of communicative capital, the growth of these workspaces over the last 20 years has been staggering, producing notable shifts in the composition of labour forces across many regions. If the factory once was symbolic of work within developed countries, call centres have taken their place alongside other occupations such as service sector work, retail employment and care giving as one of the most likely fields of employment for new generations of workers. By 1998, it was estimated that employment within them was expanding by 20 percent a year globally and that 100,000 jobs were being added every 12 months (Datamonitor, cited in Deery and Kinnie, 2004). Since then, some 15,000 call centres have opened in Europe alone, fuelling the continent's fastest-growing form of employment (Burgess and Connell, 2006; Paul and Huws, 2002). In Ireland and the Netherlands during the first decade of the twenty-first century, one out of every three new jobs was a call centre position (Datamonitor, cited in Cugusi, 2005) and in America, the country that gave us the call centre, over

3.5 million people, almost 3 percent of the working population, are said to toil in one (Head, 2003). Nor is such employment growth restricted to the developed world, as the call centre workforce has grown rapidly in India, the Philippines, Barbados, China, Malaysia, South Africa and other countries. Afghanistan, one of the most war-ravaged places on earth, has an emergent call centre sector supporting the growing market for mobile phones in that country: 'Taliban call in and the women talk to them', says Zermina, a manager at one of Kabul's call centres, illustrating how the industry has been translated into stunningly diverse settings, producing novel workforce compositions everywhere it goes (cited in Doucet, 2007).

Two main intellectual traditions have competed to explain the condition and experience of call centre work. The first emerges from business, management and occupational psychology, and drawing on Daniel Bell's (1999) post-industrial narrative of declining class conflict has presented a rather hopeful portrait of call centre employment as a form of what management guru Peter Drucker (1999) called 'knowledge work'. These researchers have stressed how call centre work can be a rewarding job, marked by autonomy, relatively high levels of employee satisfaction, and a workforce that identifies with management's objectives (Frenkel et al., 1999). Marxist labour process theorists have begged to differ with such cheery portraits. The intellectual roots of these researchers are to be found in the work of Harry Braverman (1999), who in *Labour and Monopoly Capital: The Degradation of Work in the Twentieth Century* examined how new forms of control and exploitation were being devised for those performing what he called 'mental labour'. Written as a response to the industrial sociology of his day and the 'apologetic purposes' it pursued in its celebratory discussion of labour, Braverman (1999: 241) took aim at Bell and others by cataloguing the ways management was routinizing, deskilling and dehumanizing the clerical worker's labour process. Almost 40 years after his landmark text, the labour process perspective Braverman gave life to has produced a broad set of studies into the ways that force and consent are combined in the exploitation of call centre workers' communicative abilities (Callaghan and Thompson, 2001; Taylor and Bain, 1999). Labour process scholars have seen call centre work not as a humane departure from, but instead as the latest update of the Taylorist separation of conception and execution – for these workers, post-industrial society has become not Daniel Bell's dream, but Harry Braverman's nightmare.

By the early twenty-first century, however, it began to be acknowledged that critical approaches to the call centre labour process, in their eagerness to rebut fables of knowledge work in the call centre, had paid much more attention to how workers are organized by management rather than looking for the moments when they organize for themselves. If knowledge worker theories were disingenuous in their portraits of happy call-centre workers in friction-free informational workplaces, labour process critiques had largely served up the dispiriting image of a subjugated workforce in return. Seeking to remedy this problem, this research project draws from a tradition of inquiry forged over the last half century by successive generations of theorists and militants from Italy. Autonomist Marxist analysis is a heterogeneous tradition which has become prominent in the Anglophone world since the publication of Michael Hardt and Antonio Negri's *Empire* in 2000, but has since its earliest days in post-War Italy mingled with a variety of radical currents, including American labour sociology, French post-structuralism and Regulation School political economy, radical feminism, and critical communication scholarship, becoming an increasingly transnational perspective with an associated and evolving set of political tendencies. Like labour process theorists, autonomists see relations between labour and capital as ineluctably conflictual, but they begin their analysis of this relation with labour's resistance and search for autonomy, a force which their hypothesis suggests, anticipates and provokes capitalist restructuring. Within this broader outlook, since the mid-1990s, many autonomists have proposed the term 'immaterial labour' to name what Hardt and Negri (2000: 290) define as 'labour that produces an immaterial good, such as a service, a cultural product, knowledge, or communication'. Immaterial labour describes a growing variety of forms of work in the media and communication industries and beyond: it is performed by freelancers at Viacom, by sessional lecturers at your local university, and 'permatemp' software designers at Microsoft. Not only does such labour put language, culture and communication to work with unprecedented intensity, it is usually affective and expressed through now-ubiquitous information technology. So autonomists agree with knowledge worker theorists that work has changed as capitalism has gone digital, but they also point out that the extraction of value from these professions, much like that which occurred in the car factories of Detroit during the heyday of Fordism, is by no means a friction-free matter. If videogame workers sabotage, film workers agitate and call center workers organize, the concept of immaterial labour asks us to look for these moments of conflict, to launch our inquiries into those instances when the communicative worker becomes resistant and unmanageable, to explore what Negri (2005) and others refer to as the 'self-valourization' of labour.

Inspired by this tradition, the research project introduced in these pages seeks to examine call centre work from the perspective of the resistance and collective organization it produces. And while this examination ultimately requires moving beyond Braverman, the spirit of such a project is captured by a striking passage from his work. Braverman is commonly accused of offering a sobering portrait of capital's subjugation of labour, but no analysis of how and when the latter responds. In an uncharacteristic moment, however, Braverman likens labour resistance to a 'subterranean stream', which he says will emerge 'when the conditions permit, or when the capitalist drive for a greater intensity of labour oversteps the bounds of physical or mental capacity' (Braverman, 1999: 104). Organized resistance, Braverman warns, is endemic to workers under capitalism. Their insubordination, he says, 'renews itself in new generations, expresses itself in the unbounded cynicism and revulsion which large numbers of workers feel about their work, and comes to the fore repeatedly as a social issue demanding a solution' (ibid). If management is constantly compelled to reorganize and intensify the labour process so as to better exploit the communicative powers of its workforce, Braverman warned, the latter would generate its own varieties of organization.

With these words in mind, this research project accompanies Braverman's prediction into the call centre through the worker inquiry, an autonomist method that traces its roots back to Karl Marx (Panzieri, 1965). And there is much to research, for along with the spectacular growth of call centres, an inevitable efflorescence of labour resistance in both traditional and unfamiliar forms has followed. The last section of this paper offers an overview of such resistance, moving from widespread individual acts of refusal to highly organized collective behaviours. Within them, it argues, lie the seeds of a twenty-first century unionism for the digital economy.

## THE SUBTERRANEAN STREAM: LABOUR RESISTANCE IN THE CALL CENTRE

A very different picture of call centre labour emerges when it is seen through the prism of conflict. Consider one of its defining features, the unusually high rates of employee turnover, or 'churn' as it is sometimes called. According to a recent global study (Holman, Batt and Holtgrewe, 2007: 40), call centres tend to lose a fifth of their employees on average every year, but in some countries, and particularly in the outsourced sector where labour conditions are harsher, the figure is much higher. In Irish outsourced call centres, the turnover rate is 35 percent per year, and in the United States, it is 36 percent. In India, official figures are of 30-40 percent, but the real rate has been estimated at 65 to 75 percent, and exceeding 100 percent at some companies (Bain and Taylor, 2008). This feature of call centre employment could perhaps be seen as a sign of the freedom customer service agents enjoy as mobile knowledge-economy players, perpetually moving on to even better professional opportunities in the sector. Yet, as Mirchandani (2004: 368) found in her research with call centre workers in India, despite having gone through a very long series of tests to gain such employment, they were 'unanimously unconvinced by the arguments about the quality of call centre jobs'. In other words, the spectacular turnover is not due to the fact that there is always an even better job down the street, but to the insufferable labour conditions marking the customer relations factories. If it is not a freelancer's paradise, the prevalence of churn might then be taken as a sign of the utter subordination of call centre labour, of which the disposability of the workforce is seen as a symptom. Yet, this conclusion overlooks the fact that the flight from a job is one of the most basic and common forms of resistance to exploitative labour conditions.

'Undercurrents of distrust', Mulholland's (2004: 720) exploration of informal resistance by employees at an Irish call centre, offers a very different view of the 8 percent monthly turnover she found there. Quitting one's job at the call centre, she explains, was only one part of a 'widespread pattern of work rejection' among workers. One employee Mulholland cites probably summed up the sentiments of countless thousands passing through the revolving doors of call centres around the world: 'it was a struggle for me to get to the end of the week, I got very stressed and would crash out. Just being away from the place was great, then you walk in on Monday and it starts all over again. I couldn't cope with this see-saw life and left' (ibid.). This ongoing exit from the digital assembly lines does not point to some paradoxical love of its difficult labour conditions therefore, but rather to what Taylor and Bain (2003: 1497) have described as 'a deep undercurrent of distrust of management's motives' flowing beneath its organizational surface. This undercurrent carries a range of informal strategies along with it through which employees 'collude, collaborate and cooperate' in order to resist the worst parts of their profession (Mulholland, 2004: 710). One widely reported example of this behaviour are the ingenious techniques developed in order to slow down the pace of work, ranging from elementary forms of hacking call centre technology to twenty-first century strains of industrial sabotage. In a classic example of such hacking from Australia, van den Broek, Barnes and Townsend (2008) describe team members pressing the 'transfer' button a split second before customers hung up the phone at the end of the call, a trick which gave them two or three extra minutes before the next call while it appeared to supervisors that they were still in conversation. Customer service representatives can also learn to recognize the signs of when management is spying on them in order to elude its panoptic ambitions. At the call centre Mulholland (2004: 719) examined, things had gotten so bad that a culture had developed among workers where activities such as cheating, work avoidance, and phoning in sick were all seen as reasonable responses to a bad job. Such informal acts, aimed as they are at reclaiming stretches of time from the punishing rhythms of the call centre, certainly have 'an adverse and immediate impact on profitability' as Mulholland and others have pointed out, but they can also become the basis for more organized forms of resistance (Mulholland, 2004: 713).

*Teaming up.* Academic research has only begun to skim the surface of the ways in which call centre workers are creating informal, horizontal bonds in order to resist management's ceaseless productivity push from above, but the research thus far has offered some compelling glimpses of this process. Taylor and Bain's inquiry at Excell describes how collective humour, including the public ridiculing of authoritarian team leaders and managers, fed a 'vigorous counterculture' that eventually forced the reversal of a colleague's dismissal and a 99.4 percent yes-vote for union recognition across the company's three call centres (Taylor and Bain, 2003: 1502). Their research provides an example of how management's quest for technological control and work intensification begets precisely the worker cynicism and revulsion evoked by Braverman. Within this general malaise, there are some signs that workers are repurposing the 'teams' they are frequently organized into toward wholly different ends: van den Broek, Barnes, and Townsend (2008: 257) found that Australian workers 'teamed up' not to increase productivity, but to challenge managerial directives and improve their labour conditions. In one memorable example, the researchers recount how a team of 13 customer service reps signed a petition registering their opposition to excessive monitoring and 'relentless conditions of work', transforming the 'team' structure conceived of to intensify their workload into an informal vehicle through which to strike back against work intensification. Management's facile adoption of the discourse of workplace democracy clearly carries the risk workers might begin to take it seriously. In this instance, the manager urged them to recast their complaints individually, and (in an irony not missed by the researchers) despite the impressive degree of cooperation they had displayed, the workers received low marks in the 'teamwork' category of their performance appraisal (van den Broek, Barnes and Townsend, 2008: 264).

*Embryonic unionism.* If telling the boss exactly what you think, or quitting, or finding small ways to mitigate the relentless pace of work can all be rewarding in the short run, these activities do little to challenge management's structural power in the call centre. Beyond leaving or loafing, call centre workers are also engaged in a range of relationships with established trade union structures, whether through already-existing unions or organizing drives to form new ones. Scholars have often suggested that unionism is 'embryonic' in the call centre, but they have just as frequently pointed to the dearth of academic study of union organizing (Russell, 2008: 206). A very rough picture of trade unionism in the call centre is nonetheless beginning to emerge, and it presents features that might surprise those who imagine it to be a union-free zone. Holman, Batt and Holtgrewe's (2007) study found that close to half of the workplaces they examined were already covered by some form of collective representation (collective bargaining, works councils, or both), generally as the legacy of collective agreements characterizing the industries the call centres operated on behalf of. This is the case at Canada Post for example, where call centre workers belong to (and took part in the recent strike organized by) the Public Service Alliance of Canada (Rynor, 2008). In North America, as one of this research project's case studies has examined, call centre workers employed by continental oligopolies such as Sprint, Verizon, Telus and others are part of 'convergent' unions such as the Communication Workers of America, the Telecommunication Workers Union, and the Communication, Energy and Paperworkers Union of Canada (CEP) (Mosco and McKercher 2006; Brophy, 2009). In some countries (particularly ones with higher levels of collective representation), established unions have managed to incorporate outsourced call centres into industry-wide collective agreements as the Gewerkschaft der Privatangestellten union has done in Austria (Holst, 2008). The prevailing image of call centres as union-free environments may thus owe more to ideology than it does to reality, proposing management's fantasy as if it were an actually existing state of affairs.

When a union does not already protect workers, they can always form one, and academic research has recently begun to examine the labour organizing taking place along the fault line between workers and management in the call centre. Not surprisingly, some of the best research produced in the area is a product of the growing overlap between labour activism and academic inquiry. Rainnie and Drummond (2006) describe a labour organizer's experience leading a successful unionizing campaign at an Australian call centre in the Latrobe Valley, east of Melbourne. In Canada, Guard, Steedman and Garcia-Orgales (2007) have documented the United Steelworker's successful campaign in the mining town of Sudbury, Ontario. Stevens and Lavin (2007) depict the bitter (although ultimately unsuccessful) struggle to organize a call centre in southern Ontario, and Bibby (2000) has catalogued some of the many organizing efforts at financial call centres in Australia, Germany, Austria, the Netherlands and the United Kingdom. The formation of unions also appears to be pursuing employers to the locations where they had relocated precisely in order to escape collective organization and higher wages, be it to the outsourced sector domestically, or internationally. A promising example of the latter that has received some attention is the UNITES Professionals organization in India, formed under aegis of the international umbrella labour organization Union Network International (UNI) in 2005 and now acting as an organized presence in six cities with 6,000 to 7,000 members (Taylor and Bain, 2006). However 'embryonic' the unionism driving these examples, it can make real differences for workers as far as labour conditions and job security are concerned.

*Strike.* When conditions become intolerable, call centre workers across the world have taken part in work stoppages and other forms of direct action to address their working conditions. In Mexico, 1,700 call centre workers at Tecmarketing, which provides support for the telecommunications giant Telmex, struck in February of 2008 in order to achieve a 4.4 percent pay raise (Reuters News, 2008a). The following month in Finland, some 1,200 Union of Salaried Employees call centre workers at telecom operator Elisa's subcontractor Teleperformance voted to strike over the fact that they were barred from the sectoral agreement for telecommunications workers (Reuters News, 2008b). In Durban, South Africa, Communication Workers Union (CWU) call centre workers at Telkom struck in August of 2009, achieving a 7.5 percent salary increase (Moodley, 2009). In 2008, city council call centre workers in Ipswich City, Australia rallied and struck against a proposed 'shared services' model, which aimed to bring a privately listed Australian outsourcing company, UCMS, into the provision of public services (Gardiner, 2008). Privatization frequently carries the risk of outsourcing, and for Australian companies looking to pay lower wages, sending work across the Tasman Sea to New Zealand has been a tempting move. As we saw in the introduction, however, that country has turned out to be a hotspot for call centre unrest. In September of 2008, employees of the transnational company Teletech took to the streets of Palmerston North to protest the outsourcing of their Yellow Pages inquiry assistance jobs to the Philippines (Duff, 2009). The job action has occasionally also been spontaneous in its flare-ups, such as in 2009 when United Services Union call centre workers at New South Wales electricity retailers wildcatted after the state government failed to guarantee their jobs in its decision to privatize the utility (Daily Telegraph, 2009). Customer service reps employed at the Italian call centre Omnia have been engaged in an ongoing series of actions against the company in recent years, including strikes, demonstrations outside its Turin headquarters, and (in one of the more recent tactics to emerge from European labour struggles) the kidnapping of the company's managing director in Milan, who was forced to reply to workers' questions regarding late wages and the use of temporary contracts (ANSA, 2009).

It is impossible to offer an exhaustive overview of call centre labour resistance here, but it would be remiss not to finish with a more specific mention of the organizing that has occurred around the outsourcing of work, a permanent source of managerial discipline and thus a central labour issue in call centres around the world. A perfect example of how strife arises comes from Thames Water in the United Kingdom, a privatized utility providing water to people in London that is owned by the Australian corporate banking and investment company Macquarie. In the fall of 2008, Thames announced it was raising water rates for 13.5 million customers by 3 percent above inflation for five years, allowing it to reap half-year profits of £23.2 million (Morning Star Online, 2009). But management at Thames told 282 unionized workers their jobs would be outsourced to India if they did not agree to 'family unfriendly' changes in working hours, provoking employees to ballot for a strike through the GMB union (Daily Mail, 2009). Situations like this are now commonplace. Workers at South African Airlines in the South African Transport and Allied Workers Union (Satawu) pursued similar action in 2008, threatening to strike over the airline's plan to outsource 250 call centre jobs to Dimension Data, an action that ultimately caused the company to back off (Modimoeng, 2008). Bain and Taylor (2008) have described the battles arising around outsourcing at five companies in the United Kingdom, concluding that strike action was the most likely to get companies to make concessions (including offering no compulsory redundancies) and that there was promise in the UNI's internationalist approach to call centre employment. Aiming to promote international cooperation and exchange between workers at risk of being outsourced and those in areas to which jobs are being shipped, UNI developed its Offshoring Charter in 2006 as one of the opening acts of a set of labour struggles that have clearly become transnational in scope.

Against this context, the research project introduced in this paper has followed three cases of collective organization by call centre workers in the first decade of the twenty-first century. In Ireland, an inquiry is being carried out with the O2 workers in Limerick, documenting their efforts to unionize through the CWU. The outsourcing of the company's technical department in 2006 inaugurated an ongoing low-level struggle between workers and management that has evolved against the backdrop of the Irish financial crisis. O2 offers a classic example of the transnationalization of the telecommunications industry, bought as it was from British Telecom by Spanish multinational Telefonica and now part of a wireless brand reaching from Eastern Europe to Latin America. Disciplinary management and the threat of outsourcing led workers to contact the CWU, which now has a permanent presence there and represents members in disciplinary hearings, but is still not officially recognized by the employer. Ireland is a hostile environment for union organizing and its thoroughly liberalized labour laws mean that even if the majority of workers at a company sign union cards, the employer can refuse to bargain. At a July 2009 event in Dublin, featuring an encounter between trade unionists and call centre workers, CWU organizer Ian McArdle (2009) spoke of a tipping point that had to be reached in any workplace in order to force the employer to bargain. At O2, progress has been slow as far as building the union, and members frequently operate covertly for fear of retaliation, but that tipping point appears to be getting closer. The most important achievement has been an end to the arbitrary punishments and firings that marked the call centre, something that occurred soon after workers balloted for industrial action as the first step toward a strike. As one union member summed up, 'they don't try and bully us into things now, because they know they can't ... They know the union is in the door. They know the union is staying. They would be as well accepting it'.

Across the Atlantic in the province of New Brunswick, Canada, where almost 5 percent of the labour force works in call centres, the research project has tracked the story of the Aliant call-centre workers who joined the CEP in 2001. Moncton employees of the telecommunications company (formed out of a merger of four privatized monopolists in 2000) described the restructuring of its customer contact division toward the rhythms of a call centre, a process that was soon followed by outsourcing to non-union contact centres down the road. Aiming to protect their employment and quality of work, call centre workers animated a four-month strike in 2004 for their first collective agreement. In a tactic that would feature prominently in the subsequent Telus strike on the west coast of Canada, Aliant employed private security guards to monitor and intimidate the striking workers. As one worker describes '[w]e did get harassed quite a bit by the security guards. Several tactics, fear tactics, were used and stuff like that. So it was kind of rough, you know, they showed us our home address on a piece of paper, just to rub it in that we know where you live. They delivered letters at my home about conduct and stuff, they were saying I was harassing people and all that which, you know, is kind of scary'. Yet, in the process workers won moderate pay raises and, more importantly, a protocol limiting the company's ability to outsource its inhouse call centre work. Like the O2 workers, however, their status remains uncertain, given the wider basin of non-unionized call centre labour in the region.

In Italy, an inquiry was carried out with the Collettivo Precari Atesia, a self-organized collective of workers in Rome working at the largest call centre in Europe. Atesia represents the most extreme case of post-Fordist employment: over 4,000 operators at the company were employed for years on a series of freelance, or what are called parasubordinate, contracts. For new Atesia workers answering calls outsourced from Telecom Italia Mobile, employment meant having one's contract renewed once a month, then once every three months, and then every 12 months. As freelancers, they technically rented their workstations and were paid by the call, but management set their shifts at 6 hours a day, 6 days a week. In essence, it was masked permanent employment, only without benefits, the right to unionize or to strike, paid holidays, sick days, or maternity leave. Collettivo member Federica Ballarò recounted seeing women forced to work during their eighth month of pregnancy lest they lose their position, as well as new mothers leaving the workplace on breaks to breastfeed their babies. The Collettivo was formed in 2004 and began to organize with assistance from Cobas, the rank and file union. In a form of digital sabotage, operators began to hang up on customers at the two-minute and forty-second mark when they received the greatest compensation for their calls, and over the next two years, the Collettivo organized ten strikes, deftly harnessing the flexibility imposed on them. As parasubordinate workers going on strike was illegal, yet as freelancers, they technically had the right to come to work whenever they liked during their scheduled shift, or not at all. The Collettivo organised a coordinated claiming of this right, crippling the call centre for 24 hours. By 2007, an agreement was hammered out between the then centre-left government, the confederal unions, and Atesia in order to quell the unrest that was by that point sweeping the Italian call centre industry. The plan decreed the permanent hiring of parasubordinate workers, who were to be compensated for years of benefits and back pay due to their misclassification. But their organising cost them dearly, as at the moment every original member of the Collettivo at Atesia has been fired.

Call centres have not obliterated worker resistance, but their reputation as the digital sweatshops of an informational economy is clearly well deserved. Communicative capitalism is the scene of new forms of inequality, and the call centre is a privileged space for the exploration of how the former reproduces the latter. Yet, Braverman's warning against assuming the 'acclimatization' of the worker to 'new modes of production' (Braverman, 1999) points toward the importance of exploring communicative capitalism from the perspective of the labour that fuels it, and exploring that labour by beginning with the conflict, resistance and collective organization it produces. As Foucault (2000: 329) once mused, 'in order to understand what power relations are about, perhaps we should investigate the forms of resistance and attempts to dissociate those relations'. Following the twists and turns of contemporary labour resistance and collective organization allows us to focus upon a very different digital divide, the one separating employers and the increasingly affective, communicative and linguistic workforce they have come to depend on.

## References

ANSA (2009) 'Omnia Network Late with Wages, Protest in Turin', April 3.

Bain, P. and P. Taylor (2008) 'No Passage to India?: Initial Responses of UK Trade Unions to Call Centre Outsourcing', *Industrial Relations Journal*, 39(1): 5–23.

Bain, P., A. Watson, G. Mulvey, P. Taylor and G. Gall (2002) 'Taylorism, Targets and the

Pursuit of Quantity and Quality by Call Centre Management', *New Technology, Work & Employment*, 17(3): 170-185.

Bell, D. (1999) *The Coming of Post-industrial Society: A Venture in Social Forecasting*. New York: Basic Books.

Bibby, A. (2000) 'Organising in Financial Call Centres: A Report for the UNI'. [http://www.andrewbibby.com/docs/ofcc1.html]

Braverman, H. (1999) *Labour and Monopoly Capital: The Degradation of Work in the Twentieth Century*. New York: Monthly Review Press.

Brophy, E. (2009) 'Resisting Call Centre Work: The Aliant Strike and Convergent Unionism in Canada', *Work Organization, Labour & Globalisation*, 3(1): 80-99.

Burgess, J. and J. Connell (2006) 'Developments in the Call Centre Sector: An Overview' in J. Burgess and J. Connell (eds.), *Developments in the Call Centre Industry: Analysis, Changes and Challenges*. New York: Routledge, 1-18.

Callaghan, G. and P. Thompson (2001) 'Edwards Revisited: Technical Control and Call Centres', *Economic and Industrial Democracy*, 22(1): 13-37.

Cugusi, C. (2005) *Call Center: Gli Schiavi Elettronici della New Economy*. Genoa, Italy: Fratelli Frilli Editori.

Daily Mail (2009) 'Thames Battles Union Over "Sacking Threat"', March 5: 73.

Daily Telegraph (2009) 'Power Plug Pulled', *Daily Telegraph*, July 18: 16.

Dean, J. (2009) *Democracy and Other Neoliberal Fantasies: Communicative Capitalism and Left Politics*. Durham, NC: Duke University Press.

Deery, S. and N. Kinnie (2004) 'Introduction: The Nature and Management of Call Centre Work', in S. Deery and N. Kinnie (eds.) *Call Centres and Human Resource Management: A Cross-National Perspective*. London: Palgrave Macmillan, 1-24.

Doucet, L. (2007) 'Upwardly Mobile Afghanistan', *BBC News*, November 14. [http://news.bbc.co.uk/2/hi/programmes/crossing_continents/7095388.stm] accessed May 8, 2010.

Drucker, P. (1999) *Landmarks of Tomorrow: A Report on the New 'Post-Modern' World*. New Brunswick, NJ: Transaction.

Duff, M. (2009) 'Teletech 018 Staff Are Hopping Mad', *Manawatu Standard*, January 31.

Ellis, V. and P. Taylor (2006) '"You Don't Know What You've Got Till It's Gone": Re-contextualising the Origins, Development and Impact of the Call Centre', *New Technology, Work & Employment*, 21(2): 107-122.

Foucault, M. (2000) 'The Subject and Power', in J. Faubion (ed.) *The Essential Works of Michel Foucault, 1954-1984*. London: Penguin, 326-348.

Frenkel, S., M. Korczynski, K. Shire and M. Tam (1999) *On the Front Line: Organization of Work in the Information Economy*. Ithaca, NY: Cornell University Press.

Gardiner, Y. (2008) 'Workers Will Rally at Park, Strike Today', *The Queensland Times*, December 4: 7.

Guard, J., M. Steedman and J. Garcia-Orgales (2007) 'Organizing the Electronic Sweatshop: Rank-and-File Participation in Canada's Steel Union', *Labor: Studies in Working-Class*

*History of the Americas*, 4(3): 9-31.
Hardt, M. and A. Negri (2000) *Empire*. Cambridge, MA: Harvard University Press.
Head, S. (2003) *The New Ruthless Economy: Work and Power in the Digital Age*. New York: Oxford University Press.
Holman, D., R. Batt and U. Holtgrewe (2007) *The Global Call Centre Report: International Perspectives on Management and Employment (UK Format)*. [http://www.ilr.cornell.edu/globalcallcenter/upload/GCC-Intl-Rept-UK-Version.pdf]
Holst, H. (2008) 'The Political Economy of Trade Union Strategies in Austria and Germany: The Case of Call Centres', *European Journal of Industrial Relations*, 14(25): 25-45.
Huws, U. (2009) 'Working at the Interface: Call Centre Labour in a Global Economy', *Work Organisation, Labour & Globalization*, 3(1): 1-8.
McArdle, I. (2009) *Labour's Resistance in the Call Centre*. Seomra Spraoi Social Centre, July 14, Dublin, Ireland.
Mirchandani, K. (2004) 'Practices of Global Capital: Gaps, Cracks and Ironies in Transnational Call Centres in India', *Global Networks,* 4(4): 355-374.
Modimoeng, K. (2008) 'Airline Faces Strike Action', *Sowetan*, November 27: 21.
Morning Star Online (2009) 'Thames Water Staff Vote on Massive Cull', February 18.
Moodley, J. (2009) 'Telkom Strike Puts Us on Hold', *Daily News*, August 3: E2.
Mosco, V. and C. McKercher (2006) 'Convergence Bites Back: Labour Struggles in the Canadian Telecommunications Industry', *Canadian Journal of Communication*, 31(3): 733-751.
Mulholland, K. (2004) 'Workplace Resistance in an Irish Call Centre: Slammin', Scammin', Smokin' an' Leavin'', *Work, Employment & Society*, 18(4): 709-724.
Negri, A. (2005) *The Politics of Subversion: A Manifesto for the Twenty-First Century*. Malden, MA: Polity Press.
New Zealand Press Association (2009) 'Market Research Workers Begin Hunger Strike', February 24.
Panzieri, R. (1965) *The Socialist Uses of Worker Inquiry*. [http://transform.eipcp.net/transversal/0406/panzieri/en] accessed April 12, 2008.
Paul, J and U. Huws (2002) *How Can We Help? Good Practice in Call Centre Employment*. Brussel, Belgium: European Trade Union Confederation.
Rainnie, A. and G. Drummond (2006) 'Place Matters: Organising in the New Economy in an Old Industrial Area', in J. Burgess and J. Connell (eds.) *Developments in the Call Centre Industry: Analysis, Changes and Challenges*. New York: Routledge, 136-151.
Reuters News (2008a) 'Strike Ends at Mexico's Telmex Call Center Unit', February 20. [http://www.reuters.com/article/idUSN2037146220080220]
Reuters News (2008b) 'Union Plans Strike at Elisa Customer Service', March 3.
Russell, B. (2008) 'Call Centres: A Decade of Research', *International Journal of Management Reviews*, 10(3): 195-219.
Rynor, B. (2008) 'Postal Workers Launch Strike Action', *Canwest News Service*, November 17.

Schiller, D. (2007) *How to Think About Information*. Urbana, IL: University of Illinois Press.

Stevens, A. and D. Lavin (2007) 'Stealing Time: The Temporal Regulation of Labor in Neoliberal and Post-Fordist Work Regimes', *Democratic Communique*, 22(2): 40-61.

Taylor, P. and P. Bain (2006) 'Work Organisation and Employee Relations in Indian Call Centres', in J. Burgess and J. Connell (eds.) *Developments in the Call Centre Industry: Analysis, Changes and Challenges*. New York: Routledge, 36-57.

Taylor, P. and P. Bain (2003) '"Subterranean Worksick Blues": Humour as Subversion in Two Call Centres', *Organization Studies*, 24(9): 1487-1509.

Taylor, P. and P. Bain (1999) '"An Assembly-Line in the Head": Work and Employee Relations in the Call Centre', *Industrial Relations Journal*, 30(2): 101-117.

van den Broek, D., A. Barnes and K. Townsend (2008) '"Teaming Up": Teams and Team Sharing in Call Centres', *Journal of Industrial Relations*, 50(2): 257-269.

# 7 Prospects for Trade Unions and Labour Organisations in India's IT and ITES Industries

Andrew Stevens（安德鲁·史蒂文斯）
Vincent Mosco（文森特·莫斯可）[①]

[导读] 世界媒体的注意力大多聚焦于最近印度经济的增长及其正在扩张和不断国际化的商业服务部门。但是在印度，随着信息技术部门的成长，出现了一系列新的劳工组织，以表达包括从软件工程师到呼叫中心人员的不同职业劳工的利益诉求。这篇论文以2008年对工会成员以及劳工活动积极分子的访谈为基础，考察了在印度信息技术（information technology, IT）和信息技术化服务（IT-enabled services, ITES）产业中新兴的工会和行业协会，它们包括：信息技术专业人员论坛（IT Professionals Forum, ITPF）、青年专业人员共同体（Young Professionals Collective, YPC）和信息技术化服务专业人员工会（Union for ITES Professionals, UNITES）——这些印度信息技术部门中最具代表性的劳工组织。

信息技术专业人员论坛是帮助信息技术工人追求他们专业利益的最初

---

① Andrew Stevens, 现任教于加拿大里贾纳大学（University of Regina）产业关系和人力资源管理系。他的研究方向聚焦于工作的社会学分析、劳工研究和产业关系。研究成果包括《呼叫中心和劳动的全球分工：后工业的雇佣和工会组织的政治经济学分析》（*Call Centers and the Global Division of Labor: A Political Economy of Post-Industrial Employment and Union Organizing*, 2014）等。

Vincent Mosco, 全球知名学者和传播政治经济学的奠基人之一。加拿大女王大学（Queen's University）社会学系荣休教授，前加拿大媒介和社会研究主席。其代表作《传播政治经济学》（*The Political Economy of Communication*, 2009）已被翻译成19国语言，成为世界范围内最有影响力的传播政治经济学教材。其他重要的著作还包括：《数字化：后互联网社会的来临》（*Becoming Digital: Toward a Post-Internet Society*, 2017）、《云端：动荡世界的大数据》（*To the Cloud: Big Data in a Turbulent World*, 2014）、《信息社会的知识劳工》（*Knowledge Workers in the Information Society*, 2008）、《数字化崇拜：迷思、权力与赛博空间》（*The Digital Sublime: Myth, Power, and Cyberspace*, 2004）等。

几个项目之一。论坛早期的活动积极分子主要来自高端的信息技术部门，他们关注信息技术和社会发展的议题：如弥合"数字鸿沟"、分享工资信息、建立一个关注工作中不公平的机制、实现成员的专业利益诉求。信息技术专业人员论坛有意地与印度劳工运动的传统策略和政治导向相区别，通过创造性的途径在专业人员之间培养乐观的情绪，且承诺建立一个专业性的行业协会，而非工会。论坛最终根据社团法案（the Societies Act）而非工会法案（the Trade Union Act）建立，避免了人们畏惧的、且会在招募新会员时遇到种种困难的、与工会的"刻板印象"联系在一起的"斗争形象"。

然而，论坛在集体行动上的"裹足不前"体现了商业和社会组织之间的"割裂"，在集体谈判上的缺失使得劳工薪酬的提高和工作环境的改善变得"渺茫"。定位于工会还是行业协会这个两难的选择也导致论坛内部出现了分化——年轻会员因论坛缺乏实质性的行动、对"资方"的态度过于"温和"，而渐渐失去兴趣，会员的关系也变得异常松散。除此之外，信息技术专业人员论坛早期的讨论主要集中于高端的信息技术部门，论坛人员大部分是软件工程师、医疗人员、商务流程外包企业人员等，并不包括呼叫中心人员。他们承认在整个产业内存在着某种形式的不公平现象，但他们普遍相信这些问题可以通过个体来解决，并不需要诉诸集体动员。从这个角度来看，在论坛中个体被赋权，并对企业充满期待，讨论和讨价还价取代了集体协商，成为变革的机制。论坛内部支持基础的分裂和对外部网络和组织的依赖性，使得信息技术专业人员论坛很难成为一个具有较大会员规模（包括学生，其最大会员数也未超过4300人）的劳工组织，并未能在信息技术和信息技术化服务部门"脱颖而出"。

青年专业人员共同体作为工会组织，强调信息技术和信息技术化服务部门劳工的诉求。共同体的主要领导人都来自于呼叫中心行业，致力于摆脱"工会就是福利机构"的"刻板印象"，且与政府和企业深入互动。与传统工会组织会员在工厂大门口集结的传统策略不同，青年专业人员共同体将自己打造成为一个会员分享经历、教育和赋权的平台，在这个平台上他们可以安全地讨论自己的问题并寻找解决的方法、交换思想、形成观点，甚至是改善他们的工作环境。意识觉醒是青年专业人员共同体的主要特色，但是信息技术和信息技术化服务部门对集体活动的阻挠、繁重的工作安排（尤其是夜班），以及管理层对于员工行动主义的畏惧使得青年专业人员共同体在某一具体的地点组织劳工变得异常困难。除此之外，工厂的大门真实地存在着——因为工作安排的不一致性和劳工不同的流动性，使得集体身份认同的可能性很难实现。

信息技术化服务专业人员工会的前身是建立于2004年的商务流程外包职业人员中心（the Center for Business Process Outsourcing Professionals）。工会旨在将全世界的信息技术工人、工会会员和劳工活动积极分子联合起来，尤其是帮助信息技术和信息技术化服务部门的劳工"一对一"地解决因存在于行业内的结构化问题和不公平现象而带来的种种问题——建立工会良好的公共形象。尤其是在促进性别平等和工作场所的安全方面，工会成为了标杆。工会组织了大量的劳工运动，呼吁禁止妇女在夜间工作，要求女性工作者有权选择自己的工作时间，并主张这不是公平的问题，而是女性工作者的安全问题。此外，工会还在防止性骚扰和性别歧视、支付加班工资、为女性提供更多就业机会和更好的职业发展、在企业内部建立更好的管理体制、保障劳工的就业等方面"颇有建树"。

这里特别需要指出的是，信息技术化服务专业人员工会与信息技术和信息技术化服务部门的其他劳工组织都建立了广泛的联系，这些劳工组织不仅仅局限在印度，很多在亚洲的其他国家和地区。与信息技术专业人员论坛不同，信息技术化服务专业人员工会自诩为"一个大的信息技术工会"，不仅对高端的软件工程师和信息技术专业人员有吸引力。因为它不但弥合了高度专业化分工而导致的信息技术专业人员之间的疏离，更重要的是它致力于团结与信息技术专业人员相关的劳工，包括保安人员、司机等。与其他工会聚焦于某一方面的集体行动不同（如保障工人的权利、维护妇女的权益、环境保护的议题和支持社区活动等），信息技术化服务专业人员工会通过民主的方式和社区组织加强互动；不仅在工会，而且在村落中提高女性的地位和作用；与在国家和国际层面的工会建立更为紧密的联系，这些都使其影响力不断扩大。

劳工组织的未来在哪里？涵盖包括软件工程师到呼叫中心人员在内的所有信息技术和信息技术化服务行业内不同职业劳工的利益诉求并非易事。劳工组织的核心议题就是他们是否可以和出现在印度信息技术行业外的劳工组织一起"共事"。此外,国际网络工会(Union Network International, UNI)将在印度发挥更重要的作用,作为国际网络工会在印度的"绿色试验田",信息技术专业人员论坛和信息技术化服务专业人员工会如何在完全"自给自足"的前提下,更好地组织在印度跨国公司中的劳工——这个议题随着印度经济市场自由化的加速而愈发变得重要。

## INTRODUCTION

Much of the world's media attention has focused on the recent growth of the Indian economy and its expanding and increasingly transnational business services sector. But these are also interesting times for organised labour in India. The formation of the New Trade Union Initiative (NTUI) has challenged the traditional model of trade union dependency on established political parties (Roy, 2009). Within the growing IT (information technology) sector, a variety of new worker organisations have emerged to represent workers across the hierarchy of occupations from software engineers to call-centre workers. This article focuses on this important new development. Specifically, we examine the rise of the Union for ITES (IT-enabled services) Professionals (UNITES), the IT Professionals Forum (ITPF), and the Young Professionals Collective (YPC). These organisations are leading elements of professional mobilisation in India's IT sector. The paper concludes that the new model of unionisation, as the case of UNITES especially suggests, has proven to be the most effective and sustainable model for worker representation in these industries. While the associational framework offered by the ITPF was certainly appealing to IT and ITES employees who identify as professionals, the Forum's efficacy was significantly hindered by an unwillingness to engage with management as a representative body and by the Forum's adoption of a volunteer model of membership recruitment. UNITES continues to suffer from a disengaged membership base and its influence is constrained by its ability to win only a few collective agreements with small to medium-sized enterprises. The YPC case suggests that labour advocacy through public media campaigns, transnational research projects, and legal representation can effectively support the interests of workers in these industries. We conclude that the recognition of exploitation and inequality in post-industrial workplaces, as well as the significance of cross-sector solidarity, is the central catalyst for successfully organising the IT/ITES industries.

## GLOBALISATION AND CHANGING LABOUR RELATIONS IN INDIA

Many commentators attribute India's economic successes to the dramatic reforms that began in the early 1990s under the stewardship of then finance minister and economist, Manmohan Singh in the Congress-led Narasimha Rao government. Prompted by a balance of payments crisis in 1991, India was forced to accept an International Monetary Fund bailout package with the proviso that it adopt dramatic economic reforms. This involved cutting trade barriers, lifting caps on foreign investment and ownership, dismantling the system of economic planning and regulation known as the 'licensing Raj', subjecting the government to fiscal restraint, slashing corporate income taxes, and privatising state assets. Traditional development policies that followed the import substitution industrialisation model, the hallmark of post-Independence 'Nehruvian socialism', were largely abandoned in favour of economic strategies stemming from what came to be recognised as the Washington Consensus (Fine, Lapavitsas and Pincus, 2001).

As a result of these economic transformations, long-established industrial relations practices that regulated relations between capital and labour were overturned by the forces of business-led globalisation (Hill, 2009). Moreover, as important as these structural changes were, one cannot ignore the repression and violence that workers encountered from the state, especially when labour resisted the new regime (Bhattacherjee, 1988; Bidwai, 1997, 2015). While this post-1991 shift is attributed to the end of a closed economy and the release of private economic activity, there are convincing arguments suggesting that it was the pro-business reforms of the 1980s, rather than the pro-market policies of the 1990s that launched India's productivity growth (Rodrik and Subramanian, 2001). It was during Rajiv Gandhi's time in government that special attention was focused on the software sector for the potential it held to expand domestic and export markets. It included incentives such as a ten-year tax holiday, income tax exemption on export earnings in the software sector and export subsidies, as well as the free import of both the hardware and software that these companies required (Krishna, 2005). During this period, India's IT powerhouses, such as Wipro and Infosys, began to emerge precisely when the economic climate was more favourable to domestic companies. To be sure, these and other enterprises benefited from ongoing public investments in higher education, especially the Indian Institutes of Management, Science, and Technology. In this case, pre-existing strengths were unleashed by pro-business policies enacted at the central and state levels (Rodrik and Subramanian, 2001). The entry of countries like

India into the so-called 'knowledge economy', or what Schiller (1999) has defined as 'digital capitalism', has been made possible by technological change, specifically in telecommunications, allowing for the global expansion of design, production, and distribution networks. One such example, labeled as part of India's 'tech renaissance' (Kanellos, 2005), was the use of the software tool CasePac by Tata Consultancy Services in 1995, which launched the company's outsourced services into the global technology industry.

The framework of India's labour relations model has remained largely unchanged since independence, with the state playing a leading role in the mediation of labour-capital relations. Some have concluded that trade unions have failed to develop forward-looking strategies capable of responding to changes in the economy and in work (Ackers, 2006). The erosion of the close relationship unions once enjoyed with major political parties through party-based federations, and the failure to develop a grassroots constituency capable of operating outside the confines of what was initially a deeply centralised political process, has worsened the situation (Hill, 2009). In effect, the established Indian labour movement was unable to mount a definitive challenge to the marketisation process (Roychowdhury, 2003). Indeed, some labour scholars maintain that the first unions had indeed been organisations for workers run by political leaders and not organisations of workers, controlled by an active rank-and-file (Ramaswamy, 1977). These developments called into question the ability of the main statutes that structure industrial relations in India, namely the Industrial Disputes Act 1947, the Trade Unions Act 1926, and the Contract Labour Act 1970, to protect the interests of labour.

With the growing tide of business-led globalisation, the Indian government has been unwilling to intervene in the regulation of labour in the IT and ITES sectors for fear of unsettling foreign clients and disturbing the flow of investment into these export-oriented industries. As an activist with the ITPF explains, 'labour law does not apply to the IT industry ... You are considered management. The whole labour law is framed around the kind of take-home [pay] that you have' (Natarajan, 2008). But, as a labour lawyer and activist with the Young Professionals Collective clarifies,

> The thing about existing laws is that it's not clear whether existing laws apply ... The lawmakers and the legislature and the policy people, as well as the industry, have kind of made this impression that there are no laws regulating this industry, and it's supposed to be a self-regulating industry. Which is not true, actually. All the labour laws, or all laws, are applicable to this industry. (Rege, 2008)

This state of affairs is exacerbated by industry leaders who express contempt for existing regulations. As a vice president with the National Association of Software and Services Companies (Nasscom) stated, 'The Constitution provides all participants in any industry the right to try to assemble. However, the BPO (business process outsourcing) and infotech industry is cost-sensitive. There will be a huge burden in case the industry complies with the employment laws' (Verma, 2004). Acting on this view, the government of West Bengal has banned strikes throughout the state's IT and ITES sectors (The Economist, 2004). This has made the entry of UNITES into that state far more difficult (Subramaniam, 2008).

Moreover, there is a general view that the vision of India's entry into a global marketplace would be endangered by labour activism. As one ITPF activist put it:

> Things are going pretty well, but the thing you have to understand about the Indian system is that the IT professionals – I'm talking of hardware, software, not the enabled services – are not for unionisation, including the government sector. Why? Because it is one sector that is so global. (Natarajan, 2008)

It is important then, following Bain and Taylor (2002) and Noronha and D'Cruz (2009), to examine how the resistance to unions may derive from the general perception that these organisations have become marginal and ineffective, particularly for younger workers (Batt et al., 2005; Holman, Batt and Holtgrewe, 2007). For the General Secretary of UNITES, this, as well as union reactions to technological innovation, is a leading reason why IT/ITES workers have shunned organised labour:

> The unions ... in the 1980s and 1990s strongly objected to computerisation which the younger lot did not appreciate ... (Shekhar, 2008c)

> [M]ost of the trade union centres are at a crossroads. The INTUC, the HMS, many of the communist [unions], they are at a crossroads. One, they will not attract the youngsters, and even I am unable to attract them in really big numbers. But at the same time, without youngsters you can't make [it work]. (Shekhar, 2008a)

Perhaps it is the case that, as Ramaswamy (1977) argued in the 1970s, simple bread-and-butter unionism cannot but produce membership apathy; sustained participation by an identifiable group over a period of time cannot unfold if individuals are drawn only by narrow issues.

How does this conclusion apply to unions dominated primarily by IT/ITES 'professionals', and what is the potential for solidarity in the midst of economic prosperity and hardship? As an IT manager and activist with

UNITES explains:

> Why is a union required in IT? This is a place where people are paid enough and are not bothered about anybody else. So it is seriously a self-centered kind of an industry. Okay, I am getting my money and I'm safe. I'm doing my job; I'm doing my work – why should I be bothered about anybody else? (Bhargava, 2008)

The distinction between IT and ITES-BPO professionals is important to consider. This is reflected in the contrasting opinions voiced by ITPF organisers with regard to the higher-skilled and valued engineers and designers, versus the IT-enabled services workers (Natarajan, 2008). For Upadhya (2007), class and caste positions orient socioeconomic profiles of workers engaged in the hierarchically structured IT/ITES industry. Yet, despite the well-explored sociological significance of defining labour in IT as 'professional' (Noronha and D'Cruz, 2006; Remesh, 2004a), there is a history of unionism in white collar workplaces in India. A founding member of the YPC, Vinod Shetty (2008) describes the contradictory terrain on which IT labour organising unfolds:

> I would say it's more of an identity issue. The average BPO employee and IT professional sees themselves as a 'professional'; he doesn't see himself, or herself, as a working class or even a white collar employee. Even like a bank employee or insurance employee. Because, in our country even the pilots are unionised, it's strange when you have a bunch of kids who don't believe that they are working class ... This, also, is part of the fact that ... the student movement in the country is very weak.

A joint research project conducted by Indian and US-based trade unions and labour organisations found that the collective identity of call-centre workers was prevented from reaching a politically active threshold through a socialisation process that fostered possessive individualism alongside technologically-induced surveillance methods, and various human resource management techniques (CWA et al., 2006). In the BPO sector specifically, this process of individualisation is further entrenched by creating the perception that work is fun and by constructing a human resource management (HRM) system that provides a seemingly effective outlet through which employees can air their grievances (Remesh, 2004b). Individualism is also constructed and enforced through hiring practices and secrecy surrounding pay and compensation. In the industry, employees are hired on an individual basis:

> ... [T]he company negotiates differently with each employee. The pay also differs drastically. For example, if a person is working in a company for ten years but somebody

else joins the next year and that person ... doesn't have as much qualifications, but that person gets Rs 10,000 more than this person who [has already been] working for ten years ... Everybody is told not to disclose their salaries. This is all across the industry. Naturally, because that person doesn't want to bear the brunt of being the person who gets more salary than the senior person. Automatically, this way the company discourages any kind of finding of common ground by the employees. (Rege, 2008)

HRM is established by firms as the sole means of resolving problems for individual workers, rather than as a means of enabling legitimate responses by workers collectively. Both the structure of work in BPOs and the practices of hiring and compensation inhibit collective mobilisation. There is also the issue of how management, and concomitantly HRM, practices attempt to subvert labour regulations and establish professional identities by using elaborate titles such as 'Senior Customer Service Associate' as a means both to enforce 'professionalism' and to exclude workers from the protections granted by the Industrial Disputes Act 1947.

Writing about the call-centre industry, Remesh (2004a) concluded that without an effective collective channel to empower workers, employees would resort to other methods of subversion, such as making fun of management style, disregarding the organisation's scripted conversational rules, redirecting calls, hanging up on offensive customers, and even exploiting weaknesses in the organisations' control systems so as to make free spaces for themselves. Despite the significance of these attempts at transforming the workplace, the efficacy of such actions in this and other BPO industries is questionable. Nevertheless, it worries industry supporters concerned about its appearance in the eyes of foreign investors.

The appeal to professionalism, long advocated by Nasscom, is also a disciplinary mechanism, in that labour is controlled through the construction of what constitutes 'appropriate' work identities and conduct. According to Fournier (1999), not only does this include actions and behaviour specifically designated as work-related, it also encompasses a professional ethos that aims to separate IT/ITES workers from the rest of the private and public sector in order to inoculate them against the lure of collective organisation. The structure of the IT/ITES industries also plays a role in determining the propensity for employees to organise. As Natarajan (2008) points out:

Because unionisation in the public sector, the white collar sector and the banks, they have a totally different concept of unionisation compared to the rest. Here, you don't get something, you go on strike ... In the case of the IT sector, what has happened is, the kind of pay scales they have is no match for the government sector. It's much higher. The job opportunities are also very high.

While ethnographies of the global information economy have shed light on the transformations in work, identity, sociality, and culture experienced by employees of the Indian IT/ITES sectors, as Upadhya (2008) describes, one must also consider the social reproduction of anti-union attitudes and the philosophy of managerialism developed in the elite institutions and social networks that have helped to shape a large segment of corporate managers (Srinivasan, 1989). Nevertheless, it would be incorrect to conclude that the class of professionals occupying the IT industries is homogenous. It too is divided by social inequalities, with gender taking an increasingly prominent role in the division (Remesh and Neetha, 2008).

## IT PROFESSIONALS FORUM

At the turn of the 21$^{st}$ century, the independent journalist and writer, Andrew Bibby, recognised that the organising techniques and methods adopted by trade unions needed to reflect the characteristics of call-centre life (Bibby, 2000). Bibby focused on a Union Network International (UNI)-led initiative based on the successful worker associations in the US, WashTech and Alliance@ IBM. The IT Professionals Forum was one of the first projects that sought to capture the professionally-minded interests of IT workers. 'Unity is strength', one Bangalore Forum member said, 'and when capitalists get collectively organised, why shouldn't we?' (cited in Bibby, 2002a). H. R. Hegde, the UNI Development Organisation Centre (UNIDOC) director in Bangalore, was involved with the establishment of the ITPF from the beginning. As an active member of the Federation of National Telecommunication Organisations, an Indian telecommunications union and member of Communications International (CI) before it became part of UNI, Hedge used his contacts to help recruit members to the nascent IT association. He was especially helped by Christopher Ng who is secretary of the Asia-Pacific region division for UNI.

The Forum's earliest activists, drawn primarily from the higher-end IT sector, were mainly concerned with social development causes such as bridging the 'digital divide', sharing wage information, providing a mechanism to address unfairness in the workplace, and advancing the professional interests of members (Hirschfeld, 2005). In one of its earliest interventions, the ITPF arranged legal action against a dishonest training company that promised prospective IT workers a non-existent e-commerce course and job placement services for a lofty fee of Rs 60,000 (Bibby, 2002b). In another case, Hegde worked with UNI to secure H-1B visas through the American embassy, which were promised to IT workers destined for the US, but then suddenly revoked (Hegde, 2008). Despite taking up these causes, there was still the challenge of holding the interests of a younger generation of workers who demand a different approach to organising. 'See, everywhere something new has started ... the old is substituted by the new', Hegde pointed out. '[W]e want to organise the youngsters in a new forum ... People are not liking the unions; they are not attracted by the unions because of the old story, of past experience' (Hegde, 2008).

Addressing members of the Bangalore ITPF, the head of UNI's Industry, Business and Information Technology Services (IBITS) department, Gerhard Rohde, argued that professionals need to find 'new types of organisation' and 'should be trying to find new ways of expressing their needs and demands' (cited in Bibby, 2002a). Using the financial support of UNI and several Western European unions – particularly the Belgian Union of White Collar, Technical and Executive Employees, the Union of Technical and Clerical Employees in Sweden, and the Union of Commercial and Clerical Employees in Denmark – as well as on-the-ground mobilisation in India, enough support was mustered to formally launch the Forums in Bangalore, Hyderabad, Visakhapatnam, Mysore, and Hubli (UNI, 2003). The ITPF purposefully deviated from the strategies and political directions traditionally associated with the Indian labour movement, providing a source for optimism in potentially innovative approaches and the commitment to forming a professional organisation. When rumours circulated that the ITPF would register as a trade union, Sangeeta Gupta, then vice-president of Nasscom responded, 'trade unions are formed only when employees are unhappy. Today, employers are most concerned about the employees' (cited in Verma, 2004). This sentiment was echoed by Natarajan, who remarked that there is 'no basis for unionisation. Pay as well as facilities. Unionisation comes when there is a lot of discontent' (Natarajan, 2008). Ultimately, the Forums chose to fall under the Societies Act, thus avoiding the militant image some feared would hinder their prospects of recruiting members. Natarajan, also as a research scientist who was charged with developing a women's wing called Women in the IT Sector (WITS), reinforced the importance of this approach: 'we had made it very clear ... that the question of unionisation doesn't arise. In the sense of the white collar jobs, this was an association or a forum, whatever you want to call it' (Natarajan, 2008).

The reluctance to consistently engage in collective action reflects a clash between business and social unionism. Because associations do not directly engage in collective bargaining, there are few, if any, guarantees of improvements in wages and working conditions (Mosco, McKercher and Stevens, 2008). The question of unionisation versus professional association also caused rifts amongst the groups that were part of the ITPF's initiation

(Noronha and D'Cruz, 2009). As a trade unionist, Hegde was part of a group that wanted to call the organisation the IT Employees Association and registered under the Trade Union Act. But, he emphasises, 'some people never wanted to call themselves unionists' (Hegde, 2008). As time passed, there was concern that too many young members were losing interest, due to what was perceived as a lack of action. Membership merely involved a loose affiliation based on the completion of forms. From a trade unionist perspective, Hegde noted that the ITPF's relationship with employers was 'too soft', and that communications about the Forum's activities were going to employees, 'whether they were members of ITPF or not'. Eventually, he charged, the 'ITPF started functioning [in] a different style ... like a corporate office ... [A] lot of money was spent to buy a lot of things, very posh ... Was it for trade union people or top people? ... ITPF was neither a union, nor a company, nor a society' (ibid).

The overwhelming focus of early ITPF discussion was on the most highly-skilled sectors within the Forums. When meetings were held, the attendance was comprised largely of software personnel, medical transcriptionists, and BPO employees, 'but not call-centre [employees] ... Hardly one percent [of the] membership [was] from call-centres' (Hegde, 2008). There was recognition that some inequality existed throughout the industry, but there was a widespread belief that problems could be addressed on an individual basis and without collective mobilisation. In this sense, individuals were empowered through Forums, operating with the blessing of companies; discussion and consultation replaced collective bargaining as the mechanism for bringing about change.

In addition to the complex relationship between the Forums and companies, which contributed to divisions within the Forums' support base, there is also the question of dependency on external networks and organisations. Natarajan expressed frustration about the withdrawal of the funds initially offered by the Belgian union, which had been expected to last until 2011. 'We could have done it provided we had a little bit more time,' she suggested. 'You can't expect financial sustainability in four years. We had to start from scratch, it was not possible in India' (Natarajan, 2008). For Natarajan, the initial launch fell flat shortly after the funding dried up. 'You can't start something in May of 2007 and kill it in March 2008; it's just not done.' A similar sentiment was expressed by Hegde, who asserted that the 'union's existence cannot be dependent on the project ... In a true project, you should train up your leadership and you should conduct meetings to encourage [members to join] and spread the concept and at the end of the day, you must have some presence in the workforce. This is the normal style of union functioning' (Hegde, 2008). It was, as the interview participants have suggested, the ITPF's inability to gather a sufficient membership base and create a noticeable presence in the IT/ITES sectors that resulted in the loss of funding from the Belgian union. By some estimates, the membership never exceeded 4,300, including students (Shekhar, 2009).

## YOUNG PROFESSIONALS COLLECTIVE

The ITPF was an approach to organising the IT sector through the development of a professional association, with the crucial collaboration of UNI and a number of European trade unions. Conversely, the Young Professionals Collective was an entirely Indian invention, determined to address the concerns of workers throughout the IT/ITES sectors. Founded by labour activists, lawyers, and other professionals, the YPC's initial goal, according to one of its members, was to serve as a trade union for IT/ITES professionals:

> The idea was to organise them and make sure that if there is any kind of operation happening against them in the company, and they can voice it and be a union. Like any other union, [the] objective would be to collectively bargain with the management for their own rights. (Sajjanshetty, 2008)

Like several of the founding members of the ITPF, the Collective had within its ranks trade union activists, including some who had worked with unions involved in the historic Bombay textile strike of the early 1980s and several who were currently with the Textile Workers Struggle Committee. As the founding member, Vinod Shetty recalls, 'at that time, I was a student and got a real insight to the working of trade unions and how the government treated the textile workers' (Shetty, 2008). The year-long strike, involving over a quarter of a million workers, resulted in a shattered industry and a broken union that significantly eroded the form of Fordism dominant in India (Bhattacherjee, 1988). In Mumbai, the real-estate boom fueled soaring land values, prompting mill owners to sell their properties rather than re-start the industry. More than a process of restructuring, Shetty describes it as a process of 'de-unionising'. From the vantage point of YPC activists, the post-industrial boom, of which IT/ITES is a major component, is built upon the decimation of manufacturing and the undermining of trade union strength.

Leading activists, like Ketaki Rege, were either directly involved or had close friends or relatives engaged in the IT/ITES sector, but mainly from the call-centre industry. According to Rege (2008), 'Naturally, as trade unionists and labour lawyers, we were interested in finding out ... what are the conditions of service, what are the employee-employer relations, are there any rules ... If there is any injustice done to them, any unfair practice ... then we take the matters to the court'.

From the beginning, YPC activists discovered that the organisation 'wouldn't be in the traditional model of trade unions', which '[we] were used to'. Instead, Shetty argued that although 'there have been demands from employees that a trade union be set up, [his] feeling [was] that it would always work like a welfare association, or a forum, or a platform for employees to meet, and that organisation would have to actively engage the government as well as the companies' (Shetty, 2008). Mobilisation, then, would have to be built on employee networks sustained by an association such as the YPC. Unlike the traditional tactics deployed by trade unions, YPC activists quickly realised that organising at factory gates would not be effective. 'We found out,' Rege (2008) observed, 'almost instinctively and from experience, that it would be difficult, in this industry, to have a union which is based on the traditional lines ... In this case, we realised that since the workers never identify themselves as working class who need to have any kind of bargaining power, it was not happening'. The YPC was established as a space to share experiences, educate and empower employees by giving them an opportunity to safely 'discuss their own issues and find solutions to their problems ... where they can exchange ideas, form opinions, and maybe improve their service condition' (Sajjanshetty, 2008). Consciousness raising, then, was a decisive feature of the Collective. YPC members recognised that the structure of the IT/ITES sector inhibited organising activities. Work schedules, particularly arduous night shifts, as well as the fear of management's response to employee activism, made it difficult for the YPC to organise any one location. Also, according to Shetty (2008):

> Many of these employees are migrant labour. I wouldn't say 'migrant labour' [as the term is usually used] but employees who have come from other states. ... Unlike locals or people who are already living in Bombay, who would be much more ready to take the risk or put their jobs at stake, we find that those who come from outside the state are very much apprehensive of any threat to their employment to their salaries. They don't want to show to the organisation that they are part of any such organising, a union, which they think would cause the management to terminate them. This kind of salary is very important to their families back home. They come from small towns. This is another reason why it is difficult to get employees to join a trade union.

Factory gates certainly do exist, but the potential to develop a collective identity is made very difficult by inconsistent work schedules and workers' mobility. Rege's (2008) comment is also indicative of the uphill battle facing organisers:

> The thing is, it is very difficult to approach employees in call-centres. Friends of members of YPC, we tell them, is it possible for you to get even five of your colleagues from the call-centre? It is very difficult ... Our biggest hurdle is the lack of

class consciousness. People just don't identify with having the need for any kind of association.

Along with the organisation Focus on the Global South, the YPC documented the nature of the BPO sector and the prospects for unions in their 2005 publication, *When the Wind Blows: An Overview of Business Process Outsourcing (BPO) in India*. It made the important observation that 'there are hardly any agencies representing the interests of BPO employees in India' and that the 'interests of the sector are being solely represented by the owners/managements of the BPO sector' (Young Professionals Collective and Focus on the Global South, 2005:13). For labour's perspective to be publicly recognised, organisations like the YPC, UNITES, and ITPF would be necessary. The Collective's activists came to realise that it 'would be required to lobby the government and set up best practices. This would be [the YPC's] main work, [which] would be to provide information to society at large about this industry, and work out best practices and codes for the industry so that they would self-regulate' (Shetty, 2008).

Following the tragic rape and murder of Pratibha Srikanth, a BPO employee working for Hewlett Packard (HP), women's advocacy groups and labour organisations mobilised to draw attention to what came to be seen as a structural issue within the ITES-BPO. The crime was committed by a driver who was supposed to take her from the office to her home. These organisations charged that management provided inadequate protection for its workers.

> One of the main reasons that we've found that these attacks have taken place [against] women ... [is] because the drivers are not employed full-time by the companies. Companies are trying to save money by outsourcing the supply of drivers ... So this kind of movement and turnover of drivers has caused a lot of problems, there is no verification of backgrounds ... The companies' response is to hush up any such cases ... Nor do they compensate openly, they do a hush-hush deal by forcing the family of the victim to basically not speak to the media. (Shetty, 2008)

Like the fragmented service-production chains that characterise the global BPO industry, the transportation network responsible for ferrying ITES employees from their homes to their often-remote work location is equally reliant on a complex sub-contracting system. The YPC's recommendation is that all drivers should have their names registered with the police and criminal record checks conducted, in addition to branding vehicles as BPO shuttles (The Indian Express, 2005).

These instances of labour organisations actively engaging with firms, Shetty predicted, are going to increase.

I feel that in the coming days organisations like YPC or UNITES or any other organisation or trade union, which is going to work for these employees, will have a large role in protecting the rights of workers. They will increasingly turn to such organisations because the crisis is big. This is just the tip of the iceberg. I feel that as the effects of the [economic] meltdown take place, the IT industry and BPO industry is going to be badly hit. Increasingly, companies are going to start terminating employees without following the [fair and legal] processes. (Shetty, 2008)

The YPC has emerged as a nascent regulatory agent to confront the deficiencies of oversight from government and industry bodies that are ill-equipped to effectively address problems throughout the sector, in a way that is symptomatic of liberalisation. The YPC has suggested that funds equal to 2% of corporate profits, contributed by both the government and companies, should be kept aside as a Contingency Provident Fund for retraining and retrenchment compensation (Young Professionals Collective and Focus on the Global South, 2005). In the event, Shetty (2008) explains, that companies 'leave or shutdown overnight, these BPO employees should be protected; they should have some kind of bridging of the gap between now and the next job'.

## THE UNION FOR IT-ENABLED SERVICES PROFESSIONALS

UNITES was initially launched as the Centre for Business Process Outsourcing Professionals (CBPOP) in 2004 by organisers from UNI as well as individuals associated with the ITPF who were concerned that the latter would never evolve into a genuine union (Hegde 2008; Noronha and D'Cruz 2009). In the process, UNI's Asia-Pacific Regional Office took a leading role in establishing what would eventually become UNITES. Karthik Shekhar, General Secretary of UNITES since 2006, has become the public face of the professional union in India. Shekhar began his IT career with IBM and over the years observed the changes in how the company's employees were managed as the corporate structure was transformed with liberalisation in the early 1990s. It was this transformation that prompted the programmer to investigate unionism at Big Blue.

[There was an] initial comfort level when I joined ... IBM ... Then I started seeing the winds of change. There was liberalisation, there was computerisation, and IBM was becoming more important. IBM decided to part ways with Tata, [leaving the Indian company and one-time corporate partner] with a one percent stake ... [Then] IBM was a fully IBM-owned company [after foreign direct investment caps were lifted]. That's when I ... got a rude shock of what IBM could be ... I started probing. Then I found that at IBM itself, there were these trade unions in Paris, there were trade unions in the US, there was this IBM solidarity network – so I started interacting with them. By then, again ... they made me lose one more promotion and they cut my salary. (Shekhar, 2008a)

Eventually, Shekhar encountered UNI's Hegde, who was at the time working on forming the ITPF, and both got involved with the organisation. After becoming disenchanted with the direction the Forum was heading, Shekhar started doing mobilisation work with UNI's newest project, UNITES. From there, he moved on to become the union's general secretary.

Shekhar's own experience as a knowledge worker is noteworthy. Despite the lucrative opportunities available in leading companies such as IBM, perceptions of injustice and unfair management practices opened the door to an interest in unionisation. As he was quoted in a major Indian daily, *The Telegraph*, 'There is exploitation in the BPO sector. A labour union is imperative' (The Telegraph, 2006). Furthermore, Shekhar's connection to IBM has had an ongoing importance for UNITES. When striking Australian workers at IBM forced the company to negotiate a collective agreement, Shekhar saw this as a significant breakthrough for organising efforts in India. 'To start with, we will ask IBM to make the same commitments for the company in India as they have agreed to do in Australia ... then we will take the agitation to other companies' (cited in Shankar, 2006). A year later, UNITES joined IT workers, trade unionists, and labour activists from around the world in what was billed as the first virtual strike. Using the social media programme Second Life, UNI led this cyberspace protest in solidarity with the demands being made by Rappresentanza Sindacale Unitaria IBM Vimercate (RSU), the union representing over 9,000 workers engaged in a labour stoppage at IBM in Italy.

From its inception, UNITES had been responding to the complaints raised by IT/ITES workers about a range of perceived injustices. In 2006, nearly one hundred call-centre employees with Bangalore-based Bel-Air BPO were hit by what has come to be known as the 'fly-by-night' operations, not uncommon in the industry. Workers discovered at the last minute that the operation had been shut down and they were not going to be paid (Suresh, 2006). For three years, UNITES has been pursuing the case, which has cost the union a significant amount in legal fees. The case-by-case basis of response to worker demands in the industry has raised the union's public profile. It also draws attention to structural problems in the IT/ITES sector. 'See, there have been trials, errors, and there have been spontaneous workers coming together because there is an issue', the General Secretary recalls (Shekhar, 2008a). But immediate demands and even solutions do not necessarily create a sustainable membership base. According to Shekhar (2008a):

[O]nce the problem gets solved, or the problem doesn't get solved, they [the employees looking to UNITES for advice] just disappear ... They say, 'okay fine, you guys are doing a good job so please continue doing a good job, in case there's a problem, I'll come to you'. That active involvement is not what we are seeing.

The companies also make organising difficult. They have been known to promote prospective members to team leaders or a similar position, effectively relieving them of whatever complaints that might have led them to consider joining the union. As Shekhar (2008b) remarks, 'for six months [or so], they will not be in touch with UNITES. By the time they come back, they have moved companies and we were losing membership regularly ... That was our first learning [experience] and failure also ... Getting a critical mass of about five or six thousand [in a BPO division of 16,000] becomes a big challenge'. Without a sustained membership base in particular companies, most importantly in the major multinational and Indian firms, corporations will not negotiate with the union. 'The problem', he says, 'is that the moment I speak to somebody, he becomes a member, he gets a promotion, he gets transferred, so it is like, they have never said no to us ... but by some coincidence that person moves around' (Shekhar, 2008a). It is hardly surprising that UNITES's success in negotiating six collective agreements has been limited to small to medium-sized enterprises, representing one thousand or so employees.

In its brief history, UNITES has attracted public attention by bringing to light issues pertaining to inequality and exploitation in the IT/ITES sectors. One of its earliest initiatives was a forum organised in response to the murder of Pratibha, which led to a more general campaign to draw attention to sexual harassment in the industry. After this incident occurred, Shekhar (2008a) asserts, 'that's when people actually started to talk to us and started looking us up, and ... immediately there was some kind of connect between the workers, the public in general.' Then an executive with HP, Som Mittal was noted as saying that women working at night was dangerous, confirming what the union had already been saying. While the responses to this incident were mixed – some in the labour movement were calling for a ban on women working at night – UNITES was fully in support of women's rights: 'Female IT employees should be given an option to choose their timings. It is not the question of equality, but safety of women employees working on an unsafe work schedule that matters' (Deccan Herald, 2005). The promotion of gender equality and workplace safety became a major campaign for UNITES, and the memorial service held in UNITES's Bangalore office helped build positive press for the organisation. It was shortly after this event that the president of INTUC and Governing Council member of the International Labour Organization (ILO), N. M. Adyanthaya, stated that the union federation would 'support UNITES as it is a responsible new-generation union founded on trade union philosophy' (The Hindu, 2005). Indeed, these early efforts attracted a significant number of members to the organisation (Taylor and Bain, 2008).

Hari Prasad, an HR manager and UNITES activist, has identified sexual harassment and discrimination as a leading form of injustice in the IT/ITES sector, and something unions need to pay close attention to. In one instance, a prospective female employee was sexually harassed during a placement interview that Prasad had arranged. This was a symptom, Prasad (2008) suggests, of executives failing to oversee the actions of front-line managers or, for Shekhar, evidence of corruption endemic to middle management in IT/ITES firms (Prasad and Shekhar 2008).

UNITES has also been active in combating the widespread practice of refusing to pay for overtime. With the recent economic slowdown, there are reports that global IT services firms, like Accenture, plan to increase working hours by almost an hour. Once recognised as a leader of good HR practices, Wipro has asked employees to strictly abide by the fixed 9.5-hour working day. Of course, the reality in the current global economic climate is that IT professionals are working 14-16 hours a day, with performance and timing even more strictly monitored (Mishra, 2008). Without the basic provision offered by labour laws regulating work times, unpaid overtime is an expectation (Bhargava, 2008). This was also a leading concern at a joint UNITES-UNI press conference in Delhi, when union activists reaffirmed their support for the two-hundred-year-old movement that helped to establish the 8-hour working day (UNITES and UNI, 2008).

HRM practices, from the perspective of trade unionists and Forum activists, are not able to sufficiently address the grievances presented by workers. This notion has prompted UNITES to pursue the establishment of a legal sexual harassment redressal system in the IT-BPO sector, with legal status under India's Trade Disputes Act (Acharya, 2009). Moreover, its 'Decisions for Life' project aims to raise awareness amongst young female workers about their employment opportunities and career possibilities, as well as family building and the work-family balance. For UNITES, 'their choices are key to the demographic and workforce development of the nation' (UNITES, 2009a; UNI, 2009). Along with UNI, UNITES took action against the assault of women in the South Indian city of Mangalore by Hindu fundamentalists opposed to women adopting 'Western' lifestyles (Sengupta, 2009). It also helped to organise and participate in the March 8th Women's Day midnight rally (UNI, 2009).

In the 2009 economic crisis, UNITES has been forced to contend with the consequences of fraudulent accounting practices in one of the subcontinent's largest IT firms. Labeled as 'India's Enron', in early 2009, Ramalinga Raju,

Chairman of Satyam Computer Services, admitted to committing financial irregularities, bringing down the reputation of the IT industry's corporate governance and management systems. 'The horrendous act is the biggest in corporate history', claimed a UNITES press release. 'It appears corporations have taken advantage of economic liberalisation and free market capitalism which is only a euphemism for casino capitalism' (UNITES, 2009b). In a public relations breakthrough for the union, India's major news publications reported that approximately 2,000 Satyam employees who feared for their job losses had approached UNITES. In addition, the union's website received 96,000 hits in December and that number shot up to 270,000 in January of 2009 (Mishra, 2009; Tejaswi, 2009a). While this is hardly an accurate measure of prospective membership, it indicates that the media and the wider public are beginning to pay attention to a labour organisation that emerged from obscurity just a few years earlier.

Following the dramatic plunge of India's stock market in late 2008 and what finally came to be recognised as a global recession, analysts began to question the security of IT/ITES employment. Fears of widespread job losses, estimated to be around 10,000 according to the UNITES, were quickly dismissed by Nasscom not long after the union began raising this issue in the media. In June of 2009, the influential *Outlook Business* estimated even higher figures, between 77,000 and 110,000, or 3.5% to 5% of the 2 million employed in the industry (Mahalingam, 2009). Yet, Raju Bhatnagar, a senior member of Nasscom, was quite clear in his statement, that there 'are no large-scale layoffs. There are sporadic incidents here and there. The industry is growing and in fact, needs more people' (The Economic Times, 2008). For Nasscom's president, Som Mittal, this is a time for IT/ITES workers to understand the market realities and 'reset their growth and remuneration expectations' (cited in Tejaswi, 2009b). Indeed, Bhatnagar (2008) maintained that, considering the high standards of employment, effective HR practices, and plentiful job opportunities even in the face of recession, the industry did not need government, and certainly not union, intervention.

For the first time, giants such as Infosys Technologies and Wipro cut their annual pay increases of 12% to 14% down to 7% or 8% (Sayeed and Sekhar, 2009). Even high-end designers and programmers were asked to sit on the bench, known as a 'free pool', as a disciplinary waiting area for IT workers with no work to do (Mahalingam, 2009). With companies now trying to rationalise expenditures, some call-centre employees have been asked to relocate to less expensive facilities in smaller cities or risk losing their jobs. Admittedly, UNITES can do very little to stave off unemployment, but the union does advise workers on how to resist the redundancy process and advocate for them to ensure that they receive everything to which they are entitled (Kazmin, 2009).

On May 1, 2009, the union launched a month-long 'Stop the Pink Slip' initiative aimed at collecting 100,000 signatures from IT workers to force Nasscom to pressure the Indian IT industry to stop cutting jobs (Basu, 2009). 'Instead of firing', Shekhar says, 'companies should focus on staff training, skill enhancement or learning new languages ... They should realise that bench sitters are live intellectual bodies and not perishable commodities. And getting rid of jobs via the new-found, unscientific, biased performance evaluation is unfair' (cited in Tejaswi, 2009b). In some instances, managers have resorted to verbally and physically harassing employees into quitting. One thirty-seven-year-old team leader was driven to file a harassment suit against his employer, Wipro (SiliconIndia, 2009). UNITES also questions how all of the tax-free revenues accumulated by the industry over the years have dried up. The recession, from this perspective, is being used to discipline the IT/ITES labour force and justify salary cuts and job losses. For Shekhar, other changes are possible, notably increasing lateral hiring as well as internal austerity measures that cut down on unnecessary expenditures.

The ability of UNITES to operate as an information centre and a publicly recognised advocate for IT/ITES employees has given the organisation considerable hope that it will become a more influential player with leading companies. But membership remains low, at approximately 22,000, concentrated mostly in Hyderabad and Bangalore. Only about 1,300 are covered by collective bargaining agreements. The critical mass achieved by white-collar unions in decades past has yet to be achieved and, as a result, the capacity to negotiate with multinational enterprises is restricted. As the union's leading activists have recognised, large foreign companies like HSBC and Barclays, both of which have negotiated collective agreements with unions in their home countries and have framework agreements with UNI, have never opened the door to UNITES.

> They actually, in some of the cases, they almost ... threw us out. That's when we realised that these guys are not going accept the same commitment what they have given to the European works councils or to the members there. That was an eye opener. Then we started focusing on concrete organising at these firms. (Shekhar, 2008b)

Despite these setbacks, UNITES has responded by working in solidarity with other employee groups associated with IT/ITES, with much of this building on UNI connections in India and Asia. Unlike the ITPF, UNITES presents itself as 'One Big IT Union', rather than appealing solely to the higher-value software engineers and IT professionals.

> As per our constitution, we do not demarcate between IT and ITES ... IT is treated as one set, there's nothing [between] the BPO and IT sector. We come under the IT sector. My membership can be anybody who touches computers. As per the law, if you are a computer user, you are [someone] who comes from where computers are, even cleaning, anyone can be a member. (Shekhar, 2008a)

Because of the highly-skilled workforce, flexible employment opportunities, and temporary employment, UNITES has adopted a pragmatic model. This model breaks with the strict division of labour and job protection strategy of traditional labour unions:

> We have consciously said, anybody who works with IT or ITES, are our members. We have said, whether you are typists, whether you are a programmer, whether you are a call-centre guy, there's no difference ... That is one of the reasons we are supporting also the call-centre drivers, call-centre cooks, because we know [at some point] these drivers graduate to become a call-centre employee. We know that these cooks who either move on to become a career employee, or also go on ... into the hotel industry, so it is a funny situation. What we try to do is we try to support ... as many different groups as possible. Because we know ... we will be contacted at some point of life by the same member. The membership is very dynamic. (Shekhar, 2008c)

Wages and financial benefits may not be the leading cause for IT/ITES workers to seek assistance from UNITES, so the union instead focuses on promoting a living wage campaign. In the process, security guards, drivers, and other categories of workers affiliated with IT/ITES, albeit at the lower end of the wage scale, have been helped by UNITES.

> Whatever the minimum wage is, is actually treated by the employers as the maximum wage, so we said that these employees need a minimum living wage, not just a minimum wage that the government sponsors. So, actually, it has started setting up different thought processes, especially for ... garment workers and security workers who feel that they are exploited. So our solidarity actually helps them to bring out some of the issues to the forefront. (Shekhar, 2008a)

Building solidarity amongst the various economic and social classes embedded within IT/ITES is one thing, but mobilising real activities throughout the UNITES membership base has its own set of challenges. To this end, some union activists have turned to issues-based activism such as fighting for workers' rights, women's rights, and environmentalism, as well as supporting community activities such as blood drives and marathon races. For the General Secretary, sustaining interest in helping others can be founded on the very privilege from which many of the most educated come:

> See, what we are trying to say, you say that IT industry is the 'sunshine industry'. IT and ITES workers are paid well. So, they are supposed to be the cream, the best of the educated, having good salaries ... I also get my members to participate with the feeling that I am not only doing for myself, I am doing for somebody who's downtrodden or who doesn't have a voice ... it is a mixture of an NGO and a union that we are trying to make here. So it's some kind of a convergence. (Shekhar, 2008a)

Strengthening connections to social activists by bridging relations with community organisations, functioning democratically, enhancing women's role within the union, adopting villages, and forging stronger ties with trade unions at the national and international levels have been some of the tactics deployed by UNITES to expand its influence (FES and UNITES, 2006). But what of expanding the union model and representing the interests of workers outside India? Through its connections to UNI, UNITES is expanding into Malaysia and has set its sights on an equivalent in the Philippines and Nepal. The goal is to establish IT and ITES unions in common offshore destinations.

The media tend to present an image of UNITES as a confrontational union, regularly locking horns with the industry. The reality is more complex. Indeed, UNITES models its activities on the ILO's tripartite governance structure – through which unions, industry leaders and governments address issues of mutual concern. The union recognises the importance of offshoring in the current stage of globalisation and supports regulating the sector to defend the interests of workers and the industry's financial sustainability. However, UNITES has been most active in promoting the regulation of call centres through the mechanism of the UNI Global Call Center Charter. Furthermore, it addresses the well-being of ITES professionals through collective bargaining, advocating for best practices, and providing workers with counselling services through city-level psychological forums (The Telegraph, 2006). The 'Stop the BOSS (Burn Out Stress Syndrome)' campaign showed further that UNITES could draw attention to the conditions of work without simply demanding wage concessions. As Noronha and D'Cruz (2009: 229) observe, 'UNITES aimed at becoming a forum that could reflect the professional aspirations of its key constituency'. In this respect, the union did not assume an altogether different course from that initially taken up by the ITPF, but it did so with a clear sense of the shortcomings of the Forum model and the strengths of unionisation. While still largely dependent on financial contributions provided by the Finnish Solidarity Project and struggling with the reality of collecting voluntary dues, UNITES is hopeful that the union model will establish a more stable future.

## FUTURE OF ORGANISING

The 'new generation networks', UNI's description of the latest union models, can be used to describe the leading labour organisations in the Indian IT/ITES sectors. Building on personal experiences with textile and manufacturing unions, activists and labour lawyers working with the YPC established a forum through which ITES-BPO professionals especially could engage in informational and consciousness-raising initiatives as a starting point for identifying themselves as workers and opening up the possibility of finding empowerment in union structures. With a more professional orientation, the ITPF created a service forum for the industry's most privileged stratum to address perceived shortcomings in managerial practices. Subsequent tensions within the Forum helped clear a space for another UNI-supported project, UNITES.

The stratification of the industry, marked by software engineers at one end and back-office ITES-BPO and call-centre professionals at the other, exposes strengths and limitations in the organised efforts deployed by ITPF and UNITES. ITPF's conciliatory approach to addressing problems within the sector failed to mobilise IT professionals and gain meaningful company recognition. Since it concentrated solely on professionals, ITPF could not call on back-office or call-centre workers for support. Conversely, UNITES's stronger approach has drawn wider backing but managing a diverse group of members is a difficult task that it has been able to achieve only with the support of Western labour organisations.

One of the key questions for workers' organisations in the IT sector is whether they will be able to work together with other burgeoning Indian labour groups outside this sector. One important group is the NTUI, which has broken the traditional connection to political parties by maintaining its status as an independent federation. With over 200 constituent unions and 750,000 members, the NTUI is, like UNITES, an early attempt to forge a new union movement. In 2006, the NTUI worked with the YPC, Jobs with Justice, the Communication Workers of America, and the Centre for Education and Communication in India, to produce a bi-national perspective on call-centre offshore outsourcing. Even though the NTUI has yet to enter the IT/ITES sector with an organising drive, this landmark collaboration between Indian and US labour in the sector represents an important step in building internationalism and signals the potential for creative partnerships within India.

UNI's endeavours in India also continue to grow. The Union for Commerce Employees in India, the Union for Logistics Employees, the Union for Finance Employees, and the Union for Mobile Employees, are all part of UNI's New

Generation Network and have targeted those private sector service industries that have grown since liberalisation. UNI's 'green field' initiatives in India, both UNITES and the ITPF, are setting standards for organising workers that existing unions, and existing strategies, neglected. The current economic climate has indeed offered potential for these nascent labour organisations that have already exposed cracks in the glamourised IT/ITES sectors. The challenge now is to become fully self-sufficient and make gains in organising the major Indian and foreign multinational corporations based in India.

## References

Acharya, K. (2009) 'Labour-India: Getting "Bangalored" Back', *Global Issues*, January 2. Accessed on January 12, 2009 from http://www.globalissues.org/news/2009/01/02/189

Ackers, P. (2006) 'Leaving Labour? Some British Impressions of Indian Academic Employment Relations', *Economic and Political Weekly*, September 30: 4187-4194.

Bain, P. and P. Taylor (2002) 'Ringing the Changes? Union Recognition and Organisation in Call Centres in the UK Finance Sector', *Industrial Relations Journal*, 33(3): 246-261.

Basu, I. (2009) 'IT Workers Join Unions to Fight Job Cuts', *Upiasia.com*, May 6. Accessed on May 8, 2009 from http://www.upiasia.com/Economics/2009/05/06/it_workers_join_unions_to_fight_job_cuts/9707/

Batt, R., V. Doellgast, H. Kwon, M. Nopany, P. Nopany and A. da Costa (2005) *The Indian Call Centre Industry: National Benchmarking Report*. Working Paper, School of Industrial and Labour Relations. Ithaca, NY: Cornell University.

Bhargava, G. (2008) Interview by Andrew Stevens, November 13.

Bhatnagar, R. (2008) Interview by Andrew Stevens, December 11.

Bhattacherjee, D. (1988) 'Unions, State and Capital in Western India: Structural Determinants of the 1982 Bombay Textile Strike' in R. Southall (ed.) *Labour and Unions in Asia and Africa: Contemporary Issues*. London: MacMillan Press, 211-237.

Bibby, A. (2002a) 'IT Professionals' Forums in India', *World of Work*, 42. Accessed on September 7, 2007 from http://www.ilo.org/public/english/bureau/inf/magazine/42/itindia.htm

Bibby, A. (2002b) 'Labour Organisation in India's IT Industry', *Financial Times*. Accessed on November 19, 2007 from http://www.andrewbibby.com/telework/india.html

Bibby, A. (2000) *Organising in Financial Call Centres: A Report for UNI*. Accessed on November 19, 2007 from http://www.andrewbibby.com/docs/ofcc1.html

Bidwai, P. (2005) 'For a "New Deal" for Labor', *Frontline*, 22(17). Accessed on June 11, 2008 from http://www.flonnet.com/fl2217/stories/ 20050826003310900.htm

Bidwai, P. (1997) 'Indian Labor Leader Shot', *Multinational Monitor*, 18(3): 8-9.

CWA, CEC, JwJ, NTUI and YPC (2006) *Bi-National Perspective on Offshore Outsourcing:*

*A Collaboration Between Indian and US Labour.* Accessed on November 24, 2009 from http://www.jwj.org/campaigns/global/tools/outsourcing/us_india_report_2006.pdf

Deccan Herald (2005) 'Allow IT Women Pros to Choose Work Hours', December 19.

FES and UNITES (2006) 'Organizing Strategies for ITES Workers', Hyderabad, India, April 14-16.

Fine, B., C. Lapavitsas and J. Pincus (eds.) (2001) *Development Policy in the 21st Century: Beyond the Post-Washington Consensus*, London: Routledge.

Fournier, V. (1999) 'The Appeal to "Professionalism" as Disciplinary Mechanism', *The Sociological Review*, 47: 280-307.

Hegde, N. (2008) Interview by Andrew Stevens, October 22.

Hill, E. (2009) 'The Indian Industrial Relations System: Struggling to Address the Dynamics of a Globalizing Economy', *Journal of Industrial Relations*, 51(3): 395-410.

Hirschefeld, K. (2005) *IT Professionals Forum in India: Organization at a Crossroads: Report on a Visit to IT Professionals Forums in February 2005.* Nyon, Switzerland: Union Network International.

Holman, D., R. Batt and U. Holtgrewe (2007) *The Global Call Center Report: International Perspective on Management and Employment*, Global Call Centre Project. Accessed on November 24, 2009 from http://www.ilr.cornell.edu/globalcallcenter/upload/GCC-Intl-Rept-US-Version.pdf

Kanellos, M. (2005) 'India's Tech Renaissance', *C-Net News.com*, June 28-30.

Kazmin, A. (2009) 'Vulnerable IT Workers Find Comfort in Union', *Financial Times*, February 12. Accessed on February 15, 2009 from http://www.ft.com/cms/s/0/1a6cdb42-f92d-11dd-ab7f-000077b07658.html?nclick_check=1

Krishna, S. (2005) 'India: Globalisation and IT Development', *South Asian Journal*, April-June. Accessed on August 5, 2009 from http://www.southasianmedia.net/magazine/Journal/8_it_development.htm

Mahalingam, T. (2009) 'Where Dreams End ... And Nightmares Begin', *Outlook Business*, June 27: 47-57.

Mishra, B. (2008) 'IT-BPO Union to File PIL Against "Extended" Working Hours', *Rediff.com*, November 26. Accessed on November 30, 2008 from http://www.rediff.com/money/2008/nov/26bpo-it-bpo-union-to-file-pil-against-working-hours.htm

Mishra, P. (2009) 'The Nightmare Has Just Begun', *The Economic Times,* January 27.

Mosco, V., C. McKercher and A. Stevens (2008) 'Convergences: Elements of a Feminist Political Economy of Labor and Communication', in K. Sarikakis and L. Shade (eds.) *Feminist Interventions in International Communication: Minding the Gap.* Lanham, MD: Rowman & Littlefield Publishers, 207-223.

Natarajan, R. (2008) Interview conducted by Andrew Stevens, October 20.

Noronha, E. and P. D'Cruz (2009) 'Engaging the Professional: Organising Call Centre Agents in India', *Industrial Relations Journal,* 40(3): 215-234.

Noronha, E. and P. D'Cruz (2006) 'Organizing Call Centre Agents: Emerging Issues',

*Economic and Political Weekly*, May 27: 2115–2121.

Prasad, H. (2008) Interview by Andrew Stevens, October 20.

Prasad, H. and K. Shekhar (2008) Interview by Andrew Stevens, October 20.

Ramaswamy, E. (1977) *The Worker and His Union: A Study in South India*. Bombay, India: Allied Publishers.

Rege, K. (2008) Interview by Andrew Stevens, November 20.

Remesh, B. (2004a) *Labour in Business Process Outsourcing: A Case Study of Call Centre Agents*. New Delhi, India: V.V. Giri National Labour Institute.

Remesh, B. (2004b) '"Cyber Coolies" in BPO: Insecurities and Vulnerabilities of Non-Standard Work', *Economic and Political Weekly*, January 31: 492-497.

Remesh, B. and Neetha N. (2008) 'Gender Implications of Outsourced Work in the New Economy: A Case Study of Domestic Call Centres', *The Indian Journal of Labour Economics*, 51(4): 717-730.

Rodrik, D. and A. Subramanian (2001) 'From "Hindu Growth" to Productivity Surge: The Mystery of the Indian Growth Transition'. IMF Working Paper. Washington, D.C.: International Monetary Fund.

Roy, A. (2009) Interview by Vincent Mosco, July 8.

Roychowdhury, S. (2003) 'Public Sector Restructuring and Democracy: The State, Labour and Trade Unions in India', *The Journal of Development Studies*, 39(3): 29-50.

Sajjanshetty, G. (2008) Interview with Andrew Stevens, October 18.

Sayeed, V. and A. Sekhar (2009) 'Thousands of IT Professionals Have Lost Their Jobs in the Major Cyber Cities', *Frontline*, February 28. Accessed March 3, 2009 from http://www.hinduonnet.com/fline/stories/20090313260501400.htm

Schiller, D. (1999) *Digital Capitalism: Networking the Global Market System*. Cambridge, MA: MIT Press.

Sengupta, S. (2009) 'Attack on Women at an Indian Bar Intensifies a Clash of Cultures', *New York Times*, February 8. Accessed February 9, 2009 from http://www.nytimes.com/2009/02/09/world/asia/09india.html?partner=rss&emc=rss

Shankar, B. (2006) 'Lessons from Oz: Inspired by the IBM Employees Stir in Australia, India's IT, ITES Sector Renew Their Trade Union Plans', *Mid-Day,* September 8.

Shekhar, K. (2009) Personal correspondence, December 11.

Shekhar, K. (2008a) Interview by Andrew Stevens, October 14.

Shekhar, K. (2008b) Interview by *Live Mint* reporter, October 31.

Shekhar, K. (2008c) Interview by Andrew Stevens, November 3.

Shetty, V. (2008) Interview by Andrew Stevens, November 24.

SiliconIndia (2009) 'Sacked Wipro Employee Alleges Harassment', August 20. Accessed on August 25, 2009 from http://www.siliconindia.com/shownews/Sacked_Wipro_employee_alleges_harassment-nid-60537.html/1/1/error1#success

Srinivasan, N. (1989) 'Growth of Professional Managerial Unionism: The Indian Experience', *Economic and Political Weekly*, November 25: 169-174.

Subramaniam, E. (2008) Interview by Andrew Stevens, October 30.

Suresh, S. (2006) 'This Domain Doesn't Exist: 93 Employees of Bel-Air BPO Didn't Know Firm Had Shut Down until They Saw This Message on Its Site', *Mid-Day*. Accessed on October 22, 2008 from http://www.unitespro.org/uniindia/Pres%20reports%20and%20 UNITES%20response.pdf

Taylor, P. and P. Bain (2008) 'United by a Common Language? Trade Union Responses in the UK and India to Call Centre Offshoring', *Antipode*, 40(1): 131-154.

Tejaswi, M. (2009a) 'Tension in the Air: IT Union Website Hits Rise Dramatically', *The Times of India*, February 5. Accessed on February 5, 2009 from http://epaper. timesofindia.com/Default/Client.asp? Daily=TOIBG&login=default& Enter=true&Sk in=TOI&GZ=T&AW=1233869242187

Tejaswi, M. (2009b) 'Techies Say "No" to Pink Slips', *The Times of India*, May 1: 15.

The Economic Times (2008) 'IT-BPO Union Flays Nasscom Stand on Layoffs', December 7. Accessed on December 11, 2008 from http://economictimes.indiatimes.com/Features/ The_Sunday_ET/Companies/IT-BPO_union_flays_Nasscom_stand_on_layoffs/ articleshow/3803038.cms

The Economist (2004) 'The Thin Red Line', May 8-14: 40.

The Hindu (2005) 'ITES Union Urges Staff Safety Measures', December 17.

The Indian Express (2005) 'Industry Meet in January to Formalize Code of Conduct', December 23.

The Telegraph (2006) 'Who Says BPOs Don't Have Unions?', November 5.

UNI (2009) 'A Dose of Women Power in Uniting IT Workers in India', March 28. Accessed on June 5, 2009 from http://www.uniglobalunion.org/Apps/iportal.nsf/pages/homeEn?Ope ndocument&exURL=http://www.uniglobalunion.org/Apps/UNINews.nsf/0/ABF72DAC6 DF952CEC12575870058BAE9

UNI (2003) 'Organising IT Professionals in India', Nyon, Switzerland: Union Network International.

UNITES (2009a) 'Decisions for Life Project Launch'. Accessed on June 30, 2009 from http:// www.unitespro.org/files/html/DFL%20Page/dfl_launch.htm

UNITES (2009b) 'Request to Appoint a Commission of Enquiry under Commissioner of Enquiry Act', January 7. Accessed on January 12, 2009 from http://itnitesunion.wordpress. com/2009/01/07/request-to-appoint-a-commission-of-enquiry-under-commissioner-of- enquiry-act/

UNITES and UNI (2008) UNITES and UNI press conference. New Delhi, India, December 6.

Upadhya, C. (2008) 'Ethnographies of the Global Information Economy: Research Strategies and Methods', *Economic and Political Weekly*, April 26: 64-72.

Upadhya, C. (2007) 'Employment, Exclusion and "Merit" in the Indian IT Industry', *Economic and Political Weekly*, May 19: 1863-1868.

Verma, P. (2004) 'Forum to Tackle Unfair HR Policies in BPO Industry', *The Financial Express*, July 29. Accessed on December 8, 2007 from http://www.financialexpress.com/

old/fe_full_story.php?content_id=64607

Young Professionals Collective and Focus on the Global South (2005) *When the Wind Blows: An Overview of Business Process Outsourcing (BPO) in India*. Mumbai, India: Focusweb.

图书在版编目(CIP)数据

制造和服务业中的数字劳工/姚建华主编.—北京:
商务印书馆,2017(2020.6重印)
(媒介和数字劳工研究:西方的视角丛书)
ISBN 978-7-100-13153-7

Ⅰ.①制… Ⅱ.①姚… Ⅲ.①制造工业—数字化—研究
②服务业—数字化—研究 Ⅳ.①F407.4-39 ②F719-39

中国版本图书馆 CIP 数据核字(2017)第 061384 号

权利保留,侵权必究。

**制造和服务业中的数字劳工**
姚建华 主编

商务印书馆出版
(北京王府井大街36号 邮政编码100710)
商务印书馆发行
浙江临安市曙光印务有限公司印刷
ISBN 978-7-100-13153-7

2017年4月第1版　开本710×1000　1/16
2020年6月第3次印刷　印张14.5
定价:42.00元